# Contents

# Acknowledgments

Writing and preparing this book for publication has been a long, sometimes joyous, sometimes painstaking process which fortunately I did not have to do alone.

Over the years, I have had magnificent mentors. My first thanks goes to my teacher David Novak whose work has inspired this project and whose generosity has been unwavering, for which I am deeply grateful.

A heartfelt thanks goes also to my teacher Peter Ochs who has read and commented on the manuscript (on numerous occasions, I might add) and whose insights have deepened my perspective on the project and have guided me in my writing.

I owe much to David Ford whose rich theological perspective not only contributed to improving the manuscript but whose efforts in developing Jewish–Christian–Islamic relations inspires me greatly.

I am grateful to Kenneth Seeskin for offering a careful, challenging and ever patient read of the manuscript and the chapter on Cohen in particular. Additional thanks go to Robert Gibbs, Eugene Rogers and Jamie Ferreira for helping me write the first version of the manuscript as my dissertation at the University of Virginia.

Of course no-one writes books without enlisting the aid of many dear and loyal friends. Of note are my 'Cambridge friends' Rachel Muers, Mike Higton, Ben Quash and Nick Adams whose love for theology parallels and stimulates my own. A special thanks goes to Chad Pecknold whose poignant theological sense not to mention flair for titles and covers has been a great source of support. Claire Katz, Leora Batnitkzy, Nancy Levene, Michael Gottsegen, Barbara Galli and Gregory Kaplan have all been great conversation partners at one stage or another and Brendan Corbalis provided me with a wonderful place to write in our Greenwich Village apartment. Finally, I am more than grateful for my eternal friendship with Martin

Kavka whose brilliance and rigor has influenced much of this manuscript and whose phone conversations get me through each day of every semester.

I am grateful to my family: my parents Rita and Erwin, as well as Jim, Elizabeth and my brother for their love and support of the project over the years, not to mention their humor, in particular my brother's constant reminder to 'use verbs' and my mother's tireless suggestion to mention her in the text, somewhere.

At T&T Clark I owe a mighty thanks to Philip Law for his help in the production of the manuscript and willingness to consider new theological perspectives. Sarah Douglas has proven to be the most efficient and professional editorial aid with whom I have ever worked. Thanks, too, go to the design team at T&T Clark for their terrific job on the cover.

Finally, my greatest thanks go to my ever patient and always understanding husband Andy and my wonderful and joyous daughter Anna for giving me our home. This book is dedicated to both of you.

# Introduction: Grounding a Politics of Praise

## A. Re-asserting the Labor of Reason

Ever since Stephen Carter published his *The Culture of Disbelief*, religionists in America have been challenged to re-visit the age-old question of the relation between faith and reason. More recently, this same invitation has been presented by Jeffrey Stout's highly acclaimed *Democracy and Tradition*. On the surface both books address the relation between religion and the state. There is, however, a necessary connection between the two concerns. At the heart of Carter's and Stout's arguments is the fundamental awareness of the extent to which religious beliefs are dismissed as irrational and therefore insignificant and inappropriate in the context of public discourse. Both Carter and Stout see this claim for what it is, an ideological prejudice left over from enlightenment biases against religion and more specifically against perceived impressions of unbridled ecclesiastical authority. In their own ways both Carter and Stout challenge liberal democracy in the abstract and its non-religious members to invite religionists to voice their political positions on religious grounds. Neither Carter nor Stout think religionists ought to be able to use sheer political force to assert their religiously funded positions. Rather, Carter and Stout invite religionists to expose the patterns of reasoning that emerge out of their traditions and give rise to their varying political concerns. Consciously or not, both Carter and Stout have done more than ask religionists to actively participate as religionists in public discourse. Carter and Stout have challenged religionists to identify what their reasoning practices are and how these reasoning practices emerge out of their particular religious traditions. In other words, they have challenged religionists to re-examine the faith–reason question.

Needless to say, the question of the relation between reason and faith and the extent to which the rationality of a religious tradition legitimizes its

1

participation in the public square is an old question because it is a thorny question. Neither Judaism nor Christianity are strangers to apologetic appeals to rationality that ultimately destroy the fabric of their own traditions. The primary objective of this book is take a first step in demonstrating how Judaism and Christianity fund a rationality that emerges out of their particular scriptural texts and liturgical practices by examining the theological projects of Franz Rosenzweig and Karl Barth, both of whom espouse what I refer to as a theology of testimony.[1] As will become clearer below, by rationality I mean capable of self-critique and capable of discerning the claims of those outside one's religious tradition. To the extent that this larger project succeeds, both traditions will be able to lay claim to reasoning practices that are neither parasitic on dominant strains in secular philosophy nor disguises for fanatical thinking. Moreover, equipped and aware of these reasoning practices, both Judaism and Christianity will be better suited to assert their religious positions within the political sphere without falling prey to modes of reasoning and/or ideologies that undermine either tradition.

At the outset it is important to note that this book will not attempt to convince secularists that religion in general or Judaism and Christianity in particular are rational. Neither will the book assess how the rationality of a theology of testimony is or is not commensurate with the standards of rationality at work in contemporary American discourse. This would require a more extended investigation of the scriptural and liturgical reasoning practices that follow revelation in each tradition as well as a thoroughgoing examination of the standards and practices of rationality within the contemporary American discourse, both of which exceed the bounds of this discussion.[2] Nonetheless, towards the end of the book I will suggest a number of ways that Jewish and Christian theologians may build theoretically and practically on the foundation established by Rosenzweig and Barth in order to begin to address these wider questions.

## B. Rosenzweig–Barth

In his book *Resisting History*, David Myers argues that the period of the Weimar Republic in Germany was captivated by a great 'spirit of innovation'.[3] Above all, Myers notes this spirit of innovation assumed theological expression in the work of a range of noteworthy Jewish and Christian thinkers including Franz Rosenzweig, Hans and Rudolf Ehrenberg, Eugen Rosenstock-Huessy, Emil Brunner, Rudolf Bultmann and Karl Barth. This group of thinkers, Myers argues, 'sought new outlets for their simmering discontent with previous modes of theological discourse'.[4] In the past twenty years there has been a renaissance in Rosenzweig studies reflecting his contribution to this creative chapter in theological history. Current studies have begun to reveal the truly revolutionary character of Rosenzweig's *The Star of Redemption* and later letters and essays. The list of scholars who have contributed to this renaissance in Rosenzweig studies includes Stéphane Mosès, Robert Gibbs, David Novak, Leora Batnitzky and Barbara Galli. Beyond comparisons with Buber, Rosenzweig's work has now been placed in conversation with the work of Heidegger, Levinas, Weber, Nietzsche and Benjamin among others. Much of this renaissance has consisted in placing Rosenzweig in his intellectual context.[5] Up until this point, however, there has no been no complete work comparing Rosenzweig's thought to his most methodologically similar contemporary, Karl Barth. This book offers a comparative reading of the work of Franz Rosenzweig and Karl Barth and uses this new reading as the basis for a philosophically justified theopolitics.[6]

More specifically, I argue that both Rosenzweig and Barth reject modern rationalism's efforts to link religion and rationalism as well as religion and the state. By contrast, Rosenzweig and Barth assert what I will call a 'theology of testimony' that emerges out of the context of divine election. Additionally, the book identifies both Rosenzweig and Barth as dialectical theologians whose radical re-interpretation of the Word of God allows them to present portraits of their respective traditions as both meaningful and non-dogmatic. Finally, I argue that this theology of ethical testimony has crucial relevance to contemporary Jewish and Christian work in political theology insofar as it grounds what I call a politics of praise.

## C. The Theology of Testimony

*Revelation and Theopolitics: Barth, Rosenzweig and the Politics of Praise* argues that both Rosenzweig and Barth present a theology of testimony. By a theology of testimony I mean a theology that is based on the notion that knowledge of God is possible only in the context of the ethical labor of the elect individual who seeks through her moral endeavor to testify to the loving act of the transcendent God. Although on the surface this appears to be an argument that revives Kant, I argue that the problem with Kant's account of the practical life is that it grounds ethics in a morally autonomous, rational will for whom God is no more than the guarantor of the theoretical viability of an individual's practical act.[7] More similar to Hermann Cohen's theology of correlation, Barth's and Rosenzweig's theology of testimony continues in the tradition of Cohen's practical theology but develops this practical theology through a return to the biblical sources rather than from within the system of critical idealism. In opening sections of the book I argue that Cohen's theology of revelation and acknowledgment continues and expands upon the tradition of practical theology initiated by Immanuel Kant. Nonetheless, Cohen's effort to identify moral life with religious devotion cannot express the reality of the God who loves and forgives us and whom we love and need in order to engage in the pursuit of our infinite moral task as it is enacted in our lives as members of the modern state.

By contrast, Rosenzweig and Barth reject Cohen's neo-Kantian emphasis on moral self-reliance and redirect theology away from critical idealism back to the biblical sources to provide a philosophically consistent basis for a theology of the loving and forgiving God. Both Rosenzweig and Barth share a similar phenomenology of revelation, rooted in their respective readings of scripture. According to both theologians, revelation is the irruptive encounter between a meta-rational, loving God and the individual chosen to receive this love. Furthermore, as a result of this unprecedented encounter with a loving Other, the individual called upon experiences the shock of her former ignorance of love and comes to awareness of her own sin. Consequently, in view of her sinfulness, the individual self relinquishes any trust in her own cognitive or moral abilities. In the context of this rupture of her sense of herself and her world, the individual can assert no independent knowledge of the reality she experiences. This account, although theologically superior to Kant and Cohen, still has to deal with the problem of how the believer can come to know anything about God.

The answer is found in Barth's and Rosenzweig's understanding of witness or testimony. Incapable of generating any individual response, the elected individual can only affirm or deny the reality before her. As sovereign over her, God's reality commands her to respond. But the God of revelation is not simply sovereign but loving as well, and strengthened by the love she experiences the individual feels commanded to affirm this loving God. Witness therefore is an obedient response to a loving and commanding God. This is not to say that either Rosenzweig or Barth reduce religious life to blind obedience. Rather, for Rosenzweig, theological witness is expressed and related to the world through a testimony of pragmatic verification. For Barth, witness takes place through the church's self-critical effort to articulate the Word of God in the world prior to the kingdom of God.

For Barth and Rosenzweig, witness is an essentially practical but non-linguistic deed. For both theologians, revelation is an event of divine love and not the dispensation of information about the nature of God's being. The God of revelation is the God whose being it is to act, and specifically to act lovingly toward humanity. Consequently, testimony to this reality must be practical in nature. In this context, knowledge of God can mean no more than the soul's ability to witness to the act of this divine and loving Other and thereby acknowledge its reality as transcendent to its own. Practical testimony of this kind cannot consist in the person's self-determined response, for the experience of revelation has shattered the self's autonomy. The elect individual can only acknowledge the act of this Other through an act of ethical witness that points away from the self to the transcendent reality that has affected it. Consequently, theological knowledge of testimony is not rooted in a commensurability between God's nature and ours.

## D. Theology of Testimony: The Word of God: Ritual, Sacrament and Community

If revelation is an event of a meta-rational, loving God, it would seem to exceed the bounds of language. Nonetheless, neither Rosenzweig nor Barth dismiss the significance of language for theology. On the contrary, both thinkers radically re-invent the notion of the Word of God for their respective traditions, what is Torah for Rosenzweig and Jesus for Barth. Both Rosenzweig's Torah and Barth's Jesus provide two essential functions for theology: 1) they are the necessary and dialectical medium of the revelation event and 2) they provide the basis for the forms of ritual, sacrament and community that bridge the divide between the human order and the divine covenantal order established in revelation.

Both Barth and Rosenzweig understand the Word of God to be the medium of divine revelation. Without a medium for revelation, the transcendent God remains either remote and inaccessible or, conversely, strictly incarnate and no longer transcendent. However, the medium itself must not compromise God's transcendence. As a result, both thinkers claim that the Word of God must function dialectically, i.e. it points to that which exceeds its own boundaries thereby opening up a space for the revelation of divine love or grace. In addition, I argue, both Barth and

Rosenzweig claim that it is the dialectical or finite character of the Word of God which allows this Word to be the site of the divine commandment to love and praise God.

## E. The Politics of Praise

My previously published work has shown ways in which contemporary Jewish–Christian dialogue can gain from the theology of witness presented in Rosenzweig and Barth.[8] In the final chapter of this book, I extend those arguments by drawing out the implications of a theology of witness on discussions of political theology. I claim that witness can ground a 'politics of praise' that uniquely identifies how Judaism and Christianity can contribute productively to the political environment without falling prey to either Constantinian imperialism or secular invisibility.

According to both Rosenzweig and Barth, the key to Judaism's and Christianity's productive participation in the political arena rests in their ability to engage in a covenantal life of testimony or praise of God. Since this praise is centered on the glorification of the divine name, it can never be self-interested or allied with realpolitik without ceasing to be testimony about God in God's transcendent otherness. A politics of praise posits an ongoing critique of the state in its self-understanding as a structural representation of a human moral order.

Nevertheless, this does not mean that Judaism and Christianity posit themselves as ideal moral systems or disengage themselves from the political arena. While both Rosenzweig and Barth appreciate how their traditions help us make sense of our practical faith in God's divine moral order, they also realize that these forms can never be recognized as the unique place and/or singular means of achieving this moral order. Consequently, in addition to the glorification of the name, a politics of praise requires a vigilant social criticism of all human ideological systems, Judaism and Christianity included, as well as an ongoing commitment to the pursuit of justice in the society at large.

This is not my imposition of contemporary liberalism onto Rosenzweig and Barth. In his own day Rosenzweig rejected both the assimilationist politics of Hermann Cohen as well as popular currents of political and cultural Zionism.[9] Even Rosenzweig's references to Israel as a 'blood-community' (*Blutgemeinschaft*) must be understood within the larger dialectical context of his work: Israel is only a blood community in the service of the transcendent and commanding God.

Likewise, Barth's Confessing Church also provides a powerful example of the politics of praise. Having participated in drafting the Barmen Declaration in 1934, Barth helped create the only church in Germany willing to take a vocal stand against the Nazi regime through its confessed belief in what God had done in Jesus Christ. Remarking on the Confessing Church, Barth later said, 'The Confessing Church was, so to speak, only a witness. The emphasis of everything lies in the fact that Jesus Christ has said something. The Church lives by the fact that it hears the voice of this "I" and not by its own authority.'[10]

Religious life faces enormous challenges in our time. Judaism and Christianity are challenged not only to remain alive and active, but to provide a voice of criticism and faith. The theology of testimony advanced in Rosenzweig's and Barth's work offers a valuable model to Jewish and Christian communities who strive to meet these challenges and lays the foundation for a radical transformation of Judaism's and Christianity's role in contemporary American discourse.

## Notes

1 I see my work as contributing to the effort made by a community of scholars whose work is committed to examining the character of reason exercised within religious texts and practices including but not limited to David Novak, Peter Ochs, David Weiss Halivni, Robert Gibbs, Martin Kavka, Chad Pecknold, Nicholas Adams, Oliver Davies and others.

2 Currently, I am engaged in two projects whose objective is to examine the character of liturgical rationality and its relation to religion's role in the public sphere. The first is Chad Pecknold, Randi Rashkover (eds), *Liturgy, Time and the Politics of Redemption* (Grand Rapids: Eerdmans, forthcoming 2006). This volume examines particular liturgical practices in Judaism and Christianity and investigates the relation between these practices, the hermeneutical dimension of scriptural study and the character of political activity they inspire. The second book is a monograph entitled *Ritual and the Public Square: Overcoming the Fear of Ceremonialism*. This book examines more deeply the enlightenment biases that dismiss liturgical practice as irrational and insignificant to public discourse and offers a careful analysis of the philosophical dimension of Jewish and Christian liturgical practice. Moreover, the book argues that the philosophical character of Jewish–Christian liturgical practice parallels the pragmatic modes of reasoning present in Deweyian democractic theory and when viewed together provide a basis for a new public theology that challenges the enlightenment basis for the liberal state and its dismissal of religious ceremonialism.

3  David N. Myers, *Resisting History: Historicism and Its Discontents in German–Jewish Thought* (Princeton: Princeton University Press, 2003), p. 94.

4  Myers, *Resisting History*, p. 95.

5  For comparisons between Rosenzweig and Heidegger and Cassirer, see Karl Lowith, 'Martin Heidegger and Franz Rosenzweig on Temporality and Eternity', *Philosophy and Phenomenological Research* 3 (1942/43), pp. 53–77 and Peter Gordon, *Rosenzweig and Heidegger: Between Judaism and German Philosophy* (Los Angeles: California University Press, 2003). For comparisons between Rosenzweig and Weber, Cohen and Levinas, see Robert Gibbs, *Correlations in Rosenzweig and Levinas* (Princeton: Princeton University Press, 1992). For comparisons between Rosenzweig and Levinas and Nietzsche, see Richard Cohen, 'Rosenzweig vs. Nietzsche', in *Elevations: The Height of the Good in Rosenzweig and Levinas* (Chicago: The University of Chicago Press, 1994). For an account of Rosenzweig within the wider German–Jewish community of theological inquiry see David N. Myers, *Resisting History*.

6  The work that comes closest to providing such an examination is Graham Ward, *Barth, Derrida and the Language of Theology* (Cambridge: Cambridge University Press, 1995). Ward's book compares what he calls Rosenzweig's dialogical sacramentalism to what he deems the more critical and less logocentric theology of the Word found in Barth's *Church Dogmatics*. As this book will claim, however, Ward incorrectly identifies Rosenzweig as a dialogical thinker and this failure prohibits Ward from offering an authentic comparison between Barth and Rosenzweig.

7  See Immanuel Kant, *Critique of Practical Reason* (trans. Lewis White Beck; Indianapolis: Bobbs-Merrill Educational Publishing, 1983).

8  See my 'Jewish Responses to Jewish–Christian Dialogue: A Look Ahead to the 20th Century', *Cross Currents*, vol. 50, nos.1/2, (2000), pp. 211–21.

9  My anti-Zionist reading of Rosenzweig differs therefore from the effort made by Leora Batnitzky to affiliate Rosenzweig with Zionism. For Batnitzky's argument see her *Idolatry and Representation: The Philosophy of Franz Rosenzweig Reconsidered* (Princeton: Princeton University Press, 1999). For an extended comparison between my reading and Batnitzky's see Chapter 6.

10  Karl Barth, *Church Dogmatics: The Doctrine of God*, vol. II. I. (trans. T. H. L. Parker *et al.*; Edinburgh: T&T Clark, 1994), p. 177.

## Chapter 1

# Practical Theology and the Love of God: Hermann Cohen's Influence on Rosenzweig and Barth

To assert that Rosenzweig and Barth share a vision of theology rooted in the ethical witness to an electing God is not merely to point out a coincidence. Rather, it reflects their shared inheritance of Hermann Cohen's practical theology. It has been well-documented that both Franz Rosenzweig and Karl Barth studied with Hermann Cohen.[1] Arguably the father of post-liberal Jewish and Christian theology, Hermann Cohen's work offers a stunning mix of the rigor of critical idealism and a deep insight into the religious depth of the Jewish sources and liturgical life. It is little wonder that Rosenzweig and Barth both actively sought his influence. Unfortunately, despite a tireless campaign to wed the two world-views without compromising the integrity of either, Cohen's theology prioritizes the standards and methods of critical idealism over and against his unwavering love for the prophetic rationality and morality of the Jewish sources. We begin our inquiry into the theological transformations effected by Rosenzweig and Barth by illuminating Cohen's grand effort to reconcile neo-Kantian rationalism with the sources of Judaism and marking the philosophical collapse of this effort and the religio-political alliance that results.

The centerpiece of Cohen's theology is his concept of acknowledgment (*Bekenntnis*). Cohen's notion of acknowledgment as the practical devotion to God is the crucial link between Cohen's philosophy of ethical autonomy and Cohen's philosophy of religion. Cohen's theology of acknowledgment acts as the transition between Kantian practical theology and the theologies of revelation and testimony in Barth and Rosenzweig.[2]

First, by locating theological knowledge in a moral activity which, while autonomous, expresses devotion to God as source of the holy ideal, Cohen's theology of revelation and acknowledgment continues and expands upon the tradition of practical theology initiated by Immanuel Kant. Appreciative of Kant's moral theology, Cohen nonetheless argues that Kant's theology fell short of affirming the primacy of God as well as the devotion to that God afforded through practical correlation. Still, Cohen's theology of acknowledgment does not afford a healthy marriage between critical idealism and the Jewish sources. Cohen's effort to identify moral life with religious devotion cannot express the reality of the God who loves us and whom we love. Both Barth and Rosenzweig will inherit Cohen's analysis of theology as moral action even as they transform it into what I refer to as testimony or witness.

An extension of his theology of acknowledgment in correlation, Cohen's theology of divine forgiveness also advances theologically over Kant's discussion of forgiveness in his *Religion Within the Limits of Reason Alone*. By his own admission, Cohen's theology of forgiveness through confession marks the deepest and most meaningful expression of the divine–human correlation.[3] Nonetheless, like his account of the love of God, Cohen's account of divine forgiveness and repentance reveals a tension within his application of critical idealism to the sources of Judaism. Cohen attempts to navigate between moral autonomy and divine forgiveness through his account of the relation between the self who repents and her need for a God who guarantees the success of her repentant action. Nonetheless, Cohen cannot render self-sanctification and divine forgiveness simultaneously meaningful without betraying either the language of the Jewish tradition or the categories of critical idealism.

Consequently, the argument here is that, like his appropriation of the religious language of love or devotion to God, Cohen's appropriation of the language of divine forgiveness creates problems for his overall moral and philosophical project. The tendency in modern Jewish scholarship to retain the portrait of Cohen as a strict rationalist has blurred readers' ability to appreciate this tension in his theology.[4] Read this way, Cohen's work provides a basis for Rosenzweig's and Barth's theology of testimony. Rosenzweig and Barth are both indebted to Cohen's analysis of moral theology, yet their return to a more authentic biblical account of revelation as the event of divine love and moral authority followed by and responded to by a human moral testimony allows them to bypass the problems inherent in Cohen's idealist view of religion.

## A. Cohen's Theology of Acknowledgment and the Move Beyond Kant

Although Cohen is best known as one of the leaders of the 'back-to-Kant' movement in nineteenth-century philosophy, one of his greatest contributions to the Kantian tradition was his desire and ability to more deeply investigate the God of the religious believer necessarily neglected in Kant's *Critiques*. Committed to a philosophical articulation of the God of the Jewish tradition, Cohen advances a portrait of what he calls the unique God or the monotheistic God of the Jews. David Novak makes this point. 'The problem with this [the Kantian] idea of God, for Cohen, is that it compromises the primacy of God by reducing God to functioning as the means to the end of human happiness. Such a "God" hardly satisfies the affirmation of the primacy of God insisted on by...Judaism in particular...'[5] Cohen wants to reassert a philosophical account of God without returning to either the conditions of natural theology that Kant dismissed in his *Critique of Pure Reason* or to the portrait of God as merely the product of moral need argued by Kant in his *Critique of Practical Reason*.[6]

On his crusade to rehabilitate the monotheistic God, Cohen begins his *Religion of Reason Out of the Sources of Judaism* presupposing the philosophical system he had thus far constructed in his logic and ethics. More specifically, Cohen's philosophy of religion presupposes both 1) the notion of God conceived within ethics and 2) the method of critical idealism.

First, a full appreciation of the extent to which Cohen's philosophy of religion expands Kant's practical theology requires an assessment of the theological conclusion reached in Cohen's ethics. For Cohen, the question of truth or God only arises in the context of the science of ethics. As the science that analyzes the relation between the ought as an end or an ideal and the moral activity that realizes this end or ideal, ethics assumes the continuity of the material world or nature. As the realization of what ought to be in the material world, ethical action assumes that the difference between reality as it is and reality as it ought to be may be bridged. From the vantage point of ethical action, this coordination of reality as it is and as it ought to be is an infinite task that is never fully present to it. Nonetheless, ethical action would not be reasonable unless it could assume the coordination of the 'is' and the 'ought'. Cohen calls this necessary assumption of the harmonization of nature and ethics, the idea of 'God'. 'God means that nature endures with the same certainty through which morality is eternal.'[7] This concept of God does not expand significantly beyond that presented by Kant in the *Critique of Practical Reason*. Like the God described in Kant's *Critique of Practical Reason*, the God in Cohen's ethics is postulated as the necessary condition of the rationality of moral endeavor. While Cohen rejects Kant's postulate of God as that which guarantees human *happiness,* he does not reject Kant's notion of God as postulate per se. Andrea Poma makes this point: 'Cohen never accepted Kant's conception of the idea of God as an ethical postulate, but only because his postulate was linked to the subjective end of the highest good, and thus of happiness, which for Cohen must not be part of the ethical end. He did, however, always accept the function of the idea of God as the ground of the objective unity between nature and moral action ...'[8] In order to make sense of its own infinite pursuit, ethics alone can do little more than postulate God as the necessarily assumed ground of the coordination of nature and morality.

Second, not only does philosophy presuppose the notion of God as understood in ethics, but it also presupposes the method of critical idealism in general. Cohen's application of the method of critical idealism to the study of religion is the key to the expansion of his theology beyond that conceived by ethics. By presupposing the method of critical idealism Cohen assumes three things: 1) the prior discoveries of critical idealism, i.e. what Cohen calls the 'unity of consciousness' as well as the notion that, as a part of culture, religion will contribute to the development of that unity; 2) the application of the method of critical idealism to religion – that is, religion as a reality is taken as the factual material to be analyzed and idealized in relation to the conceptual scheme above presupposed; and 3) the relevance of Judaism's literary sources as the most useful material for such analysis so far as these sources introduce elements of religious life that, when idealized, best contribute to the unity of consciousness.

It is well known that Cohen's *Religion of Reason Out of the Sources of Judaism* is a testament to his refusal to dissolve or reduce the study of religion into ethics.[9] Nonetheless, Cohen did maintain that as an aspect of human culture, religion contributes uniquely to the development of humanity toward its own fulfillment. Cohen's philosophy of religion therefore was determined by the portrait of humanity's development toward its own fulfillment as this had already been developed in the application of critical idealism to science and ethics. The study of religion is, Cohen says, guided by the concept or reason – those concepts already identified as the conditions of the possibility of various forms of human knowledge. 'Reason itself is the problem that exists for every concept, for every possible knowledge of a concept, which consequently has to be presupposed and set up as a foundation for the concept of religion and for the concept of Judaism.'[10] In Michael Zank's words, '[R]eligion is questioned as to its contribution to the constitution of the human being as a member of the human community conceived as a totality of ethical persons.'[11]

The second aspect at play in Cohen's presupposition of the system of idealism regards the application of this system to the study of religion. If philosophy is to be the practice of discerning the legitimacy or validity of any given body of facts or knowledge, it must attempt to discern the conditions of the possibility of those facts and consequently must begin with the facts as its raw material for analysis. This is as true for the study of religion as it is for law or science. 'The philosophy of religion has scientific truthfulness only when it strives objectively and impartially to refer to its sources, to excavate them through its own research and to illuminate them through its own criticism.'[12] Echoing Cohen, Michael Zank points to the necessity of the scriptural sources for philosophy of religion and says, '[I]f religion is to be understood as religion of reason, it must be "found" in a type of material analogous to the "facts" of science, law and art.'[13]

Third, Cohen's presupposition of critical idealism means not only the philosophical analysis of the raw data of religion in general, but the particular analysis of the factual or literary material of Judaism in particular. While Cohen acknowledges that all religions when idealized can be shown to contribute to the religion of reason or what is religion's contribution to the development of humanity's ultimate telos, he argues that Judaism's literary tradition provides the original source of those aspects of religion that most contribute to furthering humanity's teleological development. Judaism is, Cohen says, 'a source [which] does not shut itself off from other religious monuments, but rather becomes an original source for other sources'.[14] Not only do Judaism's literary sources offer a reliable and finite body of data available for idealization but, more significantly, these sources introduce facets of religious life that most directly coordinate with the presupposed perspective of the unity of consciousness.

The presupposition of the method of critical idealism is the key to the expansion of Cohen's theological perspective beyond that offered in the ethics. The application of the method of critical idealism to the study of religion in general and Judaism in particular, permits Cohen to introduce the religious life into his perspective of the unity of consciousness. While ethics could only appreciate God as a regulative idea from the vantage point

13

of its own finite effort to realize its ultimate end, religious believers and Jews in particular claim to directly encounter the Absolute in their religious life and document these encounters in their literary sources. The method of critical idealism guarantees that Cohen's conceptual rubric will come into contact with this literary expression of the Absolute and will consequently advance a transcendental analysis that asserts the primacy of God as experienced and described in the Jewish sources. From the perspective of ethics, God is the ground of the unity of nature and morality. But ethics can say nothing more about God as the ground of this coordination. Religion, however, confronts the Absolute qua Absolute. For religion, God is the ground of the unity of nature and morality so far as or because God is Absolute Being or the unity of the is and the ought. The application of critical idealism to religion permits an exploration (albeit a critical exploration – that is, one that strictly deduces the conditions of the possibility of the religious reality) into the character of God as Absolute Being and the relation between God as the Absolute Being and the world of nature and morality. Thus, while in the *Critique of Practical Reason* Kant could postulate God as 'cause of the whole of nature, itself distinct from nature, which contains the ground of the exact coincidence of happiness with morality ... ',[15] Kant's refusal to apply the method of critical idealism to religion denies him access to the reality of the Absolute as lived and thereby prohibits him from engaging in further reflection on the nature of God as the Absolute unity of being and ideal.[16]

It is important to note that the marriage between idea and religious phenomena will not permit Cohen to advance a metaphysical analysis. Any theological perspective afforded a critical philosophy of religion must be limited to an analysis of the conditions of the possibility of the Absolute as the Absolute is available to religious believers and not from a metaphysical perspective. This having been said, the application of critical idealism to the literary sources of Judaism inevitably expands the recognition of the Absolute and permits the assertion of God as primary in a way that remained impossible for Kant who did not apply the method of critical idealism to religion but considered religious ideas only in relation to ethics. If, Andrea Poma says, 'logic and ethics only glimpse the truth and God on the horizon since they only remain faithful to the methodological principle of the distinction between being and what ought to be, the philosophy of religion starts off from the fact of religion and, thus, from its viewpoint, that is that of the unity of being and what ought to be'.[17]

### a. *God As the Absolute Being: The Unique God*

Cohen's concept of the Unique God is the originary point of theological advance over Kantian theology. The literary sources of Judaism attest to the reality of the one God who is Absolute Being. Cohen's critical analysis idealizes this monotheistic God as the one God whose Being is the absolute inclusion of being and ideal or end. As such, this God asserts primacy over both the material and the moral orders.

As Absolute Being, the monotheistic God of the Jewish sources can never be identified with our world of spatio-temporal existence. Consequently, while Greek philosophers such as Xenophanes overcome the polytheism of earlier thought by asserting the Oneness of God, such an assertion fails to capture the transcendent reality of the monotheistic God, for Xenophanes' God remains identified with the world – united with the cosmos and thereby conditioned by temporal and spatial reality. The transcendent God, says Cohen, cannot be identical with the world. While Xenophanes was correct to identify God with the concept of Being, he could not extricate the world from these two concepts. According to Cohen, God's uniqueness is more than the oneness of his Being – it is also the transcendence of God's Being in relation to everything else. Cohen claims, '[O]nly God has Being. Only God is Being. And there is no unity that would be an identity between God and world . . . There is only one kind of being . . . God is this unique being.'[18]

However, uniqueness not only implies oneness but also exclusivity or 'incomparability'.[19] In this sense, there are no other gods than the one God and God's being transcends all existence. 'Uniqueness entails the distinction between being and existence . . . The unique being of God is such that it does not admit any mixture, any connection with sensible existence.'[20] Consequently, the reality of the unique God cannot be proven by either an ontological argument that attributes necessary existence to a perfect being, nor by a cosmological argument that recognizes God as the maker and participator in the world of things. For Cohen, God's transcendence is secured by his ideality. The transcendent and unique God must maintain purity of Being unaffected by worldly conditions. Therefore, the unique God cannot change. 'By being opposed to time, God's being also excludes change.'[21]

God's exclusivity does not, however, preclude God's relating to the world. Indeed, this relation is necessary, according to Cohen. To be unique is to be unique relative to something else, and for Cohen this something else for God is the world. But if God is Being, what is the world? For Cohen,

15

God's Being maintains logical primacy over the world. Nonetheless, one first discovers God's Being from observation in the world of becoming. The world is becoming – that which changes and, as such, poses the problem of its own origin. This is not to say, however, that God's Being is deduced from the world as its temporal or historical cause. Rather, Cohen models his understanding of God's relation to the world after Kant's categories for empirical knowledge and asserts that God's Being is the logical cause or originative principle of the world of becoming. From this perspective it makes sense to say that a principle of logical origin functions as the condition of the possibility of the existence of the world. Accordingly, this principle establishes the transcendent relation between the God of Being and the world of becoming without implicating God as a first cause in the actual substance of the world. As Being, God is the logical condition of the possibility of causality and not that first cause that participates in becoming itself. 'The unique being of God now means to us that he contains in himself the fundamental condition for causality.'[22]

After establishing this relationship between Being and Becoming or God and the world (such that God's transcendence is determined), Cohen attempts to demonstrate how this relationship accounts for the biblical tradition's understanding of creation. For help, Cohen turns to Maimonides' negative theology. Challenged by the biblical language that implicates God the Creator in the material substance of the world, Cohen looks to Maimonides' effort to rationalize the tradition and reconcile philosophy with creation.

As a logical principle, the God of Being cannot possess positive attributes which would, by virtue of either their reference to material existence or their plurality, challenge God's ideality or unity. According to Cohen, medieval philosophers knew that 'the rejection of any positive attributes of God was intended to protect monotheism against being weakened or obscured'.[23] However, this approach risks the ultimate negation of God as Being itself. Is it possible to assert the transcendence and reality of God's Being without granting God any positive characteristics?

For Cohen, the key to solving the problem rests in Maimonides' use of the concept of privation. While other philosophers struggled to assert God's originative, logical being from a negation of God's positive attributes, Maimonides began by asserting the negation of the privative attribute. Maimonides' method of negative theology guards against the subsequent assertion of any positive content after the assertion of the negative attribute. To say merely that 'God is not corporeal' suggests the possibility that God's nature retains the content of incorporeality. Alternatively, negating the negation, Kenneth Seeskin tells us, 'puts God outside the scope of the predicate or anything like it'.[24] This is to say that for Maimonides, 'It is not the positive attributes that are negated but those of privation. God is not inert.'[25] While Maimonides does not employ this method in order to argue for the doctrine of creation,[26] Cohen identifies God as the originative principle with the denial of God's inertia thereby arguing that as an originative principle, God 'is sufficient to produce things beside himself'.[27] From this, Cohen attempts to reconcile the notions of God as creator and God as logical originative principle. 'God is recognized through the attribute of being not inert, then he becomes recognizable as creator; thus the idea of creation is taken into the concept of God . . . And becoming now has its basis in this being as the originative principle.'[28] It is important to note that Cohen's theology of the creator God remains the product of a negative theology. As we will see below, Rosenzweig and Barth share Cohen's appraisal of the limits of theoretical knowledge of the Creator and agree that theology begins with a Kantian type critique of theoretical knowledge. Despite differences in their definitions of revelation, all three theologians agree that a critique of theoretical knowledge must precede an inquiry into the role of revelation and the primacy of the practical knowledge of God that will emerge from it. For Cohen, knowledge of God's attributes is not a product of our theoretical knowledge, but only derives from our moral reason.

### b. *Revelation and the Creation of Human Reason*
According to Cohen, God's uniqueness is not exhausted by its relation to the becoming of the natural world but extends to God's creation of rational human beings. While as natural beings humans have their origin in God as creator of the world, human beings are also rational and their relation to God as rational further defines God's uniqueness. For Cohen, the question of God's particular relation to human reason inaugurates a discussion of God's role not only as the origin of the physical world but also as the origin of the *purpose* of this world for, as we shall see, the ultimate purpose of human reason is to strive to realize God's holiness in the world. God is the transcendent origin of the scientific and the ethical spheres of life. Both spheres are rational and derive from God.

Cohen uses the term 'revelation' to designate the particular creation of man's reason by God – the connection between God's Being and, in this case, human beings' becoming as rational creatures. But if revelation constitutes another instance of creation, like the creation of the world, it can mean nothing other than a logical relation with God as originative principle. More specifically, revelation is the originative precondition for human beings' theoretical and moral reason. It is not a material or historical interaction between God and human beings.

> Just as being is the necessary presupposition for becoming, so is it also . . . for the becoming [of] a man. It is only by virtue of revelation that the rational creature, man, comes to be. This statement is of the same logical power as the one about the uniqueness of being as substance namely, it has to be the presupposition for becoming.[29]

By revelation Cohen means nothing other than the logical condition of the possibility of constructive human theoretical *and* moral reason, although to say that God is the originative principle of theoretical reason differs somewhat from what it means to say that God is the originative principle of moral reason. God is the creator of theoretical reason in the sense that God works as the logical first principle in what Cohen takes to be the idealist construction of the world from reason. However, as I will discuss in greater detail below, moral reason involves an action of the will and not a use of theoretical reason. Consequently, as the origin of moral reason, God functions as that primary norm or moral ideal – the condition of the possibility of autonomous human morality. Cohen's analysis of revelation affords a portrait of God as both transcendent and primary with respect to human reason, in that, as logical or teleological origin, God's being stands distinct from the becoming which it makes possible, as well as in relation to human being so far as human reason is capable of responding to divine primacy.

How does this view of revelation also incorporate a concept of the relation between humanity and God? While revelation is, Cohen says, a 'continuation of creation',[30] it differs from creation by virtue of the particular character of human reason. In revelation, Cohen tells us, 'God in no way reveals himself in something, but only to something, in relation to something'.[31] This revealing *to* man invites the possibility of the human reception of the revelation – the possibility of a human response. Furthermore, in revelation, God reveals reason. Consequently, unlike creation, revelation inaugurates a *relationship* between God as the origin of reason and a human's response to this revelation by means of her employment of that reason. Cohen calls this relation, 'correlation'.

Thus the question of creation, in the case of man now concerns knowledge. And with regard to knowledge the question concerns the relation of man to God. The serpent calls it identity; our philosophical language calls it correlation ... A reciprocal relation exists between man and God ... and in the case of man, God's being must be the presupposition for knowledge. And knowledge is concerned not only with the knowledge of nature, but is also concerned with the 'knowledge of good and evil'.[32]

Therefore, whenever human beings employ their theoretical or moral knowledge, they enter into relation with God – which is to say they exploit the possibility of constructive theoretical or moral reason provided by the originative idea, be it the theoretical principle or the moral ideal. Correlation is a *logical* interdependence of concepts and not an active relationship between God and human beings. God is the originative principle, taken up and exploited by the rational human being. '[C]orrelation ... is the term for *concepts* [emphasis mine] of reciprocal relation. A reciprocal relation exists between man and God ...'[33]

By understanding God's relation to human beings as the condition of the possibility of their theoretical or moral reasoning, Cohen enriches his concept of God as creator by identifying God as revealer. However, by equating revelation and correlation, Cohen demands that revelation be understood in strictly spiritual and not material or historical terms. Accordingly, any identification of revelation with an historical event whereby God revealed himself compromises God's pure ideality and consequently, his transcendence. The revelation event must be demythologized in order to recognize its true meaning. More significantly for the analysis to follow, Cohen's rejection of revelation as a divine act or event also reflects his interest in maintaining the possibility of ethical autonomy. Revelation cannot refer to any kind of divine act of love or command that might serve as an exterior motive for human moral action. Consequently, revelation is not to be understood as an historical event of love or command but in strictly spiritualized terms as the creation or awakening of human reason. Just as monotheism precludes the notion of a God speaking in history at Sinai, so it also means that to receive revelation is not to hear God speaking but rather to awaken to one's rational ability. 'If man is to be God's creation and if revelation is to be possible with regard to him, it can only be through his reason; consequently, revelation itself can only be thought of as the revelation to reason.'[34] The giving of the Torah, Cohen says, is not the physical offering of a speaking God, but rather the notion of the 'eternal presupposition' of the statutes and ordinances of the Jewish way of life, i.e. the originative moral norm that provides the condition of the possibility of the rational Jewish moral life. 'This eternal, as the foundation of reason in all of its content, the Jew calls revelation ... The technical term is "the giving of the Torah". This giving does not contain a mystery ... There is nothing said about a mystery, nothing about unveiling ... Revelation is the sign of reason ... '[35]

### c. *The Holy God*

Our introduction to Cohen's understanding of creation and revelation behind us, the question emerges, given correlation, what does knowledge of God mean for Cohen? Above we have discussed the extents and limitations concerning rational knowledge of the creator God. Theology as a theoretical endeavor always functions within the bounds of negative theology which, with the aid of a proper exploitation of the concept of privation, can establish God as the originative principle of all existence and specifically of human theoretical reason. For Cohen, beyond this knowledge of God as originative condition of the possibility of the world of existence or the creation of theoretical reason, there are no positive attributes that we can discern with respect to God's being. Revelation does not provide information concerning God's essence or the nature of his being, beyond this. Not even Moses, says Cohen, was privy to any additional theoretical information regarding God's being. 'God wants to reveal only the effects of his essence to Moses, not his essence itself.'[36]

There is, however, a difference, says Cohen, between knowledge of God as the originative principle of our theoretical reason and knowledge of God as the originative norm of our moral reason. As mentioned earlier, Cohen's God functions simultaneously as the condition of the possibility of both science and ethics. This God is the origin of both truth and truthfulness. In this sense, God's being correlates not only with the becoming of our knowledge of causality, but also with the becoming of our knowledge of our purpose – or the becoming of our moral action – what Cohen calls 'teleology'. The unique God links what is and what ought to be, that is, being and telos. As Andrea Poma says, 'Origin and absolute end are identical in the idea of God.'[37] This is also to say that the Unique God is the holy God – the one who 'is' holy – whose being is the ideal. As such, God is both the condition of the possibility of existence and of the ultimate fulfillment of our lives.

If our theoretical knowledge of God's being fails to provide knowledge of God's positive attributes, can moral knowledge do any better? The answer for Cohen is both yes and no. In the chapter entitled 'The Attributes of Action', Cohen begins his discussion with the Talmud's list of the thirteen attributes (*middot*) of God, which he crystallizes into two divine characteristics: holiness and goodness.[38]

What kind of attribute is holiness? What do we know when we say that God is holy? Actually, Cohen informs us, holiness is not an attribute of God's being but of God's action. Holiness, loving-kindness, graciousness, mercy, etc., all these are features of God's action and not descriptions of his essence or nature. But what could action possibly mean with respect to an unchanging, eternal, ideal being? By attributes of action, Cohen does not mean a set of divine attributes we may discern from an assessment of the 'aftereffects' that we see in the world. By divine attributes of action, Cohen does not mean to attribute to God causal characteristics. To speak of divine attributes of action is to speak less of the actions God has performed to produce certain effects, but rather to speak of the divine telos or purpose that guides human action.[39] Consequently, Cohen tells us, God's action cannot be understood without correlation with human action – which is to say, these characteristics are less attributes of God's own action but ultimately work as norms for human action which alone realizes them in the world. The attributes of action are 'norms of action, as love and justice, they originate not in causality but in the purpose of the action . . . Action in the case of God is related to the possibility of action in becoming, namely man.'[40] God provides the ideals for our moral behavior – a moral behavior only we can and must autonomously implement.

From this vantage point correlation means the relationship forged between God and us insofar as we enact the divine moral ideals. Not a so-called logical relation between being and becoming, ethics is instead a teleological relation between God's ideals and our fulfillment of them. It is a relation of purpose between God's holiness and our becoming holy through our moral action. As the origin and ideal of our morality, Cohen's God assumes primacy over our moral activity and herein retains his position as transcendent. God 'is' holy, whereas human beings can only 'become' holy. There is, according to Cohen, a fundamental asymmetry in this moral correlation and this asymmetry provides the condition that maintains God's otherness or transcendence in the relation. For human beings, holiness...is only the task and ideal of action. You desire to strive for holiness.... The latter, however, can never be completed; it can only persist in the elevating of the task ...[Therefore] the linking of the human creature to God [in the correlation] at the same time means the limitation of his action no less than the limitation of his knowledge.[41]

Working to establish the asymmetry between God and human beings, Cohen goes so far as to call God the 'lawgiver'. 'In holiness God becomes for man the lawgiver who sets tasks for him.'[42]

Continuing to trace Cohen's own argument, we may now inquire again as to the sense in which knowledge is afforded through this particular correlation. While God's holiness is not, Cohen says, an attribute of his being, it is an expression of the Absolute as an ideal that we may pursue. Consequently, although moral correlation does not provide theoretical knowledge of God's nature, Cohen does assert that it affords a practical knowledge of God. Like Kant, Cohen believes that knowledge of God (in Cohen's case, as the holy ideal), is a necessary feature of our moral action. However, while Kant maintains that the moral self must postulate knowledge of God for the sake of the rationality of our action, Cohen understands God as the very pre-condition of our morality. As we will see below, Cohen's theological expansion beyond Kant rests on the notion of holiness as the precondition and not only the postulate of our moral action. For Cohen, divine revelation means that the only possible human actions that deserve to be called moral are those that are grounded in and thereby reflect the divine. The dichotomy between divine command and moral autonomy is illusory and God's moral primacy is re-established as the law or ideal that forms the basis for the exercise of human moral autonomy.[43] Consequently, moral action inevitably implicates an awareness of God – or what Cohen calls an 'acknowledgment'[44] of God. If God's holiness is the precondition for our moral activity, we necessarily *know* it when engaging in moral action. Insofar as moral action is the means whereby we realize divine holiness in the world of our existence, God – or the ideal – is made real to us and thereby knowable in a manner that far exceeds the rational hypothesis or pragmatic acting as if characteristic of Kantian moral theology.

### d. *The Theology of Acknowledgment and Love*
Cohen's concept of 'acknowledgment' has been long neglected by scholarship. An analysis of this concept is crucial to any reading of Cohen's

religious thought insofar as it links practical reason or ethical autonomy with the love of God. What does acknowledgment of God mean for Cohen and wherein lies its cognitive value for theology?

Cohen's notion of acknowledgment is the necessary result of his notion of divine holiness and thereby a consequence of his recovery of the reality of the Absolute from out of the Jewish sources. The concept of acknowledgment is a by-product of the application of the method of critical idealism to religion. According to Cohen, to say that God's holiness functions as the precondition for our moral striving is not simply to say that God is the origin of our moral striving. God's holiness functions, Cohen says, as a model for our own moral action. God's holiness – his attributes of action – provide the 'archetype' for our own striving. Therefore God, says Cohen, commands the Jews, 'Ye shall be holy; for I the Eternal your God am holy.'[45] Cohen interprets this command to mean that God, as the archetype, *is* holy, but human beings must 'emulate' this archetype and *become* holy. As archetype, God's holiness has primacy over human moral action. Human moral action is emulation of God's holiness. While Cohen maintains belief in autonomous human moral action, i.e. the ability of human beings to discern the validity of the law themselves and thereby bind themselves to it, he also maintains that God is the source of the law. As Kenneth Seeskin explains, autonomy does not necessarily mean that persons individually author their own law. Rather autonomy means that persons are 'capable of grasping the validity of the law and choosing to act for its sake'.[46] Cohen's position navigates between heteronomy and autonomy. Seeskin articulates this point nicely when he says, 'Cohen believes the law comes from God; the duty from man.'[47]

If it is true that God's holiness functions as an ideal for us, then two points necessarily follow. First, it is impossible for us to generate this ideal for ourselves or even imitate this ideal, for it transcends us. To imitate divine holiness would be to realize divine holiness now. But, for Cohen, divine holiness is the telos or the ideal that is both the source of our moral agenda as well as that which we must infinitely strive to realize. To speak of imitation, therefore, and not emulation is to deny divine transcendence. Second, in our effort to follow it, our only choice is, as Cohen says, to 'emulate' it. 'Emulation not imitation! . . . a drawing near to God, but not a union with God.'[48] The difference between imitation and emulation is, according to Cohen, the difference between monotheism and pantheism and/or mysticism. 'God remains the goal.'[49]

Cohen makes this striking point in the section 'The Problem of Religious Love'.

It thus becomes understandable that in the fight of the Jewish tradition against anthropomorphism, one speaks only of 'attributes of action' with regard to God.... God is compassionate, so are you to be compassionate. The attribute has only the meaning of a model. But the model makes only emulation possible, and not imitation; it is only an archetype ...[50]

But in the chapter on 'Image-Worship' Cohen further explores this notion of emulation of an archetype and connects it with the concept of acknowledgment (*Bekenntnis*[51]). 'To have knowledge of God means to acknowledge God ... hence the acknowledgment ... becomes an action, a primary act of the moral consciousness.'[52] Emulation of God's holiness through our own moral activity necessarily presupposes a cognitive (though not theoretical) element for Cohen. When we emulate something − when we try to copy from a model − we must necessarily acknowledge the existence of the model and *act after* this model,[53] so far as it maintains primacy over the effort at emulation. However, this does not mean that we assert theoretical knowledge of the model.

Moral action that emulates itself after God's holiness and acknowledges God, opens up a new way of understanding the knowledge of God as what Cohen will call 'love' or 'devotion' or 'service'. Different from theoretical reason,

moral reason, as practical reason, would have to act ... love [we learn] is the self-transformation of reason, as it were, from its preliminary theoretical precondition to its ethical ripeness and maturity. Therefore the relation of man to the unique God has to *activate and attest* [emphasis mine] itself in love ... To have knowledge of God means to acknowledge God. And acknowledgment excels knowledge, as the action of the will excels the thinking of the understanding.[54]

As transcendent to human sensibility, God cannot be an object of our theoretical knowledge as other objects are. We may know God as creator. Beyond this, we know the transcendent and holy God only by acknowledgment − the knowledge of love − the knowledge implicated in our willingness to oblige ourselves to emulate God's ideal in our own moral life. As Kenneth Seeskin says, 'Cohen took the practical turn by abandoning the question of what God is and replacing it with what God does ... God should be understood as an archetype. In Cohen's eyes ... to know God is to undertake the task of purifying one's behavior.'[55] Moreover, such moral knowledge does not generate, but 'enacts' or 'attests' − a knowledge whose cognitive value is the value of 'recognition' more than cognition. 'Acknowledgment', says Cohen, 'means an action of the will, as distinguished from mere theoretical knowledge. To come to know God, therefore becomes to love God, becomes active devotion to and acknowledgment of God.'[56]

Attestation differs from Kant's act of postulation or practical belief, driven as it is, not by devotion or love, but strictly by rational need. Kant's practical postulates articulate what Kant claims are necessary conditions to the possibility of moral action – that is, their objective reality is predicated *post-facto*, strictly on the grounds of their rational necessity for moral action.[57] Moreover, Jamie Ferreira has persuasively argued that not only is the God of the *Critique of Practical Reason* nothing more than a logically required postulate, but what is postulated is not the necessary existence of God but rather only the real possibility or the necessary hypothesis of God. Ferreira bases her argument on claims like the following in the *Critique of Practical Reason*:

> The ideas of God and immortality . . . are the conditions of applying the morally determined will to the object which is given to it a priori . . . Consequently, the *possibility* of these conditions can and must be assumed in this practical context without our knowing or understanding them in a theoretical sense.[58]

Ferreira cites the *Critique of Pure Reason* to differentiate between two different uses of possibility in Kant's thought: logical and real possibility.

> I can think whatever I please, provided only that I do not contradict myself . . . This suffices for the possibility of the concept, even though I may not be able to answer for there being in the sum of all possibility an object corresponding to it. But something more is required before I can ascribe to such a concept objective validity, that is real possibility; the former is merely logical. This something more need not, however, be sought in the theoretical sources of knowledge; it may lie in those that are practical.[59]

At stake is not simply the claim that one may, on practical grounds, be able to assert the objective validity of that which remained only logically possible for theoretical reason. More significant for Ferreira is the claim that objective validity may mean only real possibility as opposed to real or necessary existence. And, according to Ferreira it is 'real possibility' and not necessary existence that best characterizes the epistemological status of our knowledge of the postulates. She says,

> Kant's references to 'practical belief' in God's existence seem to amount to the
> necessity of postulating the possibility of God's existence coupled with the desire
> for it – and this is what hope amounts to. That is, 'practical belief' in God's
> existence cannot equal 'theoretical belief' in God's existence . . . 'practical belief'
> means hope which depends on the theoretical affirmation of the real possibility of
> God and immortality.[60]

Translated into practical terms, the practical belief in the possibility of
God's existence amounts to 'acting as if (though clearly not while believing
it is false) that God exists'.[61] Ferreira continues, 'On such a view Kant
would have held that although denying the existence of God precludes
rational commitment to the Highest Good, it is sufficient for such
commitment that one unconditionally affirm the more than logical
possibility of God's existence and see oneself as unable rationally to deny
that [possible] existence.'[62] Such a God is a far cry from Cohen's God who is
not only more than a real hypothesis necessary to render our moral action
rational but the God of correlation which as Kenneth Seeskin describes is

> a dynamic relation in which each side reaches out to and takes responsibility for
> the other. God calls for the sanctification of man; by sanctifying himself, man
> sanctifies God as well . . . sanctification is not the same as simple obedience. It is
> not just that we have a law to obey but that we affirm the validity of the law and
> devote ourselves to fulfilling it. In short, the command to sanctify ourselves is
> God's way of asking for a partner.'[63]

Our moral activity is part of a divine–human partnership for Cohen and not
for Kant.[64]

Attestation or emulation is an act performed in recognition of a
something that precedes the performance. Cohen's appreciation for the prior
reality of divine holiness coupled with the fact that moral action is a
response to this prior ideal accounts for his language of love and devotion –
a language missing from Kant's account of postulation. A person loves or is
devoted to that which it seeks to emulate – that which precedes or is higher
than itself and that to which it responds. For Cohen, therefore, covenant is
correlation and correlation means autonomously drawing near to the God
who offers or is the source of the holy ideal that one seeks to realize. Cohen
uses not only the language of love but also the language of divine command
to express the height and authorial primacy of divine holiness. 'In holiness
God becomes for man the lawgiver who sets tasks for him.'[65] While Kant

does claim that from a religious point of view moral duty is understood as divine command,[66] the construal of moral duty as divine command is merely an extension of the postulate of God as that cause of nature which guarantees happiness and is therefore not necessary to activate but only to accompany moral action. In other words, for Kant, divine holiness is postulated to make moral life rational, whereas for Cohen, divine holiness constitutes the origin and meaning of morality itself.[67] Kenneth Seeskin summarizes the difference and says that for Kant 'our idea of God is derived from our idea of moral perfection, not the other way around ... [T]he fact that the moral law originates with God has no more bearing than a remark about the weather.'[68] From a Cohenian perspective, however, Kant's dismissal of the origin of the moral law is a testament to his refusal to apply the method of critical idealism to religion. Cohen's appreciation for God as the source of the holy ideal and therefore the one to whom we long to draw near in our moral activity is an appreciation made possible only by Cohen's return to the Jewish sources and their expression of the lived experience of the Absolute in the life of the believer.

Thus far our analysis of Cohen's philosophy of religion has demonstrated how Cohen's application of the method of critical idealism to religion has introduced the notion of acknowledgment whereby moral life is not simply the respect for a moral law within that requires a postulate of God as the guarantee of the coordination of nature and morality, but the loving acknowledgment of and devotion to the holy God. In this way, correlation weds practical reason and the love of God, or what may be otherwise recognized as reason and revelation, or philosophy and religion. Does it, however? It is reasonable at this point to ask whether the concept of acknowledgment reveals any tension between the religion of the Jewish sources and Cohen's notion of autonomous ethics. One may argue in fact that rather than successfully bind Jewish life to ethical idealism, Cohen's notion of acknowledgment reveals a strain between the two approaches to religious life. More specifically one may argue, as Martin Buber did, that Cohen's description of the love persons have for God cannot refer simply to a concept of God as the absolute unity of is and ought – that is, to the notion of God as the ideal of holiness. The kind of love and devotion or service that Cohen associates with the concept of acknowledgment can only refer to a personal God and not merely an idea. In Buber's words, 'He who loves God loves the ideal and loves God more than the ideal.'[69] In response to Cohen's rhetorical, '[H]ow can one love anything save an idea?' Buber responds, '[E]ven if it were correct that in ... love one loves only the idealized person,

27

that does not at all mean that nothing more than the idea of the person is loved: even the idealized person remains a person and has not been transformed into an idea.'[70]

The issue of whether it makes sense to speak of the love of God as the love of an ideal emerges in Cohen's discussion of the love for God as the basis for social concern. According to Cohen's reading of the prophets, Judaism's sources had long ago discovered the moral problem of poverty. Poverty, the sources indicate to us, calls into question the notion of divine holiness or justice and consequently stands as an obstacle to the moral development of humanity. What if, Cohen asks, a person is righteous and yet suffers from poverty? Can persons committed to the pursuit of holiness accept this reality? Wouldn't such an acceptance betray one's supposed faith in divine holiness? 'How could the misfortune of the righteous be reconciled with God's justice?'[71] Doesn't the existence and potential acceptance of social poverty give the lie to the notion that human beings are endowed with practical reason?

Cohen's answer is a clear and resounding 'No'. On the contrary, it is the prophets' ability to recognize the moral claim of those who suffer from poverty that further expands upon the meaning of moral correlation as the acknowledgment of divine holiness. If social poverty defies the success of moral life, then the inverse is true as well: that is, moral activity – or the pursuit of holiness – is possible only in an environment that forbids social poverty or economic disparity. Such an environment, Cohen tells us, is the state that issues laws protecting the poor.

> The proper historical understanding of monotheism must be based on the correct understanding of the Israelitic theocracy. Religion develops in connection with the development of the state ... The social differentiation between poor and rich poses the most difficult question for the concept of man ... This correction of society and its history is the demand of the unique God.[72]

Such laws are a direct reflection of the pity that grows into love, that citizens feel for those who suffer in poverty.

The problem of social poverty and the antidote of the law-abiding citizen who enacts laws protecting the poor enhances the meaning of humanity in the divine–human correlation. The notion of the state that cares for its poor particularizes the notion of the moral man into the law-abiding citizen who loves the fellowman. Through its laws, the state provides citizens with the opportunity to awaken to the reality of the poor person who thereby stirs the citizen to a pity that prompts compassion. In this context, devotion to God means devotion to those laws that protect the impoverished. In this sense, love for the fellowman does not transform the character of persons' love for God as an ideal but simply particularizes the ideal into specific laws that are directed toward the impoverished. 'The love of man for God is the love of the moral ideal.'[73] Analogously, the analysis of poverty deepens the character of divine holiness, which from the viewpoint of poverty is recognized as divine love. 'Only now, after man has learned to love man as fellowman, is his thought turned back to God, and only now does he understand that God loves man and indeed loves the poor man with the same favor as the stranger.'[74] Thus, the enactment of political justice reflects back on God – unveiling divine love as an attribute of action.

Nonetheless, while Cohen's analysis of political justice leads to a discussion of divine love, the divine love discussed is enacted not by God who is the archetype of this love, but by the citizen. According to Buber, Cohen misapplies the language of the love for God and the love by God to his analysis of social legislation. Beyond the question of whether it makes sense to speak of the love of God as the love of an ideal, Buber questions how Cohen can speak of loving an ideal when his discussion of social poverty unveils the character of God's love for humankind as well. He says, '[E]ven supposing that ideas can also be loved, the fact remains that persons are the only ones who love.'[75] To speak of loving or acknowledging a God who loves humankind is to speak of more than the absolute unity of the 'is' and the 'ought'. Cohen, Buber argues,

> set out to put the idea into a sequence so logical as to make it impossible for any impulse to opposition to develop and . . . was of the opinion that 'the deepest basis of the Jewish idea of God' was on his side. But even the deepest basis of the Jewish idea of God can be achieved only by plunging into that word by which God revealed himself to Moses.[76]

Buber's comments illuminate how Cohen's thought strains to translate the language and religious life found in the Jewish sources into the perimeters of ethical idealism. The result, as Buber notes, is the retention of elements of biblical theology oddly applied and/or misapplied to the categories of critical idealism.

In summary, a theological advance of Kant's practical theology, Cohen's theology of acknowledgment lays the groundwork for the theology of testimony in Rosenzweig and Barth.[77] Nonetheless, Cohen continues to view religion from the perspective of ethics or reason rather than viewing ethics and reason 'after' religion/revelation. Even a critically idealist view of religion is not sufficient to recognize religion's full worth. For this, one needs a return to the sources and to revelation.

## B. Cohen's Practical Theology: From Love to Forgiveness

Cohen's application of critical idealism to the sources of Judaism results in a theological expansion over Kant not only with respect to the notion of acknowledgment in correlation, but also with respect to what Cohen considers the deepest expression of correlation, i.e. divine forgiveness. Unlike Kant who in *Religion Within the Limits of Reason Alone* refuses to justify a belief, theoretical or practical, in a forgiving God, Cohen's *Religion of Reason Out of the Sources of Judaism* boldly asserts that 'it is the essence of God to forgive the sin of man. This is the most important content of the correlation of God and man.'[78] However, as with his appropriation of the language of love or devotion for God, Cohen's theology of divine forgiveness stands in tension with his critical idealism. More specifically, Cohen's willingness to assert that 'I am in constant need of God, as the One who forgives sin'[79] conflicts on the one hand with his account of the process of self-sanctification whereby 'forgiveness [is] replaced by self-sanctification ...'[80] On the other hand, Cohen frequently contradicts the above account and argues that persons do need a forgiving God. If, however, by a forgiving God we understand the attribute of goodness as realized in the human activity of repentance, then Cohen's language of forgiveness falls prey again to the Buberian 'can an idea forgive?' critique. If, finally, Cohen's forgiving God is, as Andrea Poma argues, a God who as more than an idea actively forgives or redeems, such a God challenges the adequacy of Cohen's own idealistic concept of God in correlation.

### a. *Kant's Theology of Divine Forgiveness*
The argument that Cohen's *Religion of Reason Out of the Sources of Judaism* advances theologically beyond Kant's practical theology and thereby sets the stage for Rosenzweig and Barth seems challenged by Kant's foray into religion in his *Religion Within the Limits of Reason Alone*. An effort to contend with the challenge of what Kant calls radical evil, Kant's *Religion Within the Limits of Reason Alone* discusses the religious issues of sin, atonement and grace. The fact that Kant openly incorporates these topics into his work

might lead readers to conclude that *Religion Within the Limits of Reason Alone* marks Kant's willingness to engage in theological discourse. In what follows I will argue that despite the presence of religious vocabulary, Kant's *Religion Within the Limits of Reason Alone* remains far more theologically skittish than Cohen's *Religion of Reason Out of the Sources of Judaism*. More specifically, Cohen not only argues for the *necessity* of the forgiving God within the divine–human correlation, he declares that forgiveness constitutes the deepest expression of the divine–human correlation. Conversely, Kant never asserts the necessity of divine aid in the process of moral regeneration but on the contrary, argues that 'we can admit a work of grace as something incomprehensible but we cannot adopt it into our maxims either for theoretical or practical use'.[81] While there are instances in *Religion Within the Limits of Reason Alone* where Kant's discussion of the hope for divine assistance sounds similar to Cohen's account, Kant's claims are restrained by greater epistemological and theological qualifications than Cohen's and thereby do not raise Kant's discourse to the level of theological assertion found in *Religion of Reason Out of the Sources of Judaism*.

In *Fallen Freedom: Kant on Radical Evil and Moral Regeneration*, Gordon Michalson argues, '[I]n the end, I think it is fair to say that Kant remains utterly agnostic on the question of the reality of grace.'[82] The great irony in the comparison between Kant and Cohen on the question of divine forgiveness is that Cohen goes to great lengths to retain the notion of a forgiving God even though his account of sin and moral regeneration does not (generally speaking) warrant a forgiving God so far as he does not posit evil as inextirpable, while Kant remains 'utterly agnostic' with respect to a forgiving God and yet Kant's account of radical evil as inextirpable generates a real warrant for a salvific or gracious God.[83] The point of the current analysis is not, however, to discern the extent to which Kant's account of radical evil ought to result in an assertion of a forgiving God. Rather it is to demonstrate that Kant is more theologically skittish in his claims regarding a forgiving God than Cohen. Kant's theological caution is evidenced in *Religion Within the Limits of Reason Alone* by his argument that while we may rationally hope for 'whatever we may need' to accompany our efforts at moral regeneration, we cannot admit divine grace into our practical reason and, therefore, divine grace remains what Kant calls a parergon that borders on but cannot be admitted as an object of rational hope.

As earlier cited, Kant argues in *Religion Within the Limits of Reason Alone* that 'the calling to our assistance of works of grace . . . cannot be adopted into the maxims of reason, if she is to remain within her limits'.[84] Divine grace differs from the postulates of practical reason identified in the *Critique of Practical Reason*. The postulates of God and immortality of the soul are contents of what Kant calls rational faith. In the *Critique of Pure Reason* Kant says that the assumption of these postulates is a 'necessary belief' so far as they constitute the *necessary* and sufficient conditions for the pursuit of the highest good. Not only can they, but they *must* be admitted into our practical maxims.

There are three reasons why Kant refuses to make the same claim for divine grace. First, according to his own account, persons suffering from radical evil do not necessarily need divine grace in order to morally regenerate. Said in other words, moral regeneration out of radical evil is 'possible' without divine assistance. How can Kant consistently argue that moral regeneration is possible if elsewhere he argued that radical evil is a free decision to assert one's sensuous interests over the moral law which functions thereafter as the basic maxim of our practical reason? Kant's answer, satisfactory or not, is that while one cannot detail precisely how an evil person can choose the priority of the moral law as her basic maxim, such a choice is theoretically possible so far as all moral decision making is free. Said in other terms, radical evil is not synonymous with devilishness – or what is the outright rejection and/or silencing of the moral law. Radical evil is a prioritizing of desires or inclinations over the moral law even though the *Wille* or the ability to act on the call of the moral law continues to reside within our reason. In fact, *Wille* or the ability to act freely on the moral law is itself a condition of the possibility of radical evil. If radical evil as the decision to subvert the law is a free choice, it must therefore be a choice over another possibility – what is the possibility of choosing to obey the moral law instead of one's desires? Consequently, radical evil cannot destroy the call of the moral law within reason and its continued presence there provides the condition of the possibility therefore of moral regeneration.[85] 'However evil a man has been up to the very moment of an impending free act . . . it was not only his duty to have been better [in the past], it is now still his duty to better himself. To do so must be within his power.'[86] In view of Kant's comments, Michalson concludes, '[I]n his rejection of devilishness, Kant had already established the possibility of moral regeneration apart from divine aid by showing it to be a duty.'[87]

A second reason why Kant refuses to postulate divine grace as a necessary element of moral activity is due to the theoretical indeterminacy of the moral individual's need. A postulate is the assumption of 'a theoretical proposition which is not as such demonstrable, but which is an inseparable corollary of an a-priori unconditionally valid practical law'.[88] Elsewhere Kant says postulates are 'necessary conditions of the possibility of that which this [moral] law requires'.[89] To postulate presupposes identification of what the moral agent needs. Radical evil, however, is inscrutable. We know neither how we fell into it nor how we will freely choose to act differently.[90] Consequently, we cannot postulate divine aid so far as we do not know what if anything we might need in order to overcome evil. Jamie Ferreira makes this point and says, 'Kant's view is that not only can we not say what the assistance would consist in, but that we cannot even say that we do need help, for that too would go beyond what we can theoretically ascertain.'[91]

A third and final reason why Kant categorizes the notion of divine grace as parergon – or that which lies on the border of reason but cannot be admitted into reason's domain either theoretical or practical – is because to do so is to encourage moral laxity when in fact the purpose of the postulates is to help make moral endeavor rational and complete. Kant says,

> [E]ven the hypothesis of a practical application of this idea [grace] is wholly self-contradictory. For the employment of this idea would presuppose a rule concerning the good which we ourselves must do in order to accomplish something, whereas to await a work of grace means exactly the opposite, namely that the good is not our deed but the deed of another being and that therefore we can achieve it only by doing nothing, which contradicts itself. Hence we admit a work of grace as something incomprehensible, but we cannot adopt it into our maxims either for theoretical or for practical use.[92]

Here Kant suggests that believers who postulate a forgiving God, who incorporate a belief in divine grace into their practical action will abandon their efforts at moral regeneration and rely instead on the belief that God will forgive their sin for them.

It is important now to distinguish between Kant's discussion of divine aid and his discussion of the hope for 'whatever aid may be necessary' for, while Kant will not postulate divine grace, he does see a role for rational hope in the process of moral regeneration. Moreover, even though Kant argues that one cannot and/or does not need to assert what in the Second Critique he calls a 'pure practical faith' in divine grace insofar as to do so is uniquely premised upon the moral necessity of the object of faith, Kant often invokes the notion of divine grace in his analyses of moral regeneration and it is these references to divine or supernatural aid that have led scholars to assert a theological turn in Kant's *Religion Within the Limits of Reason Alone*. In dealing with these instances, my goal is not to deny Kant's flirtation with theology but rather to argue that even here Kant remains more theologically cautious than Cohen on the issue of divine grace or forgiveness. In what follows I will consider three instances in *Religion Within the Limits of Reason Alone* where Kant references supernatural aid or grace and demonstrate how he either places strict limitations on the use of this grace and/or demonstrates how such grace is not necessary after all.

The first reference to the notion of God's help appears in Kant's claim that persons who work actively toward moral regeneration may hope that some supernatural aid may supplement their efforts. Early in his discussion of the 'Restoration to its Power of the Original Predisposition to the Good' Kant says, '[G]ranted that some supernatural cooperation may be necessary to his becoming good, or to his becoming better, yet ... man must first make himself worthy to receive it and must lay hold of this aid ...'[93] Kant's reference to supernatural aid here seems most debilitating to my overall argument insofar as his position seems to parallel Cohen's account of divine forgiveness. Both Kant and Cohen try to navigate between the poles of moral autonomy and divine forgiveness without allowing the one to negate the other. Their shared strategy posits divine forgiveness as both helpful and yet necessarily merited by the individual's moral effort. The question here is not whether Kant resolves the tension between autonomy and forgiveness nor why he would invoke the need for supernatural aid when above he argued for the possibility of moral regeneration without it, but rather whether or not he is asserting the same position as Cohen.[94] In fact, Kant's position is not the same as Cohen's. Unlike Cohen, who asserts divine forgiveness as the most important element in ethical monotheism, Kant qualifies his statements concerning supernatural aid. 'Granted', he says, 'that some supernatural cooperation *may* [emphasis mine] be necessary to his becoming good.' Elsewhere he re-inforces this point and says, 'It is not essential and hence not necessary for every one to know what God does or has done for his salvation.'[95] 'May' be necessary is a far cry therefore from 'is' necessary and stands in strong contrast to Cohen's claim that 'faith is fundamentally rooted in the firm trust in God as the Good One who, beyond doubt, in his goodness, forgives the sins of man'.[96] If anything, Kant's 'may be necessary' is closer, practically speaking, to 'is not essential and hence not necessary'. Whereas Cohen boldly and unabashedly asserts the reality of the forgiving God spoken of in the Jewish sources regardless of the extent to which this God is or is not mandated by his moral account,

Kant sheepishly mentions the God whose help we may need but cannot and should not practically believe in or assume.

What follows this initial hesitation to speak of divine grace as the object of rational hope are two additional references to divine grace, both of which do more to demonstrate the insignificance of any possible aid rather than assert the clear-cut need for it. The first reference is to the need for the divine perspective on the noumenal character of the morally revolutionary act. Kant invokes the possibility of divine aid in response to what he identifies as the following difficulty associated with moral regeneration: 'How can a disposition count for the act itself, when the act is always (not eternally, but at each instant of time) defective?'[97] If moral regeneration is grounded in a noumenal act, how can individuals know that their perceptible acts count as reflections of this noumenal act? To this Kant answers,

[We] may also think of this endless progress of our goodness towards conformity to the law . . . as being judged by him who knows the heart, through a purely intellectual intuition as a completed whole, because of the disposition, supersensible in its nature, from which this progress itself is derived.[98]

Kant's invocation of divine aid resembles Cohen's belief in God's willingness to see our efforts as part and parcel of a moral and not sensuously driven self. The issue seems to be one of the individual's confidence concerning her appraisal of her moral efforts and the extent to which she can trust that they reflect the moral regeneration she aspires to.

However, while Cohen appreciates the individual's need for God as forgiving redeemer to guarantee the success of her actions, in comments relating to what he calls the second difficulty facing the morally pursuant individual – the difficulty of moral happiness – Kant casts doubt on the individual's need for a divine guarantee regarding the character of her moral effort. On the contrary, Kant suggests individuals pursuing moral regeneration may draw confidence regarding their moral future from the accrued evidence of their own moral effort.[99]

If man lacked all confidence in his moral disposition . . . he would scarcely be able to persevere steadfastly in it. He can gain such confidence, however without yielding himself up either to pleasing or to anxious fantasies, by comparing the course of his life hitherto with the resolution which he has adopted. It is true, indeed, that the man, who through a sufficiently long course of life has observed the efficacy of these principles of goodness ... that is in the steady improvement of his way of life, can still only conjecture from this that there has been a fundamental improvement in his inner disposition. Yet he has reasonable grounds for hope as well ... since such improvements if only their underlying principle is good, ever increase his strength for future advances, he can hope that he will never forsake this course during his life on earth but will press on with ever-increasing courage.[100]

The inability to be certain about one's moral effort does not, for Kant, undermine one's moral confidence altogether. In fact, Kant argues that too much certainty has the opposite effect – it breeds a moral laxity that conjecture alone does not.[101]

The second time Kant references grace is in the context of his discussion of guilt. The problem of guilt emerges even for the person who has adopted a good disposition, so far as this same individual has led formerly a life predicated on a maxim of evil and is therefore accountable for her past actions, even if she has now adopted a good disposition. How can justice be done with respect to her past deeds if she is no longer the person who has committed those deeds? Would it not be unfair to punish her now for acts that she is no longer committing? According to Kant, vicarious atonement is not a possible solution. 'This is no transmissible liability which can be made over to another like a financial indebtedness ... [R]ather is it the most personal of all debts ... which only the culprit can bear and no innocent person can assume ... '[102] How can the individual bear this responsibility? The transformation from evil to good is, according to Kant, the transformation of the old man to the new man. This shedding of ways is not easy. Individuals pursuing the good must, as sensuous beings, always work to do the good and often incur obstacles or suffer for the choice to do the good. Still the individual takes on these difficulties as punishments which 'the old man would have had to regard as punishments and which he too, so far as he is still in the process of becoming dead to the old man accepts as such'.[103] If, however, Kant renders the moral striving of a sensuous physical being sufficient justification for debt accrued while evil, he must still guard against what appears to be the consequence that the good person bears the blame for deeds she has not done. To do so, Kant argues that, 'so far as he is a new man ... these sufferings are not ascribed to him as punishments at all'.[104] Despite the difficulties involved in Kant's effort to resolve the issue of guilt through this identification of different moral selves within the single moral agent, Kant bravely attempts to provide an account of atonement devoid of any external assistance. The only place where outside grace is called for concerns an individual's ability to render the punishments or sacrifices she makes daily as equivalent to a debt fully paid. This, Kant says, 'is reckoned to us by grace. That what in our earthly life . . . is ever only a becoming (namely becoming a man well-pleasing to God) should be credited to us exactly as if we were already in full possession of it.'[105] Immediately following, however, Kant recoils from this suggestion and he asks,

> [D]oes the deduction of the idea of a justification of an individual who is indeed guilty but who has changed his disposition into one well-pleasing to God possess any practical use whatever, and what may this use be? One does not perceive what positive use could be made of it for religion for the conduct of life, because the condition underlying the enquiry just conducted is that the individual in question is already in actual possession of the required good disposition toward the development and encouragement of which all practical employment of ethical concepts properly aims; and as regards comfort, a good disposition already carries with it, for him who is conscious of possessing it, both comfort and hope (though not certainty).[106]

We do not need grace. The individual who, enduring sacrifice to do the good as payment for her prior debt, may draw from the same confidence she uses to sustain her moral effort to assuage her concern regarding payment of her prior debt. This confidence, as we recall, is rooted in her own moral effort and not in external assistance.

### b. *Cohen's Theology of Divine Forgiveness*

There is a noteworthy difference between Kant's claims regarding divine forgiveness and Cohen's. Whereas Kant refuses to assert the ground for a practical belief in divine forgiveness, Cohen boldly embraces divine forgiveness as a necessary feature of the return from sin. Nonetheless, Cohen's willingness to include divine forgiveness in his moral account poses problems for his overall philosophical project.

Cohen's discussion of the need for divine forgiveness emerges out of his more focused discussion regarding the particular historical and cultural conditions required for the realization of moral life. For Cohen, philosophy of religion does more than identify an abstract notion of God as Ultimate Being who stands in correlation with an abstract humanity. The work of transcendental idealism presupposes that the concepts of God and humanity derive from transcendental analyses of the phenomena of religious life. If on the one hand these concepts lend legitimacy to religious life, on the other hand religious life is the vehicle through which these concepts are realized. Consequently a complete analysis of correlation and acknowledgment requires an analysis of the conditions or environments in which correlation is realized. Such an analysis ought to enrich and deepen the formerly abstract concepts of God and humanity and the character of divine and human love thereby further demonstrating the marriage between ethics and religion.

How do we know that correlation requires certain historical and cultural conditions in order to be realized? We know, Cohen argues, because an analysis of literary sources helps to identify what are both obstacles and aids to the realization of divine–human moral correlation. The practical correlation between the holy God and moral humanity requires two primary cultural/historical conditions: the state that protects the poor and the religious community that affords individuals the hope of divine forgiveness. Both are necessary contributions for the unity of consciousness insofar as they protect against challenges to the success of human moral pursuit. Through these analyses we learn first that divine–human correlation is a relationship between a God who loves the poor one and a human being who returns or enacts the attribute of divine love by living as a legally responsible member of a state whose laws protect the poor. Second, we learn that the divine–human correlation is a relationship between a God who forgives or redeems an individual who longs for and confesses her need for divine forgiveness. The primary focus of this discussion revolves around God's activity as redeemer and the human need for forgiveness.

Like social poverty, the problem of individual moral guilt provides an occasion to more deeply identify the character of moral life as the loving testimony to God. The task at hand is to evaluate Cohen's portrait of divine forgiveness and assess the extent to which this theological portrait will set the stage for the theology of testimony advanced by Rosenzweig and Barth.

## c. *The Problem of Sin and the Need for Forgiveness*

If according to Cohen the prophets contributed to the concept of the fellowman, it is Ezekiel whose notion of sin helps to develop the concept of the individual 'I'. While the prophets wrestled with the issue of human sin, their focus remained social sin – sin committed by the community. Ezekiel on the other hand separates the responsibility of the ancestors from the grandchildren and identifies sin as individual. Ezekiel's insight, however, raises the question, if persons/individuals are moral, how can they sin? How can we understand the individual's inclination to sin? The question, Cohen insists, is not the metaphysical question. 'What are the causes of sin?' but rather the teleological question that asks, 'What meaning has sin against God? . . . [T]he individual must be established according to the methods of ethics, within the teleological teaching of ethics.'[107] Cohen's answer that sin prompts individuals to repentance appears parallel to his analysis of social sin – namely, that individual sin, like poverty, leads the individual to a deeper mode of moral practice and thereby enriches the moral correlation with the revelatory God.

In contrast to the social sin identified by the prophets wherein members of a society engaged in behavior hurtful to other members of society, the individual's sin is a sin against God. Individual sin is a sin before God because by sinning the individual engages in behavior that prohibits her from becoming holy – prohibits her from becoming that which God absolutely is – the absolute as ideal or end. Sin is a defiance of God as the moral ideal. Still, a moral society does have recourse to contend with the individual's sin. Individuals who sin are punished before the state's tribunals and justice prevails. This does not, however, alleviate the deeper problem associated with the individual's sin: the individual's guilt over her failure to become that which she knows she ought to become. An individual's sin acts therefore as an obstacle to the unity of consciousness not because it demonstrates a failure to act on the moral law (as was the case with social poverty). Morally guided states already have laws in place that put a check on and ultimately override the tendency of persons to defy their moral nature. Unlike social poverty which, when not legislatively dealt with by a society, represents a failure by societies to recognize the character of their ultimate telos or the nature of holiness, individual sin can be adjudicated by the state and does not represent an analogous blindness. The problem of the individual's sin is guilt.

The problem of guilt is the problem of self-alienation. In the individual, sin creates a personal crisis of confidence. I know that I 'ought' to do the moral law – I know that I ought to pursue the infinite task of fulfilling my nature, I know that I ought to work towards holiness – but having sinned, I am seized by the guilt and anxiety that I am not becoming the person I ought to become. Cohen says,

> Man must gather together all his individual powers and must prepare himself in order to have mastery of his self-sanctification. But at the same time he always

feels himself to be innately infirm and defective. 'In sin did my mother conceive me'... [Nothing] can give him the certainty that the preparations for his rebirth, which are his own, will be successful.[108]

Guilt is a crisis of personal dignity. Andrea Poma says, '[B]efore the court of justice of his own consciousness, therefore, the individual sinner finds himself permanently and irreparably facing himself not as a man, but as a sinner.'[109] The individual despairs.

What is the solution to this problem? Can the individual's guilt lead, like the problem of social poverty, to a deeper appreciation of the meaning of divine–human moral correlation? As the problem of poverty can be resolved through the institution of laws protecting the poor, Cohen argues that guilt is resolved through the institution of the religious community whose ritual of confession protects the one anguished by guilt. Just as social poverty led to the discovery of care for the poor as a necessary expression and facet of the pursuit of holiness – that is, the appreciation of divine–human correlation as the correlation between the ideal of divine love and the human enactment of this love – so Cohen argues that guilt helps illuminate the meaning of divine–human correlation as the correlation between God's goodness or forgiveness and human repentance. Seen from this vantage point, the religious community who affords the opportunity for confession is culturally necessary for the pursuit of humanity's fulfillment.

How does guilt promote the deeper meaning of correlation as human repentance and divine forgiveness or what Cohen also refers to as redemption? According to Cohen, the guilty individual needs the religious community's invitation and opportunity to stand before God. 'Should confession of sin be made in the midst of the congregation...? The decision was made for the congregation...Confession is at the same time also the public expression of trust in the good God, before whom the sin of man does not endure.'[110] As we recall, through its laws the state provides citizens with the opportunity to awaken to the reality of the poor person who thereby stirs the citizen to a pity that prompts compassion. Said in other words, the state's laws act as a reminder or revealer of additional commands that are part and parcel of the pursuit of holiness. Poverty reveals the blindness of persons regarding the extent of their moral obligation and the state offers a reminder. Analogously, the congregation offers the ritual of confession that grants the individual an opportunity to repent, that is, to take responsibility for her sin and return, therefore, to the path of moral improvement.

Repentance therefore means the ability of the individual to 'walk anew in the ways of righteousness'.[111] And Cohen insists, '[I]f our basic methodological idea is correct, the autonomy of the will must remain inviolably in power . . . Now only man as I is at stake and the stake is lost if the autonomy of the will is not absolute.'[112] Generally speaking, repentance requires recognition of one's prior sinful actions and a turn toward a future of holiness or correlation with God. Again Cohen insists, '[M]an must begin and achieve the projection toward this horizon entirely him himself. Any assistance, any collaboration in repentance would make out of the return a being-turned, and would thwart the autonomous accomplishment and task of man.'[113] Consequently, Cohen says, while repentance takes place 'before God' insofar as sin means a turning away from God in correlation and repentance means the turning toward correlation, it does not take place 'with God' or through God. 'The bringing about of redemption is man's independent action.'[114]

Cohen's phenomenology of repentance includes the knowledge of sin and confession. First one must search one's past and recognize one's sin. This, however, is followed by confession which includes the 'casting away and . . . the new creation'.[115] Cohen notes that confession leads to return and the alleviation of guilt only so far as it includes penance or the self's proclamation of his own guilt. 'Thus for the return in so-called penance, the punishment must also be employed as a means of liberation.'[116] According to Cohen, confession helps the individual to relieve himself of the burden of his guilt. Such punishment, Cohen says, 'is the only consolation for the relentless consciousness of guilt. It is for him the only support for his liberation from this almost intolerable burden.'[117]

With this casting off of sin and guilt the new 'I' emerges. 'Repentance is self-sanctification . . . the turning away and the returning and creating of a new way of life . . . [S]anctification is the goal; self-sanctification is the only means.'[118] 'Thus the sin is brought up before God, not in order that the individual should remain in it but in order that he be liberated from it.'[119] Sin therefore leads to a deeper appreciation of who the human being in moral correlation must be − he must be the repentant individual who 'by turning away from the previous way of life . . . [has] the capacity to enter upon a new way of life and . . . become the master of himself'.[120] Of course, Cohen reminds readers that while human beings are not afflicted by original sin, they are always capable of departing from the moral law. Consequently, repentance is an infinite task whose solution or goal of self-sanctification remains an infinite solution. This does not mean, however, that the sinner cannot become the new creation. Rather it means that she becomes the new creation for a moment only and must continually engage in the labor of renewal. 'The subject as I is determined by the moment and by the continuity of moments.'[121] Repentance therefore, 'provides man with this new life, which to be sure, can last only in the bliss of a moment. But this moment can and should repeat itself unceasingly.'[122]

Thus far, Cohen's discussion of sin has focused strictly on what the individual can and must do to liberate herself from sin and guilt. But what role is there for God? God, Cohen says, is the redeemer or the one who forgives sin. Cohen argues, while persons may autonomously engage in the process of self-sanctification, they remain doubtful of the success of their efforts at self-sanctification. 'Man himself must cast off his sin, but whether his own deed succeeds, whether it leads to the goal, this he cannot know.'[123] To this end, God, says Cohen, views all of our sins as unwitting or *shegagah*. God, Cohen says, 'can assign no task that would be a labor of Sisyphus'.[124] Awareness of divine forgiveness provides this reassurance to the repentant individual.

Immediately following this discussion, however, Cohen challenges his own account of the need for divine forgiveness. Does the repentant individual for whom self-sanctification is both the means and the goal of her endeavor already possess sufficient confidence to engage in repentant action? Isn't it the case that given her own moral fortitude – itself a product of the holy spirit within her – she does not need God to see her sin as *shegagah* or unwitting? If repentant action is autonomous, this suggests that she locates sufficient confidence to engage in it without needing divine forgiveness. Even if, one could argue further, God's forgiveness or redemption does offer helpful knowledge of the fulfillment of one's efforts, one may question the worth of calling this action forgiveness for, as Kenneth Seeskin points out, 'God is only responding to what I have accomplished on my own'[125] and not granting by forgiveness or grace a redemption I have not brought about or could not bring about myself. Recall Cohen's earlier claim, '[T]he bringing about of redemption is man's independent task.'[126] Cohen therefore asks,

[S]hould not forgiveness be replaced by self-sanctification insofar as the latter contains in itself the infinite solution, even though it ever remains an infinite task, so that self-sanctification would be identical to forgiveness? Ezekiel says 'yes' . . . [D]oes he not thereby identify the task with forgiveness and does he not thereby eliminate redemption through God?[127]

Cohen's enigmatic answer to his own question is, '[R]egardless of whether we would be able to achieve the solution of the task by our own independent work, and to succeed in liberating ourselves from it, it is necessary ... for the concept of God himself, that he and only he be the redeemer.'[128] In other words, Cohen tells us, the notion of divine forgiveness is not necessary for persons in order to effect their own liberation. Rather it is necessary for the concept of God that we be able to attribute this characteristic to him. With this claim, Cohen enters into murky waters with his theology of divine forgiveness.

As with Kant, Cohen has difficulty navigating his way through the problem of sin and the corresponding issue of divine forgiveness or grace. However, unlike Kant, who places strict epistemological limits on the role of grace in moral life, Cohen claims,

[I]t is not doubt that creeps into the spirit of the believer ... The spiritual evidence of the soul is furnished not by doubt in God but rather by the search for God, the desire for God, the desire for nothing else but God. For nothing else concerns the soul more than God's forgiveness of its sin.[129]

Clearly Cohen's theological claims exceed Kant's guarded discussion of forgiveness. And yet, in so doing, Cohen's theology meets with a number of problems.

First, Cohen's account of autonomous self-sanctification not only challenges the repentant individual's need for divine forgiveness but, in fact, conflicts with Cohen's own subsequent claims as cited above. It is confusing at best and unreasonable at worst to on the one hand claim that 'self-sanctification is identical with forgiveness and thereby eliminate[s] redemption through God'[130] and on the other hand assert that 'nothing else concerns the soul more than *God's* [emphasis mine] forgiveness of its sin'.[131] Even if one argues that what Cohen really means when he speaks about the desire for divine forgiveness is the desire to infinitely engage in the task of self-sanctification, it nonetheless remains odd to say that persons long for a divine forgiveness or redemption, the need for which their own actions have eliminated. Why would persons long for a forgiveness that they don't need, but only God needs to provide?

Even if, however, for argument's sake, we overlook this confusion in Cohen's account, his claims concerning persons' need for a forgiving God have their own problems. If by divine forgiveness Cohen means to speak of the divine attribute of forgiveness which when correlated with human enactment is realized through repentant action, one must ask whether this adequately explains the manner by which Cohen describes persons' longing for divine forgiveness. Like our love for God, Cohen tells us that our longing for divine forgiveness is impassioned. Such impassioned longing is best expressed, he argues, by the poet(s) of the psalms who, Cohen says,

> could not sing lyrically about the love to God if he were not to have experienced, in body and in soul, the magic of human love of the sexes. But he transfers this love to the love to God and who can test whether he does not want to overcome it through this transference? He transfers it to the love of God, who should liberate him from his sin ... [132]

The sinner, Cohen says, 'is in constant need of God, as the One who forgives sin'.[133] Does it make sense, however, to say that we are 'in constant need' and long passionately for an attribute of forgiveness? Can we long and sensuously desire an idea? And if it is divine forgiveness that we seek, can an idea provide forgiveness? As with his notion of acknowledgment and the devotion to God, Cohen's effort to join the language of ethical idealism with the language of liturgical expression is awkward and unconvincing.

One may try to resolve the above tension in Cohen's language by arguing that when Cohen speaks of our need for divine forgiveness, he means to refer to a God who actively forgives and redeems our actions as a personal God and is therefore more than an ideal. Cohen says,

> God, even in the ethical sense, is not good (*das Gute*) but the Good One (*der Gute*). The object of morality is thus elevated to God's being and through this unavoidably elevated to the concept of a subject. God as the Good One must therefore accomplish a kind of personal achievement of goodness. The scope of this task cannot be circumscribed by holiness only.[134]

Andrea Poma suggests this interpretation and says,

> As we have seen, the idea of God is necessary, as origin and end, to found the process of man's self-realization ... God is the sense, the holiness, without which sin-abandonment of holiness, penitence, that is return to holiness – would have no meaning and actually would not even exist. Nevertheless, and the novelty lies here, in the case of God, of the supreme idea, the two fundamental meanings of idea, as origin and end, are insufficient to manifest its sense: the fulfillment of the idea of God lies in attribution to it of active meaning in correlation with man and this is the content of the divine attribute of 'goodness'. Up until this point,

44

Cohen's idealism moves forward to the limits of the mystery of God in history . . . Not only is idea limit, but there is also a limit of idea. This consists of its being more than the origin, and more than the end of the infinite process of improvement of reality, in its also being the 'more' that the idea of God produces in respect of the normal meaning of ground and end . . . The emergence of the divine attribute of goodness does not only represent a deeper meaning of God–man correlation, but also progress in rational critical idealism up to its limit where critical reason must recognize not only a normative principle, but also an active principle in history.[135]

Therefore, in response to Buber's criticism of Cohen, Poma argues that Cohen's language of love and longing are appropriate to his theology insofar as 'Cohen's God is the God of faith, the God of Judaism, not merely a necessary hypothesis of a philosophical system'.[136] Poma recognizes, however, that this interpretation of the notion of divine forgiveness reveals how Cohen's attempt to apply the method of critical idealism to the sources of Judaism fails to fully account for the religious life and theology of these sources. Poma says, 'Cohen's critical-idealist philosophy proves inadequate to understand God through the concept of "idea" . . .'[137] An idea is incapable of acting as a personal agent who forgives persons, and therefore is not the object of the believer's faith.

As an extension of his moral theology, Cohen's theology of divine forgiveness suffers the same tension found in his theology of acknowledgment. A significant advance over Kant's refusal to embrace religious sources and incorporate them into moral philosophy, Cohen's application of critical idealism to the Jewish sources cannot adequately express and make sense of the character of devotion and the need for forgiveness expressed in the Jewish sources.

We may now return to the question with which we began this discussion. To what extent does Cohen's theology lay the groundwork for Rosenzweig's and Barth's theology of testimony and to what extent does this contribution point to a tension in Cohen's own theology? I have demonstrated how Cohen's practical theology advances beyond Kant's practical theology by its application of the critical idealist methodology to the sources of Judaism. Moreover, I have demonstrated how this advance strains to negotiate between the language of the sources and the categories of critical idealism. In this way, therefore, Cohen's theology sets the stage for Rosenzweig and Barth. Not only does Cohen offer a theology of acknowledgment that advances practical theology beyond the limits established by Kant, but his theology of love and forgiveness calls out to be corrected by a doctrine of revelation as an act of divine love and commandment, a theology that both Barth and Rosenzweig draw directly from the biblical sources without the application of a critical idealist framework. In so doing, their methodology will provide a better basis for a theology of the loving and forgiving God.

For Barth and Rosenzweig, testimony is not simply moral action that acts after an ideal of divine holiness but moral testimony that acts after a prior divine act of love. Arguably, Rosenzweig and Barth subscribe to a different reading of covenantal life than Cohen, for whom the correlation between God and human reason (theoretical and practical) appears to constitute the basis and essential meaning of covenant as biblically described. Cohen's moral correlation between God and human beings highlights moral law or holiness as the link that binds the divine–human relationship. While Cohen's emphasis on holiness or the moral law as the link between God and humanity need not compromise divine transcendence so far as only God 'is' holy and humans 'become' holy, still, Cohen's moral correlation holds both God and humankind accountable to the law – respect for which and enactment of which constitute the basic character of covenantal existence. For Cohen the love exchanged between God and humankind is a testament to the respect and zeal with which both parties approach the moral law rather than an element in the relationship separate or somehow different from the realization of holiness.

In contrast to Cohen's moral correlation, Barth and Rosenzweig will construe covenantal relationship as a relationship of holiness grounded in a preceding and gracious act of divine love. Covenantal life is predicated upon an act of divine love and judgment that prompts or motivates its recipients to repentance and love for God. Within this context, the law or the *mitzvot* express this testimonial love for God. While for Cohen the exchange of divine and human love is a testament to the mutual adoration both parties hold for the moral law, here the performance of the law services the more primary exchange of divine–human reconciliation and love. A theology of testimony predicated on a prior act of divine love does not denounce or dismiss the significance of the holy or the good but sees both divine holiness and human moral action as rooted in and expressive of love. The theology of testimony predicated in divine love does not therefore deny the prospect of *imitatio dei* but maintains that *imitatio dei* requires a prior context and act of divine grace or love to be possible.

## Notes

1 For extensive accounts of Rosenzweig's relationship with Cohen see David N. Myers, *Resisting History: Historicism and Its Discontents in German-Jewish Thought* (Princeton: Princeton University Press, 2003), pp. 68–75. For Barth's encounter with Cohen and Marburg Neo-Kantianism see Bruce McCormack, *Karl Barth's Critically Realistic Dialectical Theology: Its Genesis and Development 1909–1936* (Oxford: Oxford University Press, 1995), pp. 31–77.

2 To date there has been no detailed account linking Cohen's moral theology to the rise of dialectical theology in both Jewish and Christian thought. While past scholarship has attended to the link between either Cohen and Rosenzweig or Cohen and Barth, no one has treated the theme of their shared inheritance from Cohen. Moreover of these analyses, little attention has been paid to Cohen's moral theology in particular. Both Bruce McCormack, *Karl Barth's Critically Realistic Dialectical Theology* and Simon Fisher, *Revelatory Positivism? Barth's Earliest Theology and the Marburg School* (Oxford: Oxford University Press, 1988) have noted the effect of Cohen's work on Karl Barth. Neither, however, have considered the relation between Cohen's philosophy of religion and Barth's later theology. Robert Gibbs, *Correlations in Rosenzweig and Levinas* (Princeton: Princeton University Press, 1992) offers a rigorous comparison between Cohen and Rosenzweig, focusing on each thinker's portrait of the I–you relation. This ethical focus draws attention away from its basis in an account of revelation which Cohen and Rosenzweig share. Associating the two thinkers as ethical monotheists, as Leora Batnitzky does in *Idolatry and Representation: The Philosophy of Franz Rosenzweig Reconsidered* (Princeton: Princeton University Press, 1999), achieves only part of the theological work to be done and demands a closer analysis of the two thinkers' theologies of revelation.

3 'Thereupon, the entire monotheistic worship is based on forgiveness of sin.' Hermann Cohen, *Religion of Reason Out of the Sources of Judaism* (trans. Simon Kaplan; New York: Frederick Ungar Publishing Co., 1972), p. 209.

4 Among the two most noteworthy efforts to secure the portrait of Cohen's successful linkage between ethical idealism and Judaism are Andrea Poma, *The Critical Philosophy of Hermann Cohen* (trans. John Denton; Albany: State University of New York Press, 1997) and Michael Zank, *The Idea of Atonement in the Philosophy of Hermann Cohen* (Providence: Scholars Press, 2000).

5 David Novak, *The Election of Israel: The Idea of the Chosen People* (Cambridge: Cambridge University Press, 1995), p. 54.

6 For Kant's famous challenge to the proofs for the existence of God see Immanuel Kant, *Critique of Pure Reason* (trans. Norman Kemp Smith; New York: St. Martin's Press, 1965), pp. 485–573. For his discussion of the postulate of God see Immanual Kant, *Critique of Practical Reason* (trans. Lewis

White Beck; Indianapolis: Bobbs-Merrill Educational Publishing, 1983), pp. 128–36.

7  Hermann Cohen, *System der Philosophie. Erster Teil: Ethik des reinen Willens* (Berlin: Bruno Cassirer, 1907), p. 446.

8  Poma, *Critical Philosophy of Hermann Cohen*, p. 166.

9  For a detailed examination of the history of Cohen's work on religion see Michael Zank, *The Idea of Atonement in the Philosophy of Hermann Cohen.* With respect to this particular point Zank says, 'The original blueprint of [Cohen's] system did not provide for a specific philosophy of religion. But nothing less is introduced here . . . [R]eason itself widens its horizon by including religion rather than "resolving it into ethics."' See Zank, *The Idea of Atonement*, p. 186.

10  Cohen, *Religion,* p. 5.

11  Zank, *The Idea of Atonement*, p. 186.

12  Cohen, *Religion,* p. 34.

13  Zank, *The Idea of Atonement*, p. 187.

14  Cohen, *Religion*, p. 8.

15  Kant, *Critique of Practical Reason*, p. 129.

16  This is true not only for Kant's *Critique of Practical Reason* but also for his more detailed account of religion in Immanuel Kant, *Religion Within the Limits Alone,* (trans. Theodore Green and Hoyt H. Hudson; New York: Harper Torchbooks, 1960). Below, I will provide a detailed comparison between Cohen's philosophy of religion and Kant's.

17  Poma, *Critical Philosophy of Hermann Cohen*, p. 168.

18  Cohen, *Religion,* p. 41.

19  Cohen, *Religion*, p. 44.

20  Cohen, *Religion*, pp. 44–45.

21  Cohen, *Religion*, p. 46.

22  Cohen, *Religion*, pp. 60–61.

23  Cohen, *Religion*, p. 61.

24  Kenneth Seeskin, *Searching for a Distant God* (Oxford: Oxford University Press, 2000) p. 46.

25  Seeskin, *Searching for a Distant God*, p. 63.

26  Maimonides regarded negative theology as a tool to promote rigorous intellectual humility regarding God's essence and therefore as a means of avoiding idolatry. Kenneth Seeskin makes this point: 'In fact, Maimonides is so rigorous on the issue of particularizing God that he thinks even negative predicates are guilty of . . . subsum[ing] God under a category.' Seeskin, *Searching for a Distant God*, p. 33. For an excellent review of Maimonides' arguments in favor of the doctrine of creation see Kenneth Seeskin, *Searching for a Distant God*, pp. 77–90.

27  Cohen, *Religion,* p. 65.

28  Cohen, *Religion*, p. 65.

29 Cohen, *Religion*, p. 71.

30 Cohen, *Religion*, p. 71.

31 Cohen, *Religion*, p. 70.

32 Cohen, *Religion*, p. 86.

33 Cohen, *Religion*, p. 86.

34 Cohen, *Religion*, p. 82.

35 Cohen, *Religion*, pp. 83–84.

36 Cohen, *Religion*, p. 95.

37 Poma, *Critical Philosophy of Hermann Cohen*, p. 193.

38 Below I will address Cohen's identification of 'goodness' as an attribute of action in greater detail.

39 Therefore, while the practical effect of Cohen's theology of attributes of action is similar to Maimonides' insofar as the attributes of action guide human moral pursuit, Cohen would not agree with Maimonides' definition of an attribute of action as that which is predicated of God by virtue of an effect that we see in the world. Maimonides gives an example: 'For instance, one apprehends the kindness of His governance in the production of the embryos of living beings ... Now actions of this kind proceed from ... a certain affection and compassion, and this is the meaning of mercy. God, may He be exalted, is said to be merciful.' Moses Maimonides, *Guide of the Perplexed* (trans. Shlomo Pines; Chicago: University of Chicago Press, 1963), p. 125.

40 Cohen, *Religion,* p. 95.

41 Cohen, *Religion*, p. 111.

42 Cohen, *Religion*, p. 96.

43 See Poma, *Critical Philosophy of Hermann Cohen*, p. 194.

44 Cohen, *Religion,* pp. 50–51.

45 Cohen, *Religion*, p. 96.

46 Kenneth Seeskin, *Autonomy in Jewish Philosophy* (Cambridge: Cambridge University Press, 2001), p. 8.

47 Seeskin, *Autonomy*, p. 162.

48 Cohen, *Religion,* p. 163.

49 Cohen, *Religion,* p. 164.

50 Cohen, *Religion*, p. 162.

51 Hermann Cohen, *Die Religion der Vernunft aus den Quellen des Judentum* (Leipzig: Gustav Fock G.m.b.H., 1919), p. 58.

52 Cohen, *Die Religion*, p. 50.

53 It is worthwhile here to make reference to Barth's concept of *Nach-denken* for, as I will discuss later on, I believe that one can discern a family resemblance between Cohen's notion of *emulation* and Barth's *Nach-denken* insofar as I will read it to be an essentially practical act in the context of election. See Chapters 4 and 5 below.

54 Cohen, *Religion*, p. 50.

55  Seeskin, *Autonomy*, p. 156.

56  Cohen, *Religion,* p. 51.

57  Kant, *Critique of Practical Reason*, p. 137.

58  Kant, *Critique of Practical Reason*, p. 4.

59  Kant, *Critique of Pure Reason*, p. Bxxvi, n.

60  Jamie Ferreira, 'Making Room for Faith – Possibility and Hope', *Kant and Kierkegaard on Religion*, eds D.Z. Phillips and Timothy Tessin (New York: St. Martin's, 2000), p. 76.

61  Jamie Ferreira, 'Kant's Postulate: The Possibility or the Existence of God?', *Kant-Studien* 74 (1983), pp. 75–80.

62  Ferreira, 'Kant's Postulate'.

63  Seeskin, *Autonomy*, pp. 170–71.

64  In his *Fallen Freedom: Kant on Radical Evil and Moral Regeneration*, Gordon Michalson poses additional doubt on the moral necessity for God in the Second Critique. There he argues that Kant postulates God because the highest good requires happiness in proportion to virtue – that is, because the highest good is not only 'complete' but 'perfect'. Such perfection however, Michalson points out, is not morally but merely rationally requisite. See Gordon Michalson, *Fallen Freedom: Kant on Radical Evil and Moral Regeneration* (Cambridge: Cambridge University Press, 1990), p. 24.

65  Cohen, *Religion,* p. 96.

66  Kant, *Critique of Practical Reason*, p. 134.

67  Here, therefore, I disagree with Seeskin's claim that 'the strength of Cohen's analysis is that ultimately the question of who is responsible for the law is beside the point ...' See Seeskin, *Autonomy*, p. 162. On the contrary, Cohen understands religious life as the effort to draw near the God who is the source of holiness.

68  Seeskin, *Autonomy*, p. 14.

69  Martin Buber, 'On Hermann Cohen', in *The Writings of Martin Buber*, ed. Will Herberg; (New York: New American Library, 1973), p. 105.

70  Buber, 'On Hermann Cohen', p. 104.

71  Cohen, *Religion*, p. 132.

72  Cohen, *Religion*, p. 128.

73  Cohen, *Religion*, p. 161.

74  Cohen, *Religion*, p. 147.

75  Buber, 'On Hermann Cohen', p. 105.

76  Buber, 'On Hermann Cohen', p. 106.

77  It is important to note, however, that to claim that Cohen's correlation of practical reason advances the seeds of a theology of testimony later developed in Barth and Rosenzweig is not to claim that Cohen's practical correlation marks a turn toward a religious existentialism. The argument here does not therefore resonate with Franz Rosenzweig's own estimation of Cohen's theology of

correlation as the turning point in Cohen's career from idealism to a burgeoning existentialism. On the contrary, as we will see below, it is precisely Cohen's refusal to describe the ideal/moral correlation of revelation in either phenomenological or existential terms that ultimately generates the tension in his work between religion and ethics – a tension that Rosenzweig and Barth correct through their account of revelation as an act of divine love that precedes human moral testimony and bypasses the commitment to autonomy.

78  Cohen, *Religion*, p. 213.
79  Cohen, *Religion*, p. 212.
80  Cohen, *Religion*, p. 207.
81  Immanuel Kant, *Religion Within the Limits of Reason Alone* (trans. Theodore Gree and Hoyt H. Hudson; New York: Harper & Row, 1960), p. 49.
82  Michalson, *Fallen Freedom*, p. 96.
83  In *Fallen Freedom*, Gordon Michalson frequently notes how Kant's account of moral regeneration asks 'how' a person can do the good, when it has not discerned 'if' a person who is evil can actually attempt to do the good by herself at all. 'Notice . . . how Kant begs his own question (concerning how someone with a corrupt disposition can become good again) by simply assuming at the outset of his answer that this transformation has already occurred. Just how someone "reverses, by a single unchangeable decision, that highest ground" of one's maxims (i.e., the disposition), is exactly what we want to understand, rather than what we can assume as a premise for discussing something else.' Michalson, *Fallen Freedom*, p. 94.
84  Kant, *Religion Within the Limits*, p. 49.
85  John Silber makes this same point and argues that for Kant freedom as spontaneity presupposes the possibility of both heteronomous and autonomous action when by heteronomous we mean the ability to choose to act against the moral law and on the grounds of my desires instead. John Silber, 'The Ethical Significance of Kant's *Religion*', *Religion Within the Limits of Reason Alone*, p. xcii.
86  Kant, *Religion Within the Limits*, p. 36.
87  Michalson, *Fallen Freedom*, p. 96.
88  Kant, *Critique of Practical Reason*, p. 127.
89  Kant, *Critique of Practical Reason*, p. 140.
90  For this argument I am indebted to Jamie Ferreira, 'Making Room for Faith'.
91  Ferreira, 'Making Room for Faith', p. 78.
92  Kant, *Religion Within the Limits*, pp. 48–49.
93  Kant, *Religion Within the Limits*, p. 40.
94  Of course, the reason Kant must invoke the notion of supernatural aid is precisely because his argument about the possibility of moral regeneration above is specious. Kant's analysis of radical evil as both inscrutable and inextirpable (inscrutable because it is an act of freedom; and inextirpable

insofar as it is the choice – the single choice by a unified will to act on one's sensuous interests instead of heeding the obligation to act on the moral laws) results in the above paradox.

95  Kant, *Religion Within the Limits*, p. 47.
96  Cohen, *Religion,* p. 211.
97  Kant, *Religion Within the Limits*, p. 60.
98  Kant, *Religion Within the Limits*, p. 60.
99  To the possible objection that in this instance Kant is assuming that moral regeneration has already transpired and that, consequently, the self-confidence available to persons now is not available when discussing the individual's effort to move from radical evil to adopting a good maxim as the basis for her action, one may reply that Kant himself refuses to make this distinction. See above discussion, endnote 83.
100  Kant, *Religion Within the Limits*, p. 62.
101  Kant makes a similar argument in the *Critique of Practical Reason* with respect to the limits of our practical knowledge. It is practically fortunate, Kant argues, that our knowledge of God and immortality of the soul are limited to practical belief. Theoretical knowledge of them would impair our moral zeal. See Kant, *Critique of Practical Reason*, pp. 152–53.
102  Kant, *Religion Within the Limits*, p. 66.
103  Kant, *Religion Within the Limits*, p. 69.
104  Kant, *Religion Within the Limits*, p. 69.
105  Kant, *Religion Within the Limits*, p. 70.
106  Kant, *Religion Within the Limits*, p. 70.
107  Cohen, *Religion*, p. 184.
108  Cohen, *Religion*, p. 211.
109  Poma, *Critical Philosophy of Hermann Cohen*, p. 219.
110  Cohen, *Religion*, p. 218.
111  Cohen, *Religion*, p. 194.
112  Cohen, *Religion*, p. 202.
113  Cohen, *Religion*, p. 202.
114  Cohen, *Religion*, p. 203.
115  Cohen, *Religion*, p. 203.
116  Cohen, *Religion*, p. 195.
117  Cohen, *Religion*, p. 195.
118  Cohen, *Religion*, p. 205.
119  Cohen, *Religion*, p. 187.
120  Cohen, *Religion*, p. 194.
121  Cohen, *Religion*, p. 204.
122  Cohen, *Religion*, p. 204.
123  Cohen, *Religion*, p. 206.
124  Cohen, *Religion*, p. 207.

125  Seeskin, *Searching for a Distant God*, p. 115.
126  Cohen, *Religion*, p. 203.
127  Cohen, *Religion*, p. 207.
128  Cohen, *Religion*, p. 207.
129  Cohen, *Religion*, p. 212.
130  Cohen, *Religion*, p. 207.
131  Cohen, *Religion*, p. 212.
132  Cohen, *Religion*, p. 212.
133  Cohen, *Religion*, p. 212.
134  Cohen, *Religion*, p. 208.
135  Poma, *Critical Philosophy of Hermann Cohen*, pp. 231–32.
136  Poma, *Critical Philosophy of Hermann Cohen*, p. 232.
137  Poma, *Critical Philosophy of Hermann Cohen*, p. 233.

# Chapter 2

# Theology and the Language of Love

About *The Star of Redemption*, Rosenzweig once said, 'I have written the first Jewish book that I know to be non-fanatical.'[1] With this retrospective reflection Rosenzweig identified the single most important characteristic of his own work – its ability to present a non-fanatical theology. Rosenzweig's passionate commitment to a portrait of a non-fanatical Judaism hearkens back to the influence of his mentor Hermann Cohen. Still, Rosenzweig's quest to overcome religious dogmatism results in the toppling of Cohen's appeal to idealism's standards of rationality and boldly announces the critical or rational moment within the phenomenology of biblical revelation itself. The inspiration for the later thought of Emmanuel Levinas and a contemporary Jewish post-liberalism, Rosenzweig's account of the non-fanatical impulse of biblical revelation stands as a beacon of light for contemporary Jews and Christians seeking a full embrace of their religious texts and practices without the myopia of religious fideism.

What does it mean to say that Rosenzweig's theology is non-fanatical? It means that Rosenzweig appreciates and articulates how theology always begins from an individual's experience of commandedness to testify to an experience of both God's love and God's absence within oneself and not from a position of absolute certainty. This theology of testimony can concomitantly assert the reality of a transcendent God without falling prey to either religious dogmatism or subjectivism.

Rosenzweig's commitment to articulating a non-fanatical theology allows him to overcome the Scylla and Charybdis of pre-Kantian dogmatism and Schleiermachian subjectivism while avoiding the Kantian critique of theology. Towards the end of *The Star of Redemption* Rosenzweig states, '[T]he question of "What is God?" is impossible.'[2] Rather than sounding a sigh of despair, Rosenzweig is simply reiterating Immanuel Kant's claim that theology can no longer inquire as to God's nature or existence because our faculty of reason is incapable of meeting the demands of such a task. By means of his critical assessment of the bounds of reason, Kant undermined theological efforts to acquire knowledge of God's nature and/or his existence. One could gain objective knowledge only about those things which could be experienced within the bounds of space and time. God's nature was surely beyond such bounds and therefore beyond the bounds of theoretical cognition. We could no longer ask, 'What is God's essence?' and expect to get an answer by means of theoretical reasoning.

If theology is no longer engaged in rational exploration of God's nature, what is its task? Out of the rubble left over from the Kantian revolution, Schleiermacher offered one potential answer. Rather than base theological work in the experience of the rational faculty, Schleiermacher asserted a Copernican Revolution of his own advocating a theology based in feeling – in a 'sense and taste of the infinite'.[3] Whether Schleiermacher's intention or not, theology informed by this new approach often posited a radical opposition between thought and feeling thereby producing a theology of subjectivism focused less on God and more on an individual's own sense of God. For Rosenzweig, however, a singular focus on an individual's own experience of God robbed theology of its ability to discourse on providence. Schleiermacher's theology 'asserted the complete independence of belief from knowledge'.[4] Where was God in this kind of work? Rosenzweig and other critics argued that given this approach God could be wherever an individual wanted him to be. Relegated to private experience, talk of God could now be subject to the whims of subjective fanaticism. Against this trend Rosenzweig sought to reintroduce a theological discourse where a real, objective and transcendent God could be found.

Like his contemporary Karl Barth, Rosenzweig understood the basis of theological work to lie in the revelation event of a God who loves humankind by commanding them to love him through an act of obedient testimony. By locating the basis of theology in this account of the revelatory event of God's love, Rosenzweig found an alternative to the rationalist, natural theology debunked by Kant. Furthermore, by highlighting the asymmetrical character of the love and command encounter between God and humankind, Rosenzweig could bypass the problem of radical subjectivity associated with the theologians of experience. In the revelation event an individual experiences a love and a moral calling unlike any he has ever located within the realm of his own subjective experience.

The basis for arguing that Rosenzweig offers a theology of testimony can be found in Part II, Books 2 and 3 of *The Star of Redemption* in the sections entitled 'Revelation or the Ever Renewed Birth of the Soul' and 'Redemption, or the Eternal Future of the Kingdom.' In what follows I will examine these sections as the basis of a theology of testimony. More specifically I will argue that, for Rosenzweig, theological knowledge emerges out of the covenantal encounter between a loving and commanding God and a beloved and obedient human recipient who testifies to this love through a life of repentance and theological desire. Additionally I will demonstrate how this appreciation for Rosenzweig's commitment to non-fanatical theology undermines the long-standing tendency to identify Rosenzweig's thought with the dialogical theology of his colleague, Martin Buber.[5] I will argue that to identify Rosenzweig as a dialogical theologian is to miss precisely how his theology is non-fanatical insofar as a careful reading of Buber's dialogical thought reveals a return to subjectivism.

## A. Revelation: Divine Love, Divine Command

The centerpiece of Rosenzweig's work is his analysis of revelation.[6] According to Rosenzweig, revelation provides the exclusive opportunity for human knowledge of a transcendent God. Knowledge of God means, for Rosenzweig, knowledge of that which transcends and is exterior to human life and, according to Rosenzweig, the only means by which human beings can access knowledge of divine exteriority is through a revelatory encounter with divine love.

Prior to examining Rosenzweig's analysis of God's love, it is necessary first to consider the epistemological basis of Rosenzweig's phenomenological description of divine love. If revelation is the unique basis of theology, on what grounds may Rosenzweig provide a phenomenological account of this event and, in particular, an analysis of God's love? The answer lies in Rosenzweig's understanding of religion and its ability to articulate the covenantal love between God and humanity. Religions, Judaism and Christianity in particular, as we will see in detail later, are guardians of the human experience of divine love. Rosenzweig's phenomenological account in II:2 is an extraction from his reading of the Song of Songs. Consequently, the phenomenology here provided by Rosenzweig is not the result of a theoretical effort, nor is it even an account of a raw human experience. Rather it is a gloss on the human experience of love as described by biblical text and tradition.[7] Rosenzweig is simply translating into prose the account of love that is already in the poetic text.

We can now examine Rosenzweig's account of the act of divine love. According to Rosenzweig, revelation is an event of divine love because divine love is the unique means by which God can exteriorize or manifest himself. Rosenzweig's analysis of the religious sources suggests that God's exteriorization is a feature of God's living participation in a world made up of relations between three elements: God, the world and humankind. On the one hand, God relates to the world through his power by positing the world, i.e. God relates to the world as its creator. However, according to Rosenzweig, the continued success of God's relation to the world and, more particularly, to humankind, requires that God manifest himself more directly than he does as the origin of the world. As creator, God can become lost behind the world he creates. God needs, Rosenzweig says, a 'second revelation'[8] which 'does not posit anything'[9] that could conceal God. In this second revelation, God exteriorizes himself by distinguishing himself from the world he has created. He reveals himself as Other through an act of love.

Divine love is revelatory because it is self-sacrificing, eventful and commanding. First, God's love is wholly self-sacrifice. In the act of loving, God exteriorizes himself by placing himself into the arms of a thou or another person. 'Only the love of the lover is such a continually renewed self sacrifice, it is only he who gives himself away in love.'[10] God manifests himself through an act of grace by offering himself as a gift to the thou.

Second, not only does the act of love allow God to make himself available to a human thou, but the act of love allows God to reveal himself specifically as something radically Other from the entirety of the created order. God does not, according to Rosenzweig, reveal himself as other from the created order by disclosing a set of unique attributes. If revelation were a propositional dispensation of information regarding divine attributes, God's nature would become part of the body of propositional knowledge that makes up human knowledge about the world, i.e. God would become a part of the created order and not distinct from it. Instead, Rosenzweig tells us, God reveals his distinction from creation by performing an act of love that is ever renewed and always momentary and therefore cannot be established as a fact. Thus, says Rosenzweig, 'love is not an attribute, but an event'.[11]

It is indeed the case that Rosenzweig also describes creation as a mode of God's coming into relationship with humans, and thus as revelation in a broader sense. Nevertheless, for Rosenzweig, revelation in its essence must be an immediate experience, distinguished from God's act of creation. When one limits revelation to creation, one reduces revelation to a set of facts about the world in which God is hidden behind them as their origin. In this case my relationship to the created world is not one in which God presents God's self to me; rather, what is present to me when I encounter the world is a series of propositional statements about the world. What has been lost is that aspect of God's existence that is over and above the world. Therefore, in its essence, revelation or God's presentation of God's own self must be qualitatively different from anything and everything in our world and our experience; it must be a challenge to any claim to individual sovereignty. Otherwise what is revealed is not God's self, but worldly beings or states of affairs that are only masks of God. These can all too easily become idols.

Since revelation must be of something that is radically and qualitatively different from the created world, it cannot be simply the disclosure of a set of divine attributes. If revelation were a propositional dispensation of factual information in this manner, God's nature would become part of the body of propositional knowledge that makes up human knowledge about the world. God would become a part of the created order and not distinct from it. In shifting from an understanding of revelation as fact to an understanding of revelation as act, the transcendence of God is protected. This is the logic behind Rosenzweig's assertion that 'love is not an attribute, but an event, and no attribute has any place in it'. For Rosenzweig, revelation does not have any conceptual referent; it does not have meaning in the way that propositional sentences do. This means that revelation is not the communication of some thing called 'love' from God to humankind. If what Rosenzweig terms 'essential revelation' cannot take place in propositional or constative language, it must be performative. The referent of revelation can only be to an act; revelation cannot communicate facts. For this reason, Rosenzweig describes revelation as 'a revelation which is nothing more than revelation, a revelation in the narrower – indeed, in the narrowest sense . . . The manifestation which we seek here must be one that is wholly and essentially revelation, and nothing else.'[12]

Finally, God's love is revelatory when it commands. If revelation is not a presentation of divine attributes, neither is it a proclamation of divine love. Like the presentation of attributes, the declaration of love provides information that gets incorporated into knowledge about the world. Consequently, a declaration of love cannot express God's exteriority. The language of divine love is the imperative.[13] Only the imperative retains the performative presence characteristic of the act of love itself. Only the imperative, therefore, manifests divine otherness. 'The indicative has behind it the whole cumbersome rationalization of materiality, and at its purest therefore appears in the past tense. But the 'love me!'is wholly pure and unprepared for present tense ...'[14]

The upshot of this account is that God's second revelation is God's act of election where election means God's unconditional and commanding expression of love to another. The theology of testimony is a theology of divine election.[15] With this analysis, Rosenzweig has restored the authentic meaning of the biblical doctrine of election as the nexus of grace and commandment.[16] The commandment to love God is not a burden on the beloved but rather a gift from God that provides the beloved with a means to participate in a covenantal bond with the divine. How do we respond in this conversation of deeds?

## B. Obedience and Testimony

There is only one way for a recipient of divine love to respond and that is to acknowledge or testify to God's love. As the expression of divine otherness, divine love nullifies the individual's return to her former self. Insofar as God's love emerges from outside of her prior experience it calls that experience and its authority into question. By challenging the individual's own authority, the radical otherness of this love asserts itself as an authority and commands her acknowledgment.[17] Without any recourse to the self, there is nothing else that the beloved can do other than acknowledge the love. It is the 'beloved's admission of love [which] responds to the lover's demand of love'.[18] While an admission of love is a response to a demand of love, the admission is none other than the obedient acknowledgment required by the lover and therefore a testimony to the collapse of the individual's autonomy. With no recourse to her own experiential resources and compelled by this loving authority, she has no choice but to obey this authority by acknowledging its power – 'the soul attests the love of God'.[19]

Rosenzweig's appreciation for the unique character of the event of divine love is the basis of his non-fanatical theology. The event of divine love simultaneously presents an individual with an encounter of a transcendent God whose very loving and commanding presence forbids the reduction of this transcendence by the individual's subjective characterization.

### a. The Phenomenology and Theology of Repentance
At this point, however, the theology of testimony meets with a new problem. If it is true that a beloved has no choice but to testify to the love of

her lover, it remains unclear precisely *how* a recipient of revelation can testify to the reality of divine love without compromising that love's radical otherness. Clearly, the beloved cannot testify to God's divine love in a way that directly mirrors or repeats this love, for a simple repetition of divine love would indicate an identity between human love and divine love and destroy the revelation of divine transcendence expressed through this event. On the other hand, the beloved's testimony or acknowledgment of divine love cannot call on a person's common stock of ethical behaviors for, as human, these cannot be rooted in or respondent to an event of divine love. The beloved's testimony must simultaneously point to the reality of divine love without however denying its radical alterity.

Rosenzweig solves this problem and thereby secures the basis of a non-fanatical theology by arguing that an individual witnesses to God's love only by concomitantly recognizing the absence of God in her own life. In order to understand how the recipient of divine love testifies to divine love, it is necessary to understand *what* the recipient experiences of this divine love. She will only testify to her experience of divine love. The human experience of divine love differs from God's experience of loving. For the beloved, divine love offers a momentary sense of security and peace that simultaneously awakens the beloved to the absence of this love in her past and her inability to provide this love for herself in her future. Consequently, the beloved testifies to divine love by testifying to the absence of this divine love in her self-determined past and in her own self-determined future. By testifying to the absence of divine love in herself, the beloved successfully testifies to God and fulfills the divine command to love God without subjectivizing God's reality. God's love is that which is pointed to but not directly expressed in the beloved's awareness of its absence within herself. More specifically, an individual testifies to divine love through a life of repentance and desire.

Let us examine the human experience of divine love in greater detail. According to Rosenzweig, revelation affords an individual an experience of love unlike any she has ever known before. Divine love grants the individual feelings of security, peace and fulfillment. Rosenzweig describes her as experiencing 'an awe ... together with a feeling of dependence and of being securely sheltered or of taking refuge in the arms of eternity ...'[20] Loved by God, the individual experiences what it feels like to be reached by another in a way that is 'wholly active, wholly personal, wholly living'.[21] This, however, is not the full extent of the human experience of divine love. According to Rosenzweig's account, the

61

individual's sense of newfound security and peace is accompanied by a pressing awareness of the absence of this love in her past. The newness of the event marks a break between that moment in time and all other prior temporal moments. While God is inseparable from his act of love, the individual has lived without this love and the event of love awakens her to a sense of responsibility for this absence. 'The beloved is conscious of wanting nothing in the future but to remain what she is: beloved. But back in the past, there was a time before she was beloved, and this time of unbelovedness, of lovelessness, seems to her covered in deepest darkness.'[22]

The beloved's experience of divine love as a sense of peace and security that awakens her to her own sinfulness constitutes the content of her testimony and she repents. 'And thus the soul which God summons with the command to love is ashamed to acknowledge to him its love, for it can only acknowledge its love by acknowledging its weakness at the same time and by responding to God's "Thou shalt love" with an "I have sinned."'[23] By repenting, the soul acknowledges the reality of a transcendent authority by announcing the absence of this authority within herself.

While, therefore, like Cohen, Rosenzweig recognizes the relationship between repentance and theological awareness, Rosenzweig's return to the biblical sources permits him to recognize the prior reality of the divine act of love. Free from the constraints of critical idealism, Rosenzweig can offer a phenomenology of the sinner who awakens to moral responsibility in response to an act of divine love. Her repentant shame and subsequent longing for God is the appropriate response to the divine act. Cohen's inability to appropriate the character of the loving God into his idealist system rendered him incapable of accounting for the character of repentance as the response to and longing for the God who loves.

### b. *The Phenomenology of Desire and Theology of Verification*

Beyond the newfound awareness of her sin, the beloved also experiences divine love in terms of her inability to control and secure future moments of the divine love – that is, she experiences divine love as that which she desires. According to Rosenzweig's account, the beloved's desire for more moments of love arises from the fact that on the one hand the love that she feels is always only momentary and must therefore always be renewed yet, as divine, she cannot control the renewal of this love. She longs for more love moments. Rosenzweig offers this account: 'Is the soul beloved? Can it be beloved? Is the love of God something from which nothing can any longer separate the soul? Can it no longer be expelled from this repose in God? Is it ever with him? . . . Is its love by God a bond so secure that it simply cannot conceive of God ever being able to loosen it again?'[24]

Not only does the beloved long for more moments of divine love in the future – but now that she experiences divine love, she longs to see her past re-constituted in view of these love moments – that is, she longs or desires to remember God's love as a basis or a ground for her belief in him. Like her hope for more moments in the future, the beloved's longing to trust in a God of her past is always only a longing. As momentary and exterior, God's love is an immemorial love. To reproduce it in memory would subjectivize it and deny its otherness. The beloved may, however, *long* for memory, long for a 'ground and a warrant'[25] to her experience.

Finally, beyond her desire to secure God's love in her own past and in her own future, the beloved seeks God's presence throughout the world as well. 'Revelation climaxes in an unfulfilled wish in the cry of an open question.'[26] The beloved cries out for the presence of God throughout all the world, now and in the future. 'The prayer for the coming of the kingdom is ever but a crying and a sighing, ever but a plea.'[27] As before, the beloved's desire grows out of her reception of revelatory love but her reception of this love is conditioned by her inability to bring this love into her world, her inability to guarantee redemption. Without divine love she could not hope for the world's redemption. With divine love she cannot guarantee it.

Here, too, the beloved's experience of divine love joins together the sense of care and shelter with a sense of God's absence within herself and this experience constitutes the content of her testimony. The beloved now testifies to God by expressing her desire for God. Like repentance, theological desire suggests the reality of God's love by pointing to the absence of this reality in the human person who desires it. Along with repentance, desire becomes the way that human beings obey the divine command to love God. What then, according to Rosenzweig, does it mean to love God? It does not mean a life of certainty and self-righteousness. Rather it means to live obediently before God, in repentance and longing for a divine love that we can never possess or control. According to Rosenzweig, the beloved testifies to God through her desire in two ways: through faith and through love of the neighbor.

What happens to the beloved who searches for assurances of God's continued love? How does she contend with this desire for God? She cannot hope to eliminate this desire by turning to God. God has already turned toward her in the only fashion possible – that is, in the ever momentary and present act of love. Revelation, Rosenzweig says, 'does not posit anything'[28] and therefore God cannot declare the ground or future of this love to his beloved. Moreover, because it is ephemeral, the experience of divine love ends after the imperative has been spoken and flows off into an immemorial past. Of course, the beloved cannot mollify this desire by herself for she desires *God's* love. The beloved cannot do anything other than express her desire and, according to Rosenzweig's account, she does so by professing faith in God. Therefore revelation does not mark an end to theological eros, but rather testifies to the perdurance of theological eros, even if the beloved has further ephemeral experiences of divine love in the future. The beloved's declaration of faith includes a belief in God as creator in the past and revealer in the present. 'By its trust, the faith of the soul attests the love of God and endows it with enduring being.'[29] How does this profession of faith express rather than override the beloved's insatiable desire for the God who loves only moment to moment?

To answer this question it is important to understand the epistemological status of the beloved's declaration. On what grounds could the beloved assert these types of claims regarding God? Certainly, as we have seen, God does not provide this information. Alternatively, the soul has no independent source of knowledge concerning the God who loves. The soul's profession of faith is rooted strictly in her experience as the beloved. She knows herself loved momentarily and she knows she desires more of this love. Her profession of faith is a pragmatic verification whereby the truth that she asserts is a truth that she wants to assert. By pragmatic verification I mean what William James meant when he argued in his essay 'The Will to Believe' that there are certain times and conditions when it is not only justifiable but absolutely necessary that 'the desire for a certain kind of truth here brings about that special truths' existence'.[30] For James, one can and must use one's desire or will to generate truths when there is no conclusive evidence either way regarding the claim and when the claim in question is very important and very real for the claimant. Since there is no conclusive evidence, one cannot use one's intellect to decide. Moreover, since the issue at hand is exceptionally important – that is, one's acceptance of this claim will impact greatly on one's life – one cannot suspend judgment on this truth. James refers to beliefs rooted in these sorts of decisions as genuine options. 'Our passional nature not only lawfully may but must decide an option between propositions, whenever it is a genuine option that cannot by its nature be decided on intellectual grounds ... '[31] Consequently, under these circumstances, there is no choice but to assert one's desire or will for this truth. Rosenzweig's account of the profession of faith fits James' account of how and when we can and must assert truths based on our will or desire for them.

In his essay *The New Thinking*, Rosenzweig describes this truth and says,

> [T]his truth [is] different from the truth of the philosophers ... '[T]he' truth changes into our truth. Truth in this way ceases to be what 'is' true, and becomes that which, as true – wants to be verified. The concept of verification of the truth becomes the basic concept of this new theory of knowledge.[32]

To verify truth is, Rosenzweig says, 'to make it my own'.[33] But to make God's truth my own is to express my desire for it. 'The personal is verified as eternal truth ...'[34] The beloved's profession of faith is not an instance of mere wish-fulfillment. She *is* loved. Rather it is a testimony to her being loved in and for a moment and her hope that this love will endure. Of course, the human articles of faith are not the whole truth or God's truth. 'The whole of the truth, the whole truth can be perceived only by being seen in God.'[35] In other words, for Rosenzweig, faith is the expression of theological desire for the God who loves me moment to moment. As the expression of theological desire, faith becomes a means of living obediently with and testifying to the transcendent God who loves me.

Rosenzweig's theology of verification is one of the most neglected aspects of his thought and arguably the most significant. Rosenzweig's theology of verification maintains the epistemological balance between assertion and doubt characteristic of Jamesian pragmatism. On the one hand, desire presupposes that which it desires and may therefore positively assert that which it seeks. On the other hand, desire is the lack of that which it seeks and is therefore never capable of inscribing an objectively stable referent for its longing. Moreover, unlike James' passion, theological desire is the desire for the infinite or that which definitionally exceeds our grasp. While according to James's *Will to Believe* it is possible for religious truths to be evidenced and objectively determined and, consequently, these truths must be subject to evidential considerations when sufficient evidence is presented, the character of the infinite as radically other in Rosenzweig's account guarantees that theological truth will never be rendered accountable or verifiable by evidential reasoning. As the desire for the infinite, theological desire guards against any form of theological positivism or what, for Rosenzweig, would amount to idolatrous belief.

As such, Rosenzweig's phenomenology of desire contributes to the development of the practical turn in theology initiated in the modern period by Kant. By locating theological knowledge within the faculty of desire Rosenzweig carries on the Kantian tradition of theological knowledge as the practical acting as if God is real.[36] The significant contribution Rosenzweig makes to this Kantian tradition consists in the difference between the category of theological desire as a testimonial response to a radically Other God and Kant's practical postulate of God premised strictly on rational need rooted in an apodictic law. According to Kant, I may only act as if God is possible insofar as I have a rational need for such an assertion.

> A need of pure practical reason . . . is based on a duty to make something the object of my will . . . In doing so, I must presuppose its possibility and also its conditions; for these conditions I am not in a position to prove by my speculative reason, though I cannot disprove them either. This duty is based on an apodictic law, the moral law, which is independent of these presuppositions . . .[37]

For Rosenzweig, I only act as if God loves me precisely because I do not have a rational need for God but because I have undergone an event of election that exceeds my reason and compels me to respond through verification of my desire. Nonetheless, Rosenzweig's theology of verification does not fall prey to charges of fideism or fanaticism so far as theological desire presupposes the element of doubt or lack within itself.[38] In this way, Rosenzweig's theological desire retains the benefit of Kant's epistemological humility without however being restricted by the terms of human rationality. The life of revelation for Rosenzweig is, therefore, not one of certainty and self-righteousness but of longing and desire, rooted in the dialectical conflict established by the experience of divine love, that between an inner sense of revelation and an outer sense of the absence of God in one's environment.

Aware of the epistemological character of desire, we may return to Rosenzweig's phenomenology of theological desire. If faith is the practical expression of one's desire for God in one's life, love of the neighbor is the expression of one's desire for redemption, what is God's presence in the world and the human community. According to Rosenzweig, to love the neighbor as oneself means, literally, to treat the neighbor like myself — that is, like one who has been loved by God. It is therefore to act as if God's love extends beyond myself. Practically speaking this means that the beloved views the neighbor as an expression or a sign of God's

66

authoritative love. To love the neighbor, for Rosenzweig, is actively to approach the neighbor as one who bears or conveys God's commandment to love God. When the beloved loves the neighbor she simply allows the neighbor to prompt her to the same kenosis she arrives at in her direct encounter with God's love, the same 'ever new self-denial'.[39] She allows the neighbor to become the occasion to testify to her own inability, and God's unique ability, to love.

How then is the love of the neighbor an expression of one's *desire* for redemption? Doesn't the fact that I can love the neighbor now and live as if redemption has already occurred suggest that I no longer have to desire it? To answer this question we must further examine the two presuppositions required for love of the neighbor: 1) that I have been loved by God and 2) that I may justifiably act as if God has also loved my neighbor. While the beloved can positively attest to the certainty of the first presupposition for she has experienced God's love, she has no experience and no other basis for believing with certainty that God has already loved others as well. Consequently, her ability to treat others as herself, as ones loved by God, is rooted in the combination of her confidence in the God who loves her and her hope or her *desire* that God loves the other person in the same way. The beloved's love of the neighbor is not the result of a confirmed belief in God's already having redeemed the world. Rather it is an expression of her desire that God will redeem the world – that she *will* be able to approach the neighbor as the occasion of her self-negation and testimony to God. The believer is not able simply to wait patiently for a future redemption; waiting would falsify her experience of divine presence in the moment of revelation. Therefore in order to trust in the futurity of objective redemption, the beloved must act as if redemption has already occurred. Like her earlier profession of faith, the beloved's love of the neighbor is an act of pragmatic verification whereby the individual asserts a truth (in this instance a practical truth, i.e. she acts in a certain way) based on her desire for this truth more than on her confidence in any evidential ground for this truth.

We can now understand why Rosenzweig says, 'The love for God is to express itself in love for one's neighbor.'[40] The love of the neighbor functions as the means by which the beloved testifies to her experience of divine love as the desire for redemption. To love the neighbor is not to act with certainty but with desire and hope. By loving the neighbor, the beloved again testifies to her particularly human experience of divine love – what in this instance is the simultaneous confidence in God's love coupled

with her desire for more of God's love in her world. To love the neighbor –
to labor for redemption – is to live covenantally, for it is a demonstration of
one's reception of divine love and the desire for God's continued love that
emerges from this reception. This leads to the development of a religious
community, predicated upon, vulnerable to and inspired by the dialectics of
theological desire.

### c. *Summary*

With this account of covenantal life Rosenzweig has provided the basis of a
non-fanatical theology. Rosenzweig's account of revelation as an individual's experience of commandedness to testify to an experience of God's care
and God's absence within oneself establishes the possibility for a theological
discourse that refers to a transcendent God and is not reducible to subjective
human experience.

Theology, therefore, according to Rosenzweig, is the knowledge a
human person acquires in the context of this encounter with God's
commanding love. To know God is to participate in this event of divine
love and command in the only way possible: that is, by obediently testifying
to or announcing one's recognition of this electing love. Theology is the
practical act of witnessing to the God who loves and elects.

Rosenzweig's theology of witness is uniquely characterized by his
analysis of the human experience of divine love as it translates into
repentance and desire. Human persons testify to their particular experience
of divine love as something that has been absent in their past and something
that they desire in their future and in their world. Theology is the act of
practical witness to God's love as expressed and verified in repentance, faith
and love of the neighbor.

## C. A New Rosenzweig–Buber Comparison

Rosenzweig has long been labeled a dialogical theologian. A dialogical
theologian is one who maintains that revelation is an event of dialogical
communication between two participants which uniquely engenders the
presence of being or spirit. This longstanding view has often shaped the
basis of the comparison between the work of Rosenzweig and Buber.[41] The
above discussion of Rosenzweig's conception of revelation as an event of
divine love and human testimony undermines this characterization of
Rosenzweig's thought. To identify Rosenzweig's thought with Buber's
dialogical theology is not only incorrect but is also a failure to appreciate the

non-fanatical character of Rosenzweig's thought. A careful analysis of Buber's dialogical relation reveals a latent subjectivism that Rosenzweig's account of divine love and testimony overcomes.

It is Buber and not Rosenzweig who espouses dialogical theology. In his classic, *I and Thou*, Buber describes the I–You encounter. The I–You encounter is one of two modes of how humans relate to the world. According to Buber, a human being can relate to her world by treating it as an object for her use (I–It relation) or a human being can relate to the world as a subject that she personally encounters or meets (I–You). Neither the I–It nor the I–You relation concern human relations exclusively but may include one's relations with animate, inanimate and/or supernatural or spiritual elements of our world.

In the I–It relation, I experience the world from the vantage point of my own ego – my own thought, my own desires and my own feelings. I separate myself from the world that I seek to experience and use. 'The ego occupies himself with his My: my manner, my race, my works, my genius . . . He sets himself apart from everything else and tries to possess as much as possible by means of experience and use.'[42]

Conversely, the I–You relation is what Buber calls a 'natural (*naturhaft*) association'.[43] The purpose of the I–You relation is not to set oneself apart but rather to participate in the encounter with the You. The I–You encounter is a reciprocal meeting or dialogue between an I and another subject that transpires through grace and will. As grace, the world offers itself to me as an occasion for an encounter. 'The You confronts me.'[44] But the world does not confront me with an exterior command. Within every person is 'the a priori of relation; the innate You',[45] a will or a drive that waits and readies itself for the real You and, when confronted by it, proceeds to meet it. 'The longing for relation is primary,'[46] Buber says. Every child naturally reaches out toward the You and 'in the relationships through which we live, the innate You is realized in the you we encounter'.[47] Therefore, the I–You encounter is neither heteronomous nor autonomous but rather the fulfillment of the nature of the person through its encounter with the nature of the world. 'Thus the relationship is election and electing, passive and active at once.'[48]

As the reciprocal movement of the I and the You toward one another, the I–You relation is a dialogue of mutual address and response. The natural association of the I and the You, the dialogue requires no mediation. It requires no outside interpretation. On the contrary, the dialogue generates eternal meaning. By meaning, Buber does not mean a specific content of discussion but rather the essence of reality. Dialogue is the site of presence, the eternal essence of all reality.

> When a man steps before the countenance, the world becomes wholly present to him for the first time in the fullness of the presence, illuminated by eternity, and he can say You in one word to the being of all beings. There is no longer any tension between world and God but only the one actuality.[49]

Rosenzweig's and Buber's descriptions of the covenant relationship are markedly different. Unlike Buber, Rosenzweig's covenant is a product of divine love. Unlike the summons of the I–You encounter, divine love is radically new to the beloved. God's love does not, for Rosenzweig, greet a ready and waiting recipient. It emerges from outside of its recipient and shocks the beloved with its newness.

As radically exterior, God's love presents the beloved with an authority that challenges her sovereignty. God's love commands the beloved heteronomously. Divine love does not correlate with the beloved's a-priori nature but commands the beloved to recognize a love it formerly lacked and now desires from outside of itself. The beloved receives God's love in the context of its life and its world and testifies to God's love from its position in this world. Through repentance and desire, human beings bring God into their world. Covenant is not a mutual dialogue that generates being. It is an exchange of divine and human love within the context of divine election and human imperfection.

Buber's covenant begins with the natural, i.e. the subject's potential to greet the You within every human being, and not with an act of divine love. For Buber, therefore, covenant is not a vehicle for an encounter between a person and a radically Other God but the occasion for persons to realize their existential actuality by speaking with another person.

Buber's failure to appreciate the role of divine love within revelation spirals into a failure to appreciate the commanding character of this divine love and the obedient testimony of the one who is loved. While scholarly comparisons between Buber and Rosenzweig have focused on the differences in their view of Jewish law (*Gesetz*)[50] or the differences in their view of the relation to the neighbor[51] scholars have neglected to appreciate the difference in their view of the relation between revelation and commandment. Buber and Rosenzweig announce this as one of their central differences in their famous exchange of letters entitled 'Revelation and Law'. Rooted in an event of divine love, revelation is necessarily commanding for

70

Rosenzweig. Rooted in the meeting between equal speakers, revelation cannot be commanding for Buber. Far beyond simply denying that revelation produces particular laws, Buber maintains that the sense of revelation as command is itself a human imposition. It is, Buber says, 'the fact of man that brings about transformation from revelation to what you call commandment (*Gebot*)'.[52] In response Rosenzweig replies, 'For me too, God is not a Law-giver. But He commands...Could this, then be the difference between us?'[53]

Despite his emphasis on relation, Buber's dialogical thought perpetuates the modern concern with selfhood. Buber locates the origin of the I–You within the potential of the self and claims therefore that in the I–You encounter, the I finds its true actuality, its true personhood. Underneath the language of relation is nothing more than a self in pursuit of its own fulfillment through another person. By focusing on the centrality of divine love, Rosenzweig boldly distances himself from Buber's dialogical theology and opens up a new, non-fanatical basis for understanding the meaning of a person's life with God.

## Notes

1 Nahum N. Glatzer, *Franz Rosenzweig, His Life and Thought* (New York: Schocken Books, 1972), p. 136.
2 Franz Rosenzweig, *The Star of Redemption* (trans. William W. Hallo; New York: Holt, Rinehart and Winston, 1971), p. 390. Franz Rosenzweig, *Der Stern der Erlösung* (Frankfurt: Suhrkamp Verlag, 1988), p. 434.
3 Friedrich Schleiermacher, *On Religion: Speeches to Its Cultured Despisers* (trans. John Oman; New York: Harper & Row, 1958), p. 27.
4 Rosenzweig, *Star*, p. 101/112.
5 Samuel Hugo Bergson, *Dialogical Philosophy from Kierkegaard to Buber* (New York: State University of New York Press, 1991) is in part responsible for the identification of Rosenzweig as a dialogical thinker. The most recent scholarly identification of Rosenzweig's thought as dialogical can be found in Graham Ward, *Barth, Derrida and the Language of Theology* (Cambridge: Cambridge University Press, 1995).
6 The central argument here, that one must read *The Star* from the perspective of the revelation event described in Book II, challenges a recent trend, largely prompted by Leora Batnitzky's *Idolatry and Representation: The Philosophy of Franz Rosenzweig Reconsidered* (Princeton: Princeton University Press, 2000), to read *The Star of Redemption* backwards, as a socio-linguistic analysis of religious life. While Batnizky's method of reading *The Star* allows her to appreciate

Rosenzweig's interest in the ritual and hermeneutical life of religious communities, it nonetheless keeps her from appreciating Rosenzweig's interest in the essentially covenantal character of these same communities. A cultural linguistic reading of *The Star* cannot account for Rosenzweig's interest in a revelatory God and therefore runs the risk of portraying religious communities as social or cultural institutions rather than dialectical expressions of the effort to live in obedience to a commanding God. For a more complete comparison between my reading of *The Star* and Batnitzky's see my 'Roseznweig's Biblical Theology: An Encounter with Jon Levenson's *Sinai and Zion*', *Journal of Jewish Thought and Philosophy*, vol. 11, no. 1 (2002), pp. 75–88.

7  I will discuss Rosenzweig's biblical hermeneutics in Chapter 3. See also my 'Rosenzweig's Biblical Theology', for a detailed analysis of Rosenzweig's biblical hermeneutics.

8  Rosenzweig, *Star*, p. 161/179.

9  Rosenzweig, *Star*, p. 161/179.

10  Rosenzweig, *Star*, p. 162/181.

11  Rosenzweig, *Star*, p. 164/183.

12  Rosenzweig, *Star*, p. 161/179.

13  It is the unique relation between love and command that permits Rosenzweig's divine command theory to be both authoritative and rational. As unprecedented, divine love commands. As loving, divine command provides persons with a reason for obedience that is more than fear of the command. Rosenzweig's theology of divine command is vulnerable neither to charges of irrationality nor charges of subjectivitization. Alasdair MacIntyre's 'What God Ought We Obey,' *Philosophy of Religion* (eds Peterson *et al.*; Oxford: Oxford University Press, 2001) offers a vital critique of divine command theory as irrational and attempts on Thomistic grounds to argue for a divine command theory that is rational and authoritative. MacIntyre's Thomistic account fails to adequately account for the character of revelatory transcendence in the event of divine command. For a detailed analysis of how Rosenzweig's divine command theory offers a powerful response to MacIntyre see Randi Rashkover and Martin Kavka, 'A Modified Jewish Divine Command Theory', *Journal of Religious Ethics* 32.2 (2004), pp. 387–414.

14  Rosenzweig, *Star*, p. 177/197.

15  It is important to compare Rosenzweig's theology of divine election to subsequent theologies of divine election, most importantly that developed by David Novak in his *Election of Israel: The Idea of the Chosen People* (Cambridge: Cambridge University Press, 1995). While Novak's biblical retrieval of the theology of election bears much in common with Rosenzweig's, the central difference between the two concerns Rosenzweig's insistence on the non-propositional character of revelation. According to Rosenzweig, divine command is only exterior and thereby commanding if it is non-propositional.

Consequently, Rosenzweig's God does not issue specific commands. For Novak, however, revelation is an event wherein God speaks specific commands to the Jewish community. For a detailed comparison between Novak's theology of election and Rosenzweig's see Kavka and Rashkover, 'A Modified Divine Command Theory'.

16 To say that there is an inextricable tie between commandment and grace is not to suggest that there is an inextricable tie between grace and law for, according to Rosenzweig, the divine command to love God is not classifiable as law. Nonetheless, Rosenzweig was not antinomian like Buber. Rather, Rosenzweig maintained that 'law must become commandment which seeks to be transformed into deed at the very moment it is heard. It must regain that living reality.' Franz Rosenzweig, 'The Builders', in *On Jewish Learning* (ed. N. N. Glatzer; trans. W. Wolf; New York: Schocken, 1965), p. 85. For a detailed discussion on what it means to say that law must be transformed into commandment but that commandment cannot be transformed into law, see Chapters 3 and 4 of this work.

17 Rosenzweig's notion of testimony to the command of the infinite offers the basis for Levinas' phenomenology of the trauma of the infinite and testimonial response. Levinas' theology of testimony is most evident in Emmanuel Levinas, 'God and Philosophy', *The God Who Comes to Mind* (trans. Bettina Bergo; Stanford: Stanford University Press, 1998) pp. 55–78. Unlike Rosenzweig, however, Levinas deduces the idea of the infinite out of his phenomenology of self while Rosenzweig's phenomenology of revelation emerges out of his interpretation of the biblical text.

18 Rosenzweig, *Star*, p. 178/199.

19 Rosenzweig, *Star*, p. 171/191.

20 Rosenzweig, *Star*, pp. 168/187–88.

21 Rosenzweig, *Star*, p. 202/226.

22 Rosenzweig, *Star*, p. 179/199.

23 Rosenzweig, *Star*, p. 179/200.

24 Rosenzweig, *Star*, p. 169/189.

25 Rosenzweig, *Star*, p. 183/204.

26 Rosenzweig, *Star*, p. 185/206.

27 Rosenzweig, *Star*, p. 185/206.

28 Rosenzweig, *Star*, p. 161/179.

29 Rosenzweig, *Star*, p. 171/191.

30 William James, 'The Will to Believe', in *The Will to Believe and Other Essays in Popular Philosophy* (New York: Dover Publications, 1956), p. 24.

31 James, *Will to Believe*, p. 11.

32 Rosenzweig, Franz, 'The New Thinking', in *Franz Rosenzweig's 'The New Thinking'* (eds and trans. Alan Udoff and Barbara E. Galli; Syracuse: Syracuse University Press), p. 98.

33  Rosenzweig, *Star*, p. 393/437.

34  Rosenzweig, *Star*, p. 394/438.

35  Rosenzweig, *Star*, p. 394/439.

36  For a consideration as to whether Kant's practical belief is the acting as if God is really existent or really possible, see my discussion in Chapter 1.

37  Immanuel Kant, *Critique of Practical Reason* (trans. Lewis White Beck; Indianapolis: Bobbs-Merrill Publishing Company, 1956), p. 148.

38  Not only does Rosenzweig's theology of verification develop the Kantian and Jamesian traditions of practical theology, but it anticipates the theologies of desire developed by later thinkers including Emmanuel Levinas, René Girard, John Milbank and Graham Ward. Rosenzweig's contribution to this discussion has been neglected and warrants attention that exceeds the bounds of the current work. For a comparison between Rosenzweig's and Milbank's categories of theological desire see my 'Judaism in the Work of John Milbank', American Academy of Religion, 2002. Rosenzweig's theology of desire also permits a feminist re-consideration of covenantal theology in general. For a discussion of the significance of theological desire for feminist Jewish discourse see my 'Theological Desire: Feminism, Philosophy and Exegetical Jewish Thought', in Hava Tirosh Samuelson (ed.), *Women and Gender in Jewish Philosophy* (Indianapolis: Indiana University Press, 2004).

39  Rosenzweig, *Star*, p. 212/237.

40  Rosenzweig, *Star*, p. 214/239.

41  The most recent scholarly identification of Rosenzweig's thought as dialogical can be found in Graham Ward, *Barth, Derrida and the Language of Theology* (Cambridge: Cambridge University Press, 1995). According to Ward, Rosenzweig's use of language or 'Redensphilosophie' promotes a view such that 'in revelation . . . there is an experience of immediacy, of the present . . . dialogue here is conceived as a sacramental act'. Ward, *Barth, Derrida*, p. 68. Ward's reading of Rosenzweig fails to account for Rosenzweig's analysis of the difference between divine love and the human reception of divine love characterized in part by the human awareness of the absence of divine love in itself. Consequently, Ward overlooks Rosenzweig's analysis of repentance and theological desire and mistakenly accuses him of logocentrism.

42  Martin Buber, *I and Thou* (trans. Walter Kaufman; New York: Scribner, 1970), p. 114.

43  Buber, *I and Thou*, p. 112.

44  Buber, *I and Thou*, p. 124.

45  Buber, *I and Thou*, p. 78.

46  Buber, *I and Thou*, p. 78.

47  Buber, *I and Thou*, p. 78.

48  Buber, *I and Thou*, p. 62.

49  Buber, *I and Thou*, p. 157.
50  According to David Novak, the main point of difference between Rosenzweig and Buber concerns their view of Jewish law (*Gesetz*). 'Both Rosenzweig and Buber seem to be saying that revelation is just that, revelation and nothing else.... Nevertheless, Rosenzweig and Buber come to almost opposite conclusions concerning the relation of traditional Jewish law (*halakha*) to this foundational revelation. Buber insists that the dichotomy between the direct divine commandment (*Gebot*) and the continuing, transmitted law . . . (*Gesetz*) is unbridgeable. Rosenzweig, on the other hand, insists that the dichotomy is bridgeable.' David Novak, *The Election of Israel: The Idea of the Chosen People* (Cambridge: Cambridge University Press, 1995), p. 86. The argument I present here differs from Novak's analysis insofar as I do not believe that Rosenzweig and Buber agreed on the notion of commandment (*Gebot*) and only differed with respect to their view of *halakha*. In fact, I will argue subsequently, (Chapter 3) that Rosenzweig's understanding of *halakha* is a direct outgrowth of his understanding of commandment. Consequently, the difference between Rosenzweig's and Buber's view of *halakha* is a result of this more fundamental difference.
51  For a discussion comparing Rosenzweig, Cohen, Buber and Levinas with respect to their analyses of the love of the neighbor, see Robert Gibbs, *Correlations in Rosenzweig and Levinas* (Princeton: Princeton University Press, 1992), Chapter 8.
52  Rosenzweig, 'Revelation and Law', in *On Jewish Learning*, p. 114.
53  Rosenzweig, 'Revelation and Law', p. 116.

Chapter 3

# Publicizing the Miracle: Philosophy and the Word of God in Rosenzweig's New Thinking

If Rosenzweig's theology of testimony stands at the center of his efforts to expose the non-dogmatic character of biblical revelation, what he calls his New Thinking crowns this effort by offering a radically innovative and philosophically plausible theology of the Word of God. Granted that revelation is an event of a meta-rational, loving God, it would seem to exceed the bounds of language. Nonetheless, neither Rosenzweig nor Barth dismissed the significance of language for theology. On the contrary, Rosenzweig's interest in language motors his proposed new method of analyzing revelation and its relation to both philosophical thought and religious life. Generally speaking, Rosenzweig held that an analysis of how humans use language with respect to their world and with respect to their response to God could be enlisted in an effort to offer a viable apologetics of revealed religion. A believer's account of revelation must be defensible philosophically. Rosenzweig further maintained that only an alliance between philosophy and theology could succeed in providing this analysis. Theologians need philosophy in order to establish the epistemological viability of an irruption of divine transcendence in our world and the testimonial verification that it prompts. Equally importantly, philosophers need theologians in order to articulate the human response to this irruption and the manner by which the human response is performed through acts of testimonial verification expressed in religious texts and liturgy. Ultimately, Rosenzweig's New Thinking develops a new scriptural and liturgical hermeneutics that augments the theology of testimony by demonstrating how religious texts and liturgy can be a meaningful and yet non-dogmatic expression of a covenantal life with God.

## A. The Miraculous Defense of Revealed Religion

Rosenzweig's New Thinking is his particular antidote to what he considers a contemporary crisis in the apologetics of revealed religion. Participants of revealed religions have long sought to defend the viability of their belief to non-believers, and in this defense commonly pointed to the existence of miracles as a basis for their defense. 'When Augustine or some other Church Father had to defend the divinity and veracity of revealed religion against heathen attacks and doubts, he scarcely failed to point to miracles.'[1] According to Rosenzweig, therefore, the recognition of miracles within our natural world provides a philosophical basis to revealed religion.

Miracle, Rosenzweig tells us, is 'substantially a sign [and] miracle and prophecy belong together'.[2] Despite common thinking, a miracle is not an aberration from nature but rather the recognition 'of that predestined lawfulness of the world'[3] which suggests or points to the reality of divine providence. The notion that a miracle is an aberration of nature is unique to a modern mentality. Pre-modernists appreciated miracles not as departures from natural law but as signs or predictions of providence or divine will. Like the parting of the Red Sea or the miracle of the empty tomb, miracles indicate or point to God.

In Rosenzweig's estimation then, miracles are philosophically significant.[4] By recognizing this world or something in this world as a sign of transcendence, the proclaimer presupposes the possibility of divine reality and, more specifically, a divine reality that may be revealed in or at least to our world. As signs of divine providence only, miracles do not objectify divine reality. They permit only a recognition of the possibility of God without offering any secure knowledge of God whose reality, as transcendent, will exceed the knowledge we have of our world. Miracles' apologetic value rests in their ability to discount objections concerning the possibility of divine transcendence in our world.

Unfortunately, Rosenzweig explains, contemporary theology has renounced the value of miracles and has, therefore, left itself vulnerable to challenges concerning the viability of faith in the God of divine revelation. According to Rosenzweig, doubt regarding miracles became debilitating when the means by which miracles are proven, i.e. eye-witness accounts, was challenged. The modern theologian, says Rosenzweig, attempts to distance his theological belief from the phenomenon of miracles so far as historical inquiry calls their overall veracity into question. Not wanting to fall prey to historical critique, the modern theologian (best exemplified for Rosenzweig by Schleiermacher) attempts to base theological truth in either the believer's radically present experience of revelation or by demonstrating how the believer's experience of revelation contributes to an overall course of human progress that culminates in the establishment of the human moral order. 'Thus the enduring value of the past was denied and the ever present experience of religious emotion was anchored in the eternal future of the moral world.'[5] However, reliant on an unrealized future, such meaning is only hoped for and thereby spurious.

While we have seen in our prior discussion that Rosenzweig does appreciate how the human response to revelation can result in faith in the future of human moral life, Rosenzweig insists on securing the philosophical viability of this future hope by detailing both a theory of verification emergent out of an authentic analysis of revelation as testimony as well as by demonstrating how transcendence is philosophically possible in view of our knowledge of the world.

In Rosenzweig's estimation the modern theologian lacks both a philosophical analysis of the possibility of revelation within the world as we know it as well as a proper analysis of revelation and the subsequent theory of verification. The modern theologian cannot demonstrate how the event of revelation relates to the world of the non-believer, leaving believers ill-equipped to translate their subjectively-based belief into terms that a non-believer can deem at least plausible. This is a deplorable and unacceptable situation. Somehow, Rosenzweig maintains, a believer's account of the truth of revelation must be defended philosophically. On the one hand, this means that theology must recover the traditionalist's notion of miracle. On the other hand, theology must illuminate the theory of verification at work in the believer's religious language and ritual. This, according to Rosenzweig, is the task of the New Thinking.

### a. *Recovering the Miracle: The Task of the New Philosophy of Language*

The ultimate objective of the New Thinking is to demonstrate how revealed religion is more than an individual's subjective experience, incommunicable to or with other persons. But, according to Rosenzweig, language is the means by which human beings render their experiences meaningful – that is, more than my personal experience. My love for my friend is meaningful not simply when I feel it but when I tell my friend how I feel. Consequently, Rosenzweig's New Thinking is that alliance between a philosophy of language and a theology of the Word of God that traces the relationship between a believer's experience of divine transcendence and

79

language. Since all human experience of the world is linguistic, the New Thinking's analysis of the relationship between transcendence and human language demonstrates how revelation relates to the world as humans know it. The New Thinking therefore provides a new method of religious apologetics.

According to Rosenzweig, the first task of the New Thinking is to establish the possibility of transcendence within the world, i.e. recover the perspective of miracle formerly held by traditional apologists. In other words, the *possibility* of transcendence must be grounded in or related to our knowledge of the world. However, according to Rosenzweig, our knowledge of the world is always a knowledge of the past for, as he says, 'truth is always that which has been'.[6] Consequently, Rosenzweig identifies human propositional knowledge with what he calls the knowledge of creation, the ultimate past. 'The connection between knowledge and the concept of the past shows itself in this relationship to creation.'[7] When I say 'The mountain is high,' or 'The world is spherical,' I'm not saying that the mountain just grew or that the world just got remolded. I'm making claims about the past. And the New Thinking, Rosenzweig says, 'calls upon philosophy to build a bridge from creation to revelation'.[8]

By claiming that philosophy bridges between creation and revelation, Rosenzweig does not want to imply that philosophy uncovers the reality of divine transcendence within the bounds of propositional knowledge. On the contrary, just as miracles only succeeded in pointing to or suggesting a transcendence beyond themselves, so philosophy's task is to demonstrate how the language we use to describe and live in the world points to or suggests transcendence without objectifying it.

> From theology's point of view, what philosophy is supposed to accomplish for it is thus by no means to reconstruct theological contents, but to anticipate them or more correctly, to supply them with a foundation, to demonstrate the preconditions on which it rests ... [R]evelation is providentially 'foreseen' in creation ... [P]hilosophy becomes a prognostication of revelation ...[9]

Consequently, the New Thinking begins by describing our linguistically conditioned knowledge of the world. As we will see, this is a world of objects and living beings whose origin and destiny remains unknown. This world stands differentiated from the created order of the natural theologian, an order that may provide immediate knowledge of God.[10] Neither, however, is it the Buberian I–It realm that stands incommensurate with the reality of God. In Rosenzweig's analysis the world we know is a world of questions that suggest but cannot determine their correlative answers.

### b. *Language and Existence*

According to Rosenzweig, the created order is the order of existence and the order of life. In the first place, the created world is like the Heideggerian world, a world of things which questions its Being.[11] 'Its creatureliness presses under the wings of a Being such as would endow it with stability and veracity.'[12] In constant search for stability, the created world is the ephemeral world which 'must continually become new in order to maintain itself.'[13] The created world awaits the discovery of its source of Being.[14] In constant search of the source of its being, the created world is the world of distinct objects. Given the absence of stable being, the objects of the created world can only assert their essence in the particularity of their existence in time. Existence maintains an essence only insofar as it exists, here and now.

> In the world which manifests itself as creature, this enduring essence is converted into a momentary essence 'ever renewed' and yet universal. An unessential essence thus . . . The world has embarked on the current of reality, and this its essence is not 'always and everywhere' . . . It is: existence . . . which is full of the distinctive . . .[15]

### c. *Narrative – the Language of Existence*

On what grounds does Rosenzweig describe reality this way? For Rosenzweig we apprehend reality through language. Only language can apprehend and articulate the contours of the incomplete world of creation. Created existence is unstable and insecure in its origin. By contrast, a philosophy based in ontology hides from this truth and posits a rational, conceptually ordered account of being and existence. Ontologically-based philosophy consequently offers an inauthentic description of reality as existence. More an assertion of the pride of human thinking, a philosophy of generation, says Rosenzweig,

> is supposed to accomplish the same as creation. It is supposed to give . . . the fixed point from which [the world's] multiplicity closes ranks and arranges itself as unity. Only thereby could the world be lifted out of the uncertainty of the Perhaps and gain outwardly the stability of what is attested as real . . .[16]

Such an effort however is doomed to failure for

at its zenith idealism ... gave itself over completely into the power of its own creature, logic. At the same time it could not help but sense how it was losing touch with that living existence which it had undertaken to substantiate and to comprehend ...[17]

Ontology loses touch with the maelstrom-like nature of existence. Unlike idealism, language obediently follows reality, unveiling its contours without supplementing it.[18] Stéphane Mosès relays this fact when he says that for Rosenzweig, 'language does not constitute the real, it unveils it. The world is objective not because the categories of language as narration are so ... In fact, these categories are objective because the world they describe had always been present, even before we begin to know it.'[19]

Accommodating to the reality at hand, language passes through a number of stages of development. The first is narration. Narration articulates the reality of existence. As human beings, our most primary mode of experience, according to Rosenzweig, concerns our relationship or apprehension of the objective world around us. But for Rosenzweig our relationship to the world around us is largely a relationship of care or value.[20] According to Rosenzweig, we initially apprehend the world in terms of its value for us and we thereby articulate it through categories of value or qualities. Upon our first apprehension, then, the world as 'there' is 'good'. Soon thereafter, however, we identify different elements in the world apprehended not only through adjectives but through pronouns, indefinite and definite articles and finally nouns. The objective world comes into view for us as the world of things at our service.

Things as they are defined at first by pronouns – this or that – presuppose a 'here' against which they are 'this' or 'that'. Language apprehends space as this backdrop for all things, 'the general prerequisite for looking at the thing'.[21] But furthermore, 'these' things with their particular qualities, as they are apprehended within sentences, also presuppose time. In a sentence with its predicates, a thing either 'is' or 'is not'. But whether it 'is' or 'isn't' can change over time. That a thing is or isn't through its own changes or through movement functions as an additional qualification of its objectivity. Movement, for Rosenzweig, expressed through the presupposed 'is' and later developed by particular verbs or participle expressions, further qualifies the value of the object.

Finally, however, the thing achieves its greatest value for us when it reaches its greatest level of objectivity. The noun, the thing identified as an individual thing, is most objective when it both connects with a fixed or regular space and is securely established there in the time of the past. The 'thing' is most valuable to us when it is locatable in space and stable in time, what in Heideggerian terms might be referred to as 'ready to hand' .[22] It is not difficult for things to be fixed to a regular space. But a thing's stability is not promised if the thing 'is' only now. Neither is it secured by the hope that it 'will be'. Rather, the thing is ready to hand as what it is – only insofar as it 'has been' that way. 'It is the past which "stands ever at rest," objective, object-like, in thing-like stillness.'[23]

The created world is rendered most intelligible through narration, the description or articulation of the world as it has been in the past. According to Rosenzweig, scientists use narration to describe the world. By means of narration, the world gains objectivity through the temporalization of causality. The world here and now is real so far as it has been, i.e. so far as it is the effect of the past. But just as existence remains disconnected from its original source, correlatively, the language that articulates existence cannot lend apprehension to a first cause. Here language reaches a limit. However, with this limit language demonstrates its epistemological authenticity, for unlike idealism it does not pretend to provide intelligibility where no intelligibility exists. Language, unlike philosophy, keeps a space open for the first cause.

### d. *The World as Life and the Language of Proper Names and Culture*
The created world consists not only of existent objects but also of living things, and according to Rosenzweig we employ a different form of language in order to apprehend or articulate the world of the living. While it is the case that apprehension of the objective world identifies objects as distinctive things which have use for us, even the distinctive object belongs to a category from which it derives its full meaning. I may be sitting on 'this' chair – here and now – but still the chair gleans its meaning from its category. The situation is different with regard to living beings. While living things like objects are partly recognized by virtue of their category, i.e. Jim is a person, my dog Sam is a dog, living things also maintain the will to preserve their own existence. This will to sustain themselves reflects a level of individuality absent in the distinct object. 'What then does it mean to be alive as against merely being in existence? It really means . . . a form of one's own, forming itself from within and enduring.'[24]

But the difference between living things and objects extends beyond this dimension of individuality. While objects influence each other through cause and effect, only living things (though not necessarily all living things) create environments in which they relate to and with each other. According to Rosenzweig, living things relate to other living things because they need them to supplement their own efforts for survival against death, the common enemy. Consequently living things often form societies or communities as patterns for relating with each other. As Robert Gibbs nicely states, 'Overcoming the death of temporality is not achieved by denying death, but by forming a society where others continue to live after my death.'[25] Such forms of life are endemic to the created order. Thus, Rosenzweig tells us, 'blood kinship, brotherhood, nationhood, marriage, in sum all human relationships are established in creation ...'[26]

Unlike inanimate objects, living things seek eternal duration and assert individuality and relationships. However, despite this desire, living things inevitably lose to the forces of time and death. The very law of life, Rosenzweig tells us, is that 'all that lives must die ...'[27] Whether animals, individual persons, or societies, all life is finite and as creature will perish. As human beings with the gift of language, we seek to apprehend this reality.

Language first distinguishes between our apprehension of another person and our apprehension of an object. While it is possible to apprehend a person as an object – 'He went to the store, for example – we express a person's characteristic individuality by virtue of calling him by his proper name. 'Adam went to the store', i.e. Adam with his own will to live and his own destiny assumes a meaning beyond the meaning associated with the connection of a verb and a simple object-noun.

The proper name then provides a new linguistic building block that can be used to name larger groups of individuals in societies. We name people not only by virtue of their own destiny but also by virtue of the destiny of the group with which they associate. 'Sam is an American Indian who lives in Alberquerque.' Sam's destiny connects to the destiny of the American Indians in New Mexico. More specifically societies express identity through the linguistic forms of customs or laws. Through customs or cultures peoples carve out and apprehend the particular modes of life they assume in the world with each other. A completely different set of practices is conjured up by saying, 'Sam is an American Indian who lives in Chelsea.' Customs or cultures are the means by which we express our will to live as individuals and within groups. Furthermore, customs and laws often get expressed through ritual and social practices which in their hourly, monthly and yearly execution organize the world in the interest of the preservation of life. As we will discuss more later, the repetition of practices carves out a human dimension of reality and time that in the face of the flux of life offers a degree of continuity and duration to life forms. Whether it is the farmer who attempts to regulate yearly the planting of his crops, exploiting the earth in the interest of his own preservation, or whether it is the development of a culture's system of law which, so far as it lasts, represents the preservation of a people and its individual citizens, culture and social practice are language's means of apprehending existence as life.

'For the peoples of the world, language is the carrier and messenger of time-bound, flowing, changing ... transitory life ... For a people lives out its day in these two: in custom and law, in what has been handed down from yesterday through force of habit, and in what has been laid down for the morrow.'[28]

However, customs and laws must change with the constant flux of life. In its never-ceasing growth, life produces new types of individuals and new relationships. In order to preserve themselves cultures too must change, lest they fall prey to the inevitable pull of time. Ironically, in order to live, they must forfeit some of their 'name', some of that identity which they seek to preserve. 'Thus, in the life of nations, today is a moment which passes fleet as an arrow. And so long as this arrow is in flight, so long as new custom is added to the old, new law outstrips the old, the river of a people's life is in flux, alive ...'[29] By virtue of their willingness to alter with the flux of life, cultures establish themselves in 'history'. A people establishes itself in 'history', the story of the preservation of cultures, by establishing itself in its 'own history' – by writing and constantly re-writing the story of its own battle to sustain itself.

That cultures can transform themselves through changed customs and laws once again illustrates language's unique capacity to articulate the created order without working to define or control it. Cultures whose customs change facilitate the quest for sustained life without ignoring life's inherent tension with time or providing a false solution to this quest. Successful cultures offer what Rosenzweig calls the 'earthly analogy of eternity'[30] without pretending to have the formula for eternity itself. In other words, they present a means by which they secure their own preservation. Accordingly, the language of cultural change maintains a space for and points to the promise of eternity.

In *The Star* Rosenzweig tells us that the successful nation state is the collective formed by individuals who hope to secure their own individuality by identifying with a societal 'name' or people whose chances for preservation exceed those of any individual. According to Rosenzweig, non-fanatical states realize that they cannot secure immortality for any of their citizens. Consequently they are not totalizing in their culture, customs and laws but recognize that they must change with time.

Cultural life is neither the reflection nor the antithesis of the kingdom of God, but a condition or ground for the possibility of the kingdom of God which the act of love itself requires. It is the 'articulated life' on which the soul, be it Jewish or Christian, 'exercises its freedom . . . animating it in all its individual members, and everywhere inseminating this ground of the living structure with the seeds of immortality'.[31]

As such, religious life cannot afford to bracket itself off from a culture's self-expression but must appreciate this self-expression as a sign of the possibility of the kingdom of God. There is for Rosenzweig a dialectical relationship between a society's culture – its art, literature, science and politics – and covenantal religious communities. Covenantal communities need culture as the basis and landscape for the labor of redemption, and culture needs covenantal communities to recognize their particularity as a sign of the possibility of God's redemptive order. Within the context of carving out a philosophical defense of revealed religion, Rosenzweig's New Thinking paves the way for a fruitful relationship between culture and theology.

### e. *The Modern State*

To claim that language can authentically apprehend life as the prophecy of God's revelation and redemption is not to say that it always does. According to Rosenzweig, in the modern state we find an example of how language attempts to control life and reality rather than unveil it.[32] Compelled by the need to proclaim itself messenger of eternity, the modern state often resorts to coercive measures to unnaturally preserve or control its laws and customs in the face of the ever present current of life that threatens the state's omnipresence. This modern state, Rosenzweig argues, follows upon the coat-tails of the medieval church and assumes the early church's interest in self-preservation. Both institutions often manipulate their own customs and laws in efforts to identify their own history with salvation history.[33] But neither the church nor the state are convincing. As participants in the created order they must succumb to the fate of death and rebirth. The church and the state can access eternity only by accepting their position in the created order.[34] Like Goethe, they must learn to pray the prayer of 'hope', for 'where that prayer is recited, there commences that vitality of creaturely life which renders this life directly ripe for the irruption of eternal divine life'.[35]

Our journey through the landscape of the created order now done, we can assess the findings of the New Thinking's linguistic analysis up until this point. Thus far, the world as described by the linguistic analyses of the New Thinking is the incomplete world, unaware of its origin and in search of its final, eternal destiny. In other words, the New Thinking has provided a kind of 'critique of pure language', indicating the limits of our knowledge of the things beyond our world in the spheres of propositional logic, individual human existence, and the socio-political order while leaving open a space, and thereby pointing to that which transcends the world as its origin and its destiny. By enlisting the aid of a philosophical analysis of language, the New Thinking has demonstrated how our world points to or suggests an origin and a meaning or destiny that transcends it. It has re-claimed the meaning of miracle.

> As practiced by the theologian, philosophy becomes a prognosticaton of revelation .. but thereby revelation regains before our amazed eyes the character of authentic miracle ... [T]heology for its part therefore looks longingly to philosophy ... In these circumstances the authentic miracle, belief's dearest child, which it had given up for lost, is brought back to its arms by knowledge.[36]

## B. Theology's Share in the New Thinking: Re-Thinking the Word of God

Rosenzweig's identification between a philosophy of language and the traditional notion of miracle re-crowns philosophy without forcing it to return to either an enlightenment foundationalism or a Hegelian absolutism. Philosophy's responsibility is to carve out a space for the possibility of transcendence and lend plausibility and thereby meaning to the believer's theological testimony. Consequently, philosophy plays a key role in Rosenzweig's effort to defend religious belief as meaningful and non-dogmatic. As the surveyor of human linguistic apprehension, however, philosophy is for Rosenzweig a broad term that, as demonstrated above, can reach into studies of human psychology, sociology and political theory.[37]

However, just as theology looks back to and needs philosophy to provide a basis for the possibility of transcendence, so philosophy anticipates and needs theology to provide expression of the human encounter with transcendence. Philosophy bears no independent or supercessionist role.

Truth emerges from the revelation event alone, as lived by the believer who fulfills the divine command and testifies to God through her life of repentance, longing, faith, and love of the neighbor. *The Star of Redemption* is Rosenzweig's effort to demonstrate how meaningful theological knowledge transpires uniquely within election communities. 'What is truth?'[38] Rosenzweig asks. '[T]ruth is the essence of reality as well as of God.'[39] But Rosenzweig then asks, 'What is God? God is the Nought.'[40] God is he/she whom we don't know as we know other things in our world. But then, what does this mean to say that 'God is the Nought'? Such a question, Rosenzweig tells us, is impossible to answer. There is no answer to the question, 'What is God?' for there is no knowledge of God for us save in the 'Truly'[41] with which we answer the God who commands us. There is no philosophical route to truth. Philosophical propositions cannot provide theological knowledge.

> That God is the Nought becomes as figurative a proposition as the other one, that he is the truth. Just as the truth turned out to be simply the consummation of what we had already discovered with the palatable and visible presentness in the love of God, namely his revelation, so too the Nought can be none other than the prophecy of that Revelation. . . . Divine essentiality is none other than God's revealing himself . . . to us . . . [and consequently we find that] the apparent knowledge concerning his essence becomes the proximate, immediate experience of his activity: that he is truth tells us in the final analysis none other than that he – loves.[42]

There is no Hegelian triumph of philosophical knowledge here. The effort to reinstate confidence in theological truth leaves us at our final destination – the return to religious life.

> We had been forced to reject the truth as it presented itself to us at the beginning ... We denied that philosophy which rested on such a belief in the immediacy of cognition to the All and of the All to cognition. Now ... we find that the truth which had wanted to press itself on us as the first, is the last, there at the goal. In viewing it, we comprehend the eternal truth. But we do not view it, like philosophy, as basis ... but as ultimate goal ... And in seeing the truth ... it dawns on us at the same time that truth is after all none other than the divine revelation which occurred to us too who hover in the middle between basis and future. Our Verily, our Yea and Amen with which we answered God's revelation – at the goal it stands revealed as the beating heart of the eternal truth as well. We find our way, find ourselves in midst of the fire of the farthest star of

the eternal truth, ourselves in the truth and not – to reject here for the last time the blasphemy of philosophy – the truth in us.[43]

## a. *The Word of God as Dialectical Vehicle of Revelatory Command*

In our previous analysis of revelation we have seen how human beings encounter divine transcendence through the event of divine love and how the human experience of divine love differs from God's experience of loving. According to Rosenzweig, human beings encounter divine transcendence as a calling to obedient testimony which they enact through repentance and desire for God's love, what is covenantal life.

Nonetheless, Rosenzweig's theology of testimony requires an analysis of how the human experience of and response to revelation becomes expressed in language. There are several warrants for this analysis. First, Rosenzweig appreciates the linguistic character of human life. As linguistic beings, human beings necessarily render their experiences meaningful through language. Consequently, an account of their life of testimony would be incomplete without an examination of the forms of this linguistic interpretation. Second, an analysis of religious language or a theology of the Word of God is a necessary aspect of Rosenzweig's apologetic effort to defend the meaningfulness of revealed religion. In order to demonstrate the philosophical plausibility of revealed religion, the New Thinking needs to augment philosophy's account of the possibility of transcendence with an account of revelation, its philosophical plausibility and how it is rendered meaningful through language. Previously (Chapter 2) we examined how Rosenzweig's phenomenology of revelation results in a theology of verification. Rosenzweig's theology of verification accounts for how an encounter with a transcendent God can lead to a firm belief in a revealing, creating and redeeming God. Rosenzweig's analysis of how covenantal life is expressed through religious language and ritual augments the theology of verification so far as it demonstrates how believers successfully communicate their belief to and with others. Together the theology of verification and the analysis of religious language and ritual ground Rosenzweig's effort to defend the meaningfulness of revealed religion without betraying the transcendence that spawns and vitalizes it.

At the heart of my discussion of Rosenzweig's analysis of religious language is the claim that, more than simply provide a defense of revealed religion, Rosenzweig's New Thinking radically re-invents the meaning of the concept of the Word of God in a way that liberates revealed religions from dogmatism. According to Rosenzweig, 'the Word of God and the

Word of man are the same'.[44] While Rosenzweig scholars have often interpreted this to mean that revelation offers an occasion wherein God's speaking and human hearing and response are uniquely linked,[45] this interpretation overlooks the truly radical character of Rosenzweig's conception of the Word of God. On the contrary, what Rosenzweig means is that there is no Word of God other than the word of human beings. When we consider the possible meaning of this claim in view of Rosenzweig's theology of testimony, it becomes clear that Rosenzweig's loving and commanding God cannot and does not speak, if by speaking one means utter specific words and issue specific propositions. God's revelation is not available to humankind through language for, Rosenzweig says, there is no content to revelation other than revelation itself.[46] By identifying the Word of God and the word of human beings, Rosenzweig means that all language concerning revelation, e.g. what is Torah and Torah life for Jews and Christ and Christian life for Christians, is a reflection or expression of the human being's experience of and testimony to revelation rather than a direct expression of God in language.[47]

a.1. *The Inner Power of the Word of God*
According to Rosenzweig, religious language or the Word of God performs two distinct functions. On the one hand, the Word of God provides a linguistic expression of the experience of divine revelation and command. Religious language functions dialectically in this capacity. On the other hand, the Word of God or religious language lends expression to the human response to this experience of divine love and command. Here the function of religious language is pragmatic. I will discuss these two functions of the Word of God in turn.

First, human beings experience revelation as an unprecedented event of love that commands them to acknowledgment. If, however, revelation is an experience that judges all former human experience and commands acknowledgment of that which transcends human experience, how can human language signify or express this event? Rosenzweig contends with this issue by appreciating the dialectical character of religious language. By dialectical I mean that, for Rosenzweig, human language cannot positively reference or express divine transcendence but can refer to divine transcendence by pointing to the absence or negation of this transcendence in itself. Furthermore, as the dialectical expression of transcendence, the Word of God not only negatively points to divine transcendence but, by highlighting the absence of divine transcendence within human language and experience, also generates an awareness of divine judgment or command to acknowledge the transcendence whose exteriority challenges human experience and sovereignty.

Rosenzweig's appreciation for the dialectical character of the Word of God is most evident in his discussion of dialogue. According to Rosenzweig, dialogue is a grammatical form often used by recipients of revelation to express their response to revelation. Both Torah and Christ can be appreciated as places or occasions of dialogue between human beings and the divine. In *The Star of Redemption*, Rosenzweig offers a description of a divine–human dialogue that he draws mostly from his own reading of *The Song of Songs*. Upon first reading, Rosenzweig's description of dialogue seems to portray the Word of God as a place of loving union or merger between two impetuous lovers. 'Where art Thou?' God asks. As called, the individual prepares herself to hear from another. 'Here is the I, the individual human I as yet wholly receptive . . . pure readiness, all ears . . .'[48] And the other responds with the imperative, 'Love me.' One would expect the human being, seized by this love, to immediately rejoin, 'I am Yours.' Such an attestation would suggest the person's understanding of the love expressed and the love she now declares. It would suggest that the dialogical exchange between the two successfully enabled the divine and the human to merge as one in their shared conveyance of love. Applied to the Torah and to Christ this would mean that Torah or Christ are opportunities for a divine–human love dialogue that when either read aloud or proclaimed would invite listeners to participate in this event of loving union.

However, Rosenzweig's dialogue does not immediately record the human's declaration of love. The person responds, 'I have sinned.'[49] According to Rosenzweig, this response results from the person's inability to recognize or understand the divine expression of love. 'Back in the past,' Rosenzweig says, 'there was a time before she was beloved.'[50] The dialogue is not the vehicle for the shared understanding and love of the two participants and does not convey divine presence to the human beloved. Conversely, the dialogue breaks with the beloved's proclamation that she has sinned. By returning to a moment of self-reflection, the beloved's testimony to sin reveals her inability to absorb the imperative of the other within her linguistic frame of reference. In this way the dialogue becomes a testament to its own inability to access the Other. By so doing, however, the dialogue succeeds in pointing to the exteriority of the Other's reality.

The remainder of Rosenzweig's description of dialogue further attests to the dialectical character of the language as the unique vehicle for illuminating the transcendent Other. In conversation, generally, we rely on the other person to respond to or challenge our claims: 'No, Randi, your room is not clean.' However, according to Rosenzweig's description, God's participation in the dialogue ends with the imperative, 'Love me!' Rosenzweig's subsequent account of the dialogue indicates its repeated failure to access the divine. Despite the beloved's desire, her 'I have sinned' is not followed by a response from God but only by a stronger expression of divine absence in the beloved who proclaims, 'I am a sinner.'[51] Rosenzweig says, '[O]nly the summons by name and the commandment to love had reached the soul from God's mouth, and not any "declaration" of love ...'[52] Once again the dialogue breaks. The failure of the dialogue reaches its climax in its final moment. The beloved cries out to God but, Rosenzweig says, 'this cry is not answered from the mouth of the lover'.[53] Not the poetic expression of the merger of divine and human presence, the dialogue is the dialectical means whereby the beloved turns to language to express language's inability to describe or reference the Other.

Furthermore, Rosenzweig's dialogue not only negatively points to the beloved's sense of this radical Other, it also lends linguistic expression to the beloved's sense of being commanded. By its failings the dialogue points to the *authority* of that which it cannot express. The dialogue's failure to express the divine promotes the moral awakening of the person in that it alerts the person to a reality, a love, which exceeds her understanding. The beloved is humbled by this judgment and compelled to acknowledge or testify to this Other. For Rosenzweig, then, the Word of God becomes the vehicle of the divine commandment to testify to God's love by virtue of its very finitude. The essence of the Word of God is commandment or *Gebot*. The Word of God has what Rosenzweig calls an 'inner power (*Kraft*)'[54] to compel or summon persons to testify to God's love. It does this not by directly expressing God's presence and laws but by divesting itself of its own subject matter, silently commanding its readers or proclaimers to a life of future testimony. Rosenzweig says, 'Teaching begins where the subject matter ceases to be subject matter and changes into inner power (*Kraft*). The way to the teaching leads through what is "knowable", but the teaching itself is not knowable.'[55] In other words, teaching begins with the commandment silently and dialectically pointed to through the content or the what is 'knowable' in the text.[56] The teaching, however, is not the same as the content of the text, but rather that which the content dialectically points to in its own inadequacy and finitude.

Rosenzweig's dialectical conception of the Word of God is further

92

evidenced in his discussion of the Jewish and Christian festivals of revelation. Shavuot commemorates God's revelation to the Jewish people through the Torah. Shavuot marks the reception of the Torah when the 'people is wholly immersed in its togetherness with God'.[57] Still, Rosenzweig maintains, the Toraitic intimacy celebrated in Shavuot breaks. The intimacy of Sinai does not result in a sustained divine–human merger but rather in the people's lonely wandering in the wilderness. 'The people is not allowed to linger in the sheltering shade of Sinai . . . it must leave the hidden togetherness with God.'[58] Shavuot is followed by Sukkot and the Shavuot reading of *The Song of Songs* is replaced with the 'book full of corroding doubt, Ecclesiastes'.[59] As the culmination of the festivals of revelation, Sukkot negates the intimacy between God and the Jews through Torah and instead points to 'something beyond the community of the common word, something higher'.[60]

Like Shavuot, Easter commemorates God's call to election for Christians. As such, 'not the manger of Bethlehem, but Golgotha and the empty tomb count as the beginning of the way for Christianity'.[61] At Easter every Christian commemorates the closeness to God she first experienced through her individual encounter with the revelation of the cross. Here is the dialogue with God through the Word of Christ. While Jews draw near and respond to God through Torah, the Christian draws near to God through Christ who, as the bearer of God's loving compassion on the cross, meets each individual Christian as a loving friend. 'He is near to this individual in that form to which his brotherly feelings can most readily direct themselves.'[62] In Christ crucified and risen the individual sees the articulation of her own suffering finitude taken on and comforted by him who bears it in his compassion. However, this intimacy with God through the Word of Christ is soon superseded by the Pentecostal awakening to God's absence. 'That is the story of the Pentecostal season: the Lord leaves his charges, ascending to Heaven, while they remain behind on earth . . . Now they must learn to believe without seeing him with their own eyes; they must learn to behave as though they had no Lord at all . . .'[63] Following by the ascension of Christ to the right hand of the Father, Pentecost negates the intimacy with the Word. In this way, however, it conveys the divine commandment that is beyond Word and Christians are exhorted to go out into the world and testify to or acknowledge the God above the Word.

It is for Rosenzweig, therefore, the dialectical character of Torah and Christ that calls Jews and Christians to religious lives of testimony or witness. The Jewish life of Torah and the Christian life of Christ differ in the languages or forms of their testimonies. Still, they are both covenantal traditions whose founding texts or Words become bearers of divine revelation only through their negation and their conveyance of the divine commandment to a life of communal testimony. 'We [have] raised the question of the formative element in the community of Judaism, which Jewish dogma might have answered with "the Torah". But we were not entitled to be satisfied with that answer, and the dogmatic answer "Christ" would avail us no more here.'[64]

a.2. *Value of Dialectical Theology of the Word for Jewish and Christian Thought*
Contemporary theology has much to gain from Rosenzweig's appreciation for the dialectical character of the Word of God. Most specifically a dialectical conception of the Word of God permits acknowledgment of textual fallibility but highlights this fallibility as the link or vehicle to the divine. A dialectical theology undermines religious positivism or dogmatism without strictly humanizing the Word of God. The Word of God retains revelatory significance, not despite but because of its fallibility.

Furthermore, Rosenzweig's particular conception of the dialectical character of the Word of God promotes a praxis or witness-oriented approach to religious traditions. Rosenzweig's approach offers contemporary, liberal Jewish thought an invaluable theological ground for participation in and creative contribution to the tradition of Oral Law. While, generally speaking, orthodox Jews comply with the laws included in the rabbinic or Oral tradition on the grounds of a belief that these laws were uttered by God at Sinai, contemporary liberal Jews do not share this conception of God's Word at Sinai and yet continue to follow and develop the Oral tradition. Rosenzweig's theology of command and testimony affords a new way of understanding a commitment to Oral tradition. Seen from the point of view of a dialectical theology, the rabbinic tradition of extra-textual commentary and law is the Jews' testimonial response to the commandment issued through the finitude of the sacred text. Rosenzweig's dialectical theology helps account for what David Weiss Halivni has identified as the paradox of the *peshat* and *derash* readings of Hebrew Scripture. How can, Halivni asks, the rabbinic tradition develop an extra-biblical tradition that not only adds to the sacred text but often departs from it?[65] From a Rosenzweigian perspective the extra-textual tradition is the expression of testimony to the commandment issued forth by the text's finitude. If the Torah is the Word of God for Jews by virtue of its finitude, it does not force those who encounter it to locate their redemptive praxis from within the bounds of its particular claims. On the contrary, the dialectical model allows Jews to acknowledge and embrace the limitations of the Torah text as the summons to an extra-exegetical life of commandment and witness. From this perspective the Oral tradition is the particular rabbinic effort to service the God first encountered in the finitude of the text.

A dialectical approach to the Word of God affords similar benefits to Christianity. More specifically it affords Christians an opportunity simultaneously to appreciate the revelatory significance of the New Testament while recognizing its essential fallibility. From this perspective the New Testament becomes the site of divine judgment and the divine commandment to testify to the God who loves. Rosenzweig's dialectical theology therefore permits Christians to distinguish between the form and the message of the New Testament in a way that inspires an essentially praxis-oriented tradition. Said in other language, it offers the theological basis for a truly postmodern Christian hermeneutics.

To bring this benefit of Rosenzweig's theology of the Word into clearer focus, let us apply it to a contemporary effort in Catholic theology: the work of Elizabeth Schüssler Fiorenza. Fiorenza's now classic text, *Bread Not Stone*, argues that the New Testament is an historically conditioned text subject to the prejudices and values of its time as well as the bearer of an essential message of love and salvation from a transcendent God. Fiorenza seeks to outline a Christian hermeneutic that encourages Christians to commit themselves to the religious value of the New Testament text all the while permitting them to critique the text in its social failings. On the one hand, Fiorenza argues, 'a feminist hermeneutics must seriously take into account the androcentric character of biblical language and the patriarchal stamp of all biblical traditions . . . [A] feminist critical interpretation begins with a hermeneutics of suspicion . . .'[66] On the other hand, Fiorenza suggests that one may combine a hermeneutics of suspicion with a hermeneutics of love, based in what she calls 'the liberating Word of God finding expression in the biblical writings'.[67]

Ultimately Fiorenza uses this scriptural hermeneutic to defend her claim that authentic Christianity happens, not in the words of the text, but in practices of love and care found in contemporary church communities. Fiorenza argues that a feminist interpretation of the Bible 'subjects the Bible to a critical feminist scrutiny and to the theological authority of the church of women'.[68] Nonetheless Fiorenza argues that the theological authority of the church of women derives from the essence of the Bible as the Word of God itself, namely, its salvific message. In support of her claim she cites Vatican II which says, '[T]he books of Scripture must be acknowledged as teaching firmly, faithfully and without error that truth which God wanted put into the sacred writings *for the sake of our salvation*.'[69] Fiorenza italicizes what she takes as the fundamental criterion of the truth of the biblical message, 'for the sake of our salvation'.

Fiorenza's effort to negotiate between a retrieval of the New Testament and contemporary biblical criticism is an important effort to ground a non-dogmatic and yet meaningful retrieval of the Christian scripture. Nonetheless Fiorenza's two-pronged approach combining historical critical method with a hermeneutics of divine love does not pass theological tests. Fiorenza does not explain how the essential message of the New Testament is God's love. While she rightfully can use historical criticism to underscore the fallibility of the text, she does not succeed in demonstrating the revelatory character of the text because she offers no theological criterion for revelation and its relationship to human language. Elsewhere Fiorenza sketchily points to the role of the incarnation in her understanding of the dialectical character of the church as liberating and subject to the cultural influences of its time.[70] However, she fails to provide a full account of the doctrine of incarnation and how it applies to her scriptural hermeneutics. Consequently Fiorenza's effort to locate authentic Christian life in the praxis or testimony of contemporary church communities also lacks theological justification. If Fiorenza cannot theologically account for the liberating power of the Word of God, she also cannot account for the theological credibility of the churches whose witness she claims derives from this Word. The testimony of these churches amounts, therefore, to nothing more than wishful thinking. A successful effort to combine the historical critical method with a religious retrieval that is the postmodern theological effort requires a proper theology of language.

Applied to Fiorenza's project, Rosenzweig's dialetical theology of the Word accounts for how the New Testament text can be subject to the historical prejudices of its day and retain revelatory significance. From a Rosenzweigian perspective the text's historical conditionedness is a testament to its fallibility and consequently the dialectical site of the divine judgment and commandment to acknowledge and love God. As such, the text summons its readers to testify to the God it dialectically reveals. The text is no longer religiously inspiring *despite* its historical fallibility but precisely *because* of its historical fallibility, so far as this fallibility commands the testimony of its readers now and in the future. In this way the text becomes the revelatory inspiration to the life of church communities.

## b. *The Word of God and Testimony*

Rosenzweig's dialectical conception of the Word of God presents Torah and Christ as finite human expressions which provide a primarily negative function, alerting those who encounter them to divine judgment and the summons to acknowledge the transcendent Other. The question remains, however, can religious language assume a positive meaning as more than the site of judgment and summons without overreaching itself into theological positivism?

### b.1. *Rosenzweig's Hermeneutics of Desire*

According to Rosenzweig's account, religious language is not strictly the finite or negative vehicle of divine commandment but also lends expression to the human testimony or obedient acknowledgment of the divine. For Rosenzweig, human beings testify to God through theological desire and repentance and they lend expression to these religious practices through the language that comes to constitute their religious traditions. Consequently, religious language or the Word of God assumes positive meaning when it is the expression of human testimony or what philosophically amounts to a praxis of theological verification.[71] As the expression of theological desire and repentance, religious language does not pretend to refer directly to the transcendent and loving God and therefore does not override or negate the dialectical character of religious language. In what follows I will trace how the Word of God lends positive testimony as the longing for God and as repentance.

Earlier we examined Rosenzweig's analysis of theological desire as one of the two ways human beings have of testifying to their encounter with divine love. Since human beings can only testify to their own experience of divine love and since humans experience divine love as a momentary infusion that they cannot secure for themselves, testimony to divine love becomes, in part, testimony to one's desire for divine love. By desiring God a person simultaneously acknowledges the reality of the love she has encountered as well as her inability to control or secure that love. More specifically, by desiring, a person testifies to the reality of God's love and her desire for more of God's love. On the one hand, she yearns for an assurance of God's love in the past as a warrant and ground for her future hope. She desires a God of creation. On the other hand, she desires more of God's love

97

in the future – she yearns for or hopes for a redeemer. As we recall, Rosenzweig's account suggests that human beings express their desire for the God of creation and the God of redemption through pragmatically justified pronouncements of faith and the practical love for the neighbor. In other words, according to Rosenzweig, human beings testify to God by affirming God's loving presence in human time. Of course, proclamations regarding God as creator and the practical testimony to God as redeemer are pragmatically justified and qualified. They must always be recognized as true only when truth is pragmatically understood. In other words, religious expressions of God's presence in human time are expressions of human longing for God justifiably elevated to the status of a working truth.

*The Star of Redemption* provides numerous examples of religious language that lends expression to our testimony to or desire for the God who loves. Rosenzweig's hermeneutics of scripture is governed by his understanding of theological desire. To illuminate this hermeneutics let us return to his reading of *The Song of Songs*. For Rosenzweig, *The Song of Songs* provides not only an example of the dialectical character of the text as a vehicle of revelation but also an example of how religious language lends positive expression to the beloved's testimonial response to the divine command. *The Song of Songs*, Rosenzweig says, expresses 'the transitory in its temporal form'.[72] In it one hears the testimony of a soul seized by an unprecedented, all consuming, momentary love. 'Everything is equally present, equally fleeting and alive – "like a gazelle or a young stag upon the mountains".(2:9)'[73] Still, *The Song of Songs* also recounts the beloved's longing to trust this fleeting love, to know or remember that this love has come before and therefore will return again. *The Song of Songs* expresses faith in a God who has loved in the past. In *The Song of Songs* the lover himself asserts this claim 'with his quiet, ever-recurring address "my sister, my bride".(4:9) Thus he lifts his love above the fleeting moment. For him, the beloved was once "in times gone by my sister or my wife".' In this assertion, the lover establishes the 'historicity, ... or ground ...'[74] of this love. Such historicity or ground is, of course, born of the beloved's desire but, rather than diminish the strength of the claim, the desire of the beloved fuels this faith. For Rosenzweig the same desire and faith feeds the Jewish people's faith in or 'knowledge' of the Exodus, or a Christian's faith in or knowledge of the birth of Jesus as Christ, without sin. In this way, scriptural accounts of God's participation in history achieve verification not through historical-critical or anthropological discovery but through the fire of the love and desire that gives rise to them.

The desire for a God who loves in the present now verified, the beloved desires still more. 'Does not something ultimate still separate them, at the pinnacle of love – beyond even that "Thou art mine" of the lover?'[75] The beloved cries out for the presence of God throughout all the world, now and in the future. Rosenzweig recounts the text and says,

> O that you were like a brother to me!' (8:1) It is not enough that the lover calls his bride by the name of sister . . . The name ought to be the truth . . . It should be heard in the bright light of 'the street . . . who would grant that!' . . . And the sobs of the beloved penetrate beyond love, to a future beyond its present revelation.[76]

But here, Rosenzweig says, *The Song of Songs* closes. It ends in a cry. Positive testimony to a God who consoles these tears will have to be expressed elsewhere in scripture.

If faith in an historical God enacts the beloved's longing to remember God's love in the past, love of the neighbor enacts the beloved's desire for God's future presence in the world and, for Rosenzweig, the psalms lend the greatest expression to this testimony. As we may recall, love of the neighbor is the act whereby the beloved, stirred by her desire for more of God's love in the future and in her world, acts as if God has already redeemed the world. By loving the neighbor, the beloved allows the neighbor to pose as a sign of God's redeeming love. As a sign of God's redeeming love, the neighbor provides an analogue of God's command and motivates the beloved to respond in a way that resembles her response to God's love, that is, through loving acts of self-divestment. In this way, God's presence as redeemer is testified to in the community of those who love and are loved by the neighbor. The beloved testifies to the neighbor who, as beloved, becomes a sign of the redeeming God. Of course the community-wide testimony to God's reality as redeemer is always tensed by the dialectical character of the desire for divine love. That is, the loving performative proclamation of God's redemption is always both a positive testimony born of the certainty of divine love as well as a cry for this redemption born of the uncertainty regarding the future of a love that is transitory and exterior. The psalms capture this dialectical character of the community's performative testimony.

In particular, Rosenzweig points to the 'Let us praise him for he is good'[77] that is implicitly or explicitly expressed by the psalms. In place of the narrative of the past tense or the dialogue of the present, the psalms use the grammar of the cohortative. The cohortative 'let us' uniquely expresses the exhortation to praise and thank God which the community as the sign of God's redemption can and must convey. Furthermore the psalms permit the community to declare its trust in and praise for the God who 'for the sake of his steadfast love' is their 'help and shield' from 'this time forth and to eternity'.[78] So chanted, the psalm textually express the pragmatically verified truth of God's redemption. 'The congregational thanksgiving is already the fulfillment of all that for which it is possible to pray communally . . . the kingdom.'[79]

Still, just as the beloved's testimony is always at once a proclamation of certainty and a cry of desire so, the psalms also express the fragility of the community's chant. If the kingdom were present, there would be no need for mutual exhortation – no need for the 'let us' to rouse the community. And if the kingdom were present, the psalms would not assume a prophetic tone and distinguish between a community of 'we' and a community of 'ye', between those 'who fear the Lord'[80] and those who do not. 'A not-yet is inscribed over all redemptive unison.'[81] 'God himself must speak the ultimate word which may no longer be a word . . . For God the We's are like the Ye's.'[82] The chant presents God in communal action/love but, because it is human language, that divine presence is also negated. For now redemption lives in the heart of the beloved who longs for God's redemption and faithfully chants in the company of all who testify to God's redeeming love.

### b.2. *Rosenzweig's Hermeneutics of Repentance and Liturgical Time*

If, as we have discussed, Rosenzweig sees religious life as testimony to a loving God, this testimony assumes two distinct forms; the testimony of desire and the testimony of repentance. We may recall that, according to Rosenzweig's account, the individual who receives divine love experiences a newfound security and peace accompanied by a pressing awareness of the absence of this love in her past experience. The newness of the event marks a break between that moment in time and all other prior temporal moments. While God is inseparable from his act of love, the individual has lived without this love and the event of love awakens her to a sense of responsibility for this absence, and she repents. Religious language lends expression to this testimony through what Rosenzweig, calls proper prayer or the liturgical cycle. According to Rosenzweig liturgical cycles challenge the temporalization of all human experience, including the very temporalization that the faith acts expressed through narrative and chant have offered. Consequently the ritual cycle as a whole repentantly testifies to the negation of God in the world of our human, and therefore temporal, experience. With these two notions of time – the one, the time of pragmatic verification and the other, the liturgical time that anticipates eternity – Rosenzweig offers a new theology of history located in the unique relationship between the liturgical messianism and scriptural labor of redemption. On the one hand, Rosenzweig argues that eternal life rests on the reading and writing of scripture as verification. On the other hand, narration or temporalization of divine revelation requires the Messianic anticipation performed liturgically. If it is the case that the liturgical repetition challenges and always humbles our temporalization of the divine Word, it is also the case that the divine Word is only realized when it is the inexhaustible source of our scriptural testimony. Rosenzweig's recognition of the unique character of theological time challenges modern theology's quest to ally itself with the goals of the secular order.[83]

According to Rosenzweig, religions afford liturgical cycles that guard believers from securing their own temporalized vision of redemption by providing a new model of time based on the structural unit of the hour. Unlike the concept of time as the progressive sequence of ever-passing moments, the hour constitutes a structure of time expressive of a 'now' which does not simply pass into a new moment but which upon its passing is recreated as another 'now'. As constitutive of a moment that in its passing returns to its beginning, the unit of the hour tenses between the present and the future. Every hour is followed by another hour. Nonetheless the very hour which follows the hour is none other than a recreation of that which it follows. The first hour is a 'representative', an 'anticipation' of the next hour so far as the next hour is only a rebirth of the first. The hour resembles the today which is not yet here – and yet which is presaged in a moment representative of it. 'It is not enough that it come ever anew. It must not come anew. It must come back. It really must be the same moment . . . When an hour is up, there begins not only a "new" hour . . . rather, there begins "again an hour" . . .'[84]

But the hour is constitutive of the day and the day of the week and the week of the year. These units free human beings from the constraints of time determined by the passing of life in nature. As mentioned earlier, peoples who seek to cultivate their land through regular hourly, daily and yearly enactment of farming activities can overcome the natural changes otherwise inevitable to their crops. These opportunities for regulated activity within hours, days or years also allow for the development of human culture and its ability to challenge the dictates of nature. The regular enactment of laws and customs in particular provide a societal order and regulation that

101

protects individuals from the contingencies of nature. 'In the service of the earth, constantly repeated day in day out and year in year out, man senses his earthly eternity within the human community.'[85]

Given this portrait of cultural life, why do religious believers need to enact unique liturgical cycles in order to testify repentantly? Why can't believers use the customs of their own cultures to challenge their tendency to temporalize experience? Is there, in other words, a difference between human culture and custom and religious ritual?

According to Rosenzweig, the central difference between religious and secular custom concerns the focus or purpose of the ritual or custom. As we recall from our earlier discussion, individuals endowed with their own name or destiny look to tie their destiny to that of a group of individuals or a society and its name in the hopes of extending the range of their own lives. We will also recall that, according to Rosenzweig, the identity or name of a group is reinforced by that group's particular social practices or cults which represent the particular way in which a given culture embraces and confronts life and existence. Lastly we must recall, however, that social practices, caught in the ever-changing flux of life, often change to meet the changes in the world and consequently do not always replicate the social themes of the group they represent. A society, if healthy, will inevitably change its own identity with the necessity of changes in the life and times of which it is a part. If unhealthy, a society will attempt to preserve its customs and commemorations, often using coercion, in order to overcome the flux of time. In either case, however, secular societies are motivated by the desire to offset their inevitable dissolution within time – that is, they seek their own self-preservation. Conversely, religious societies seek to testify repentantly to the God who loves. Religious ritual is not an effort to preserve a religious society. On the contrary, the liturgical year questions all human experience, both temporal and customary. Secular customs are as vulnerable to a theological or religious critique as any other human expression insofar as God's love exceeds and is exterior to all past human experience and expression.[86] Liturgy introduces believers to 'a silence which no longer has any need of the word . . . Liturgy frees gesture from the fetters of helpless servitude to speech . . .'[87]

Rosenzweig's description of the Jewish and Christian liturgical cycles shows how their repetitive ritual cycles effect a testimony of repentance. Both traditions establish festivals that mark and proclaim their faithful and desirous temporalizations of God's presence in our world. Judaism commemorates God's historicity through Pesach, his revelatory love through Shavuot and his redemptive promise in Simhat Torah. Like Pesach, Christmas grounds the possibility of God's redemptive presence in the world via the birth of the child Jesus and commemorates this through the readings of the gospels' birth narratives. Like Shavuot, Easter commemorates the absolute miracle of God's call to election. Finally, on Pentecost, the Christian commemorates the communion of those in the church whose common chant testifies to God's redeeming love.

Nonetheless, both Judaism and Christianity contextualize these commemorations and temporalizations in the context of a yearly liturgical cycle whose repetition challenges the linearity and therefore the proclamations within the story they tell. For example, the Sabbath is, according to Rosenzweig, the 'static foundation of the year'[88] which establishes and provides a weekly reminder of the meaning of the liturgical year. The Sabbath is a day of rest during which Jews refrain from their regular affairs and reflect upon 'the entire course of the day of God'.[89] Silently reflecting on the day of God is different from proclaiming the day of God. The Sabbath is not a day of proclamation but a day of listening. 'Six days he has uttered the many useful and useless words . . . but on the seventh he lets his tongue rest from the talk of everyday, and learns silence and listening.'[90] Additionally, the very regularity of Sabbath rest and reflection challenges the linearity of the tale that the Jews tell about the God of creation and revelation and redemption. In contrast to this story, Sabbath observance testifies to the singularity of divine transcendence over and above any human effort to speak or experience otherwise.

Of course, for Rosenzweig, the Sabbath is not the only festival that occurs regularly. All Jewish festivals occur regularly within the Jewish liturgical cycle and this regularity offsets the temporal story they proclaim. If the Sabbath is the static foundation of this annually repeated cycle, Yom Kippur is its culmination, the Sabbath of Sabbaths, the ultimate day of repentance. On Yom Kippur, the meaning of the liturgical cycle reaches its most profound expression. On Yom Kippur there is neither proclamation nor restful reflection of the God who creates, reveals and redeems. On Yom Kippur 'there is no more waiting, no more hiding behind history'.[91] On Yom Kippur the Jew sacrifices the 'Word' and kneels together with the community of humankind, in the silent and repentant testimony to the transcendent God.

> The individual confronts judgment without any intermediary fact. He stands in
> the congregation. He says 'We' . . . But the 'We' of this day are not the 'We' of

103

the people in history . . [T]he 'We' in whose community the individual recognizes his sin, can be nothing less than the congregation of mankind.[92]

Bracketed on the one side by the Sabbath and on the other by Yom Kippur, the Jewish liturgical year quiets the Jewish people's proclamations and allows them to repent for the absence of God in their human experience of the world. The silence afforded through the liturgical cycle challenges all and any human proclamation concerning God's reality, regardless of the dialectical character of the proclamation itself. Of course Rosenzweig is not espousing a silent mysticism. Rather, Rosenzweig appreciates how, coupled with the desirous and faithful proclamations of the festivals themselves, the silence afforded by the liturgical calendar reminds believers of the not-yet of divine reality within the context of the still human, all-too-human world in which they dwell.

Like Judaism, Christianity's liturgical year also offsets the Christian believer's proclamation of the God of the past, the present and the future and permits believers to testify repentantly to God's absence in their human experience. For Christianity as for Judaism the clerical year is 'a curriculum of communal silence'.[93] Rosenzweig readily admits that a superficial review of Christian history would negate this claim. Christian history portrays a church clearly not committed to communal silence, but actively committed to pronouncing and extending its Word. At times the church has acted like the unhealthy state, committed singularly to its own preservation and willing to bully its members into adhering to its unchanging customs. Christianity's sometimes tainted history is a testament to the particular character of its experience and expression of divine love.

According to Rosenzweig's account, Christianity's experience and particular expression of and response to divine love varies from Judaism's experience and expression of divine love. While Jews experience and respond to divine love as a community and therefore verify God's presence in the past, present and future of this self-same community, Christians experience and respond to divine love as individuals. Consequently, for Jews, the love of the neighbor means love of the fellow Jew, who simply by birth participates in the chain of all Jews from Sinai. For Christians, love of the neighbor means love of another individual who may or may not be Christian. Christian community is a product of the outreach and testimony of individuals who qua individuals have experienced God's revelatory love. As a result, while Jewish life naturally reaches in, Christian life and testimony naturally reach out. Christianity's testimony necessitates involvement with temporal, historical reality. Consequently, Christianity often confuses its outreach and testimony for God with persuasion and domination. When this happens the church mimics the state's efforts at self-preservation and coercion. This does not mean that Christianity must fall prey to the ways of the world. On the contrary, Rosenzweig appreciates the Christian Word as an expression of theological desire and the Christian liturgical cycle as repentant testimony. Rosenzweig recognizes that Christianity has had to traverse a two-thousand-year history to reach its true expression in what he calls the Johannine church. Nonetheless, like Judaism, Christianity is essentially a tradition rooted in testimony to a loving and commanding God whose Word is the dialectical expression of this love and the vehicle of human theological desire and liturgical repentance.

Christians, like Jews, temporally sequence or narrate their proclamations of the God who loved in the past, the God who loves in the present and the God whose redeeming love will complete the world in the future. Like Jewish festivals, Christian festivals mark these various proclamations, in turn commemorated on Christmas, Easter and Pentecost. Stéphane Mosès remarks, 'For Rosenzweig, the general structure of the Christian liturgical calendar is identical to that of the Jewish one.'[94]

Like Judaism, however, these festivals are bound to a liturgical calendar which regulates annually their commemoration and offsets the progressive narrative they tell. For example, like the Jewish Sabbath, the Christian Sabbath regularly interrupts Christianity's story of progressive mission to the world. More specifically, the Christian Sabbath commemorates the intrusion of the Christ event into human time. According to Christianity, the truth concerning the historical and temporal period we currently live in is lodged in the epoch-making reality of the birth of Christ. A unique event whose own beginning is beyond time, Christ's birth defines the character of all subsequent time. Every Sunday, Christians are reminded of this epochal context of their testimonial lives. Every Sunday, Christians are reminded that their mission, their journey, their efforts to amass a world community are none other than efforts of a 'single hour, a single day ... ever in the event, ever au courant'.[95] In this way, Sabbath observance qualifies Christian tendencies to historicize or temporalize their journey and prompts a posture of repentance and humility concerning human efforts to testify to God's reality.

According to Rosenzweig's account, the repentant tenor of the Christian liturgical year is anchored in the Sunday Sabbath and consummately expressed in the celebration of New Year's. On New Year's, Christians relinquish their claims to a future coming together of all peoples. On New

Year's, Christians commemorate their detachment from their own march toward redemption, their own missionizing proclamation by participating in the secular New Year's festivals celebrated by the individual nations of the world. Anonymously dancing together with non-believers in the secular festivities, Christians liberate themselves from their own proclamations in an act of ultimate self-critique and repentance. In this moment of radical self-othering, Christianity sheds its testimony to the Word and dissolves into the wordless exchange of all who celebrate these secular festivals. The church's anonymous merger with other peoples and customs does not signal the church's fall into secularity. The church does not simply substitute one vocabulary of human culture for another. 'For only gesture is beyond word and deed – gesture which has become wholly free, wholly creative and which is no longer directed at this or that person or thing . . . There the word may evaporate.'[96] Rather, by fusing with these others, the church dances wordlessly – that is, without word, testifying to the limitation of all human language before the God who loves.

Still, Rosenzweig argues, one can appreciate fully the meaning of the dance between the believer and the non-believer only if one understands the meaning of the baptism ritual. 'Accordingly the sacrament by which the Church completes the preparation provided by those folkoristic spectacles, those offshoots of the dance, can only take the form of a consecration of the beginning.'[97] According to Rosenzweig's account, infant baptism is the ritual that commemorates the reality and independence of God's unconditional love from any form of human testimony. Every baptism allows those who witness it to recognize a baby as a child of God, even before she can utter the Word of Christ. The baby is loved not because of her beliefs or testimony, but only as God loved Jesus, that is, by virtue of the very finitude of her existence. Consequently, baptism commemorates the reality of God's grace for a humanity that has not and cannot directly proclaim God's Word itself and calls those who witness the baptism to repentant testimony. 'It allows the defenselessness of the minor child, unconscious of itself, to count as the defenselessness of the supreme consciousness of silent adoration.'[98]

## C. Re-Claiming the Center: Rosenzweig's Philosophical and Theological Renewal of Revealed Religion

Rosenzweig's hermeneutics of theological desire and repentance completes his dialectical theology of the Word. Together they offer an invaluable model for postmodern theological hermeneutics. Above we discussed the value of Rosenzweig's concept of the finite character of the Word of God for Jewish and Christian life. Rosenzweig's dialectical concept of the Word of God permits Jews and Christians to simultaneously appreciate the revelatory significance of Torah and Christ and recognize the fallibility of these central Words. Furthermore, Rosenzweig's radical re-interpretation of the revelatory significance of the Word of God promotes a praxis- or witness-oriented approach to Jewish and Christian life. As fallible, Torah and Christ become the site of divine judgment and the divine commandment to testify to the God who loves. Rosenzweig's dialectical conception of Torah and Christ offers a groundbreaking analysis of the revelatory yet non-dogmatic character of Torah and Christ as the Word of God.

Nonetheless, Rosenzweig's theology of the Word of God recognizes the strictly finite or negative significance of Torah and Christ, and cannot alone provide a viable basis for Jewish or Christian life. Rosenzweig must demonstrate how religious language can assume a positive meaning as more than the site of judgment and summons without overreaching itself into theological positivism. As we have seen, religious language assumes positive meaning when it expresses human testimony to the commanding God revealed in the finite text of Torah and Christ.

In Jewish terms, Rosenzweig's analysis of religious language as human testimony lends meaning and credence to the Jewish tradition of Oral law. From a Rosenzweigian perspective, the Oral tradition of biblical and rabbinic commentary, interpretation and legislative development are expressions of Jewish covenantal testimony or theological desire. Consequently the beloved who testifies obediently to God's love testifies to her desire of this love – a desire that proclaims both 'Where is God's love?' and 'God's love is here and I have experienced it in the past and will experience it again tomorrow.' This is one of Franz Rosenzweig's greatest and most neglected insights regarding the nature of Jewish narrative. For Rosenzweig, Jewish narrative is the expression of Jewish theological desire. Jewish narrative is, therefore, always tensed by a desire that positively proclaims God as creator, revealer and redeemer but also sometimes painfully longs for God's gracious offering. And this is the difference between Rosenzweig and Lindbeck and others for whom narratives are closed cycles of telling and re-telling. Jewish telling, Jewish memory, Jewish proclamation, are always Jewish hoping and Jewish longing, faithfully and longingly proclaimed as telling.

With this analysis of divine love and desire we have unveiled the contours of Jewish covenantal life. Jewish covenantal life is proclamation of Jewish desire as a cry and a testimony to God's love. Jews live covenantally in study and in practice and both therefore are driven by theological desire.

Jewish theological desire propels rabbinic exegetical practice. Rabbinic exegesis is the proclamation of God's love through a perpetual series of questions and expressions of faith. On the one hand, rabbinic exegesis is the relentless pursuit of justice – an endless asking 'Why?' For the rabbis, the assertion of reason and the pursuit of justice are closely allied. To ask for (rational) justification regarding a point is to ask whether the point reveals God's love or not. In rabbinic exegesis one can ask for justification of another's point or require justification for one's own claim. The 'Why?' does not have to be self-sacrificing to be religious. When a rabbi in the text or a Jew studying the text inserts doubt and asks, 'Is this position correct?' she is not asking, 'Is this position evidentially justifiable?' but rather, 'Is God's love present in this position?' One cannot understand a Rosenzweigian perspective on rabbinic exegesis without understanding how it is propelled by theological doubt – a doubt not born of atheism but born out of the human desire for more experiences of God's love. From the perspective of a Rosenzweigian hermeneutics of theological desire, rabbinic doubt is a testament to the difference between God and humanity *and* a testament to the uniqueness of God's love. Rabbinic doubt runs through the narrative and not above it. Rabbinic doubt honors the difference between God and humanity within the religious experience itself, and therefore permits rabbinic Judaism to confront instances of God's absence without departing from the context of its covenantal life with God.

But, of course, rabbinic exegesis and study is a testament to one's faith in God as well. Rabbinic disagreement and doubt meet always with rabbinic faith in God. No doubt, no question, no disagreement transcends or undoes the awareness of divine love that sponsors desire. Consequently, rabbinic engagement with Jewish texts becomes communities' ways of addressing injustice and responding through faithful action. The text permits its readers to say, 'Where is God?' and to testify, 'God is here.' Rabbinic engagement with Jewish texts permits the proclamation of God's donative love in the context of human communities whose experience of that love can be limited.

Rosenzweig presents this portrait of Jewish learning in an essay entitled 'Renaissance of Jewish Learning'. There Rosenzweig portrays this theological pragmatism in the context of the community of those who study texts together.

There is one recipe alone that can make a person Jewish ... [T]hat recipe is to
have no recipe ... [O]ur fathers had a beautiful word for it that says everything:
confidence. Confidence is the word for a state of readiness that does not ask for
recipes ... [I]t lives in the present, it crosses recklessly the threshold leading from
today to tomorrow.'[99]

Later in the same essay Rosenzweig speaks of theological desire as it is
shared among those who study the texts as the basis of this faithful
confidence. 'And words will come to the listener, and they will join together
and form desires. And desires are the messengers of confidence.' Who then is
the greatest teacher, Rosenzweig asks?

Those who know how to listen to real wishes may also know perhaps how to point
out the desired way ... For the teacher able to satisfy such spontaneous desire
cannot be a teacher according to a plan; he must be much more and much less, a
master and at the same time a pupil. It will not be enough that he himself knows or
that he himself can teach. He must be capable of something quite different – he
himself must be able to 'desire.' He who can desire must be the teacher here.[100]

From a Rosenzweigian perspective then, *halakhic* action is the expression
of these proclamations in Jewish life. For orthodox Jews *halakhic* change and
adaptation to questions of justice is slow – although it happens. For liberal
Jewish communities *halakhic* change can be more radical, can address more
provocative challenges to God's presence and can issue more innovative
proclamations of faith. In either case the dynamic between doubt and faith
woven through rabbinic study and practice reveals the pattern of justice and
divine command ethics that Jewish theological desire permits. In this way
*halakhic* life mediates between the cries for justice and the proclamation of
faith in the God who creates and reveals and redeems. Consequently
*halakhic* life is a doxological practice that writes the Word of God here on
earth in the way that humans elected and loved by God can write it – with
their own hand and with their own sense of faith.

Participation in the Oral or Rabbinic tradition is not, therefore, the
exclusive right of Jews who maintain a belief in the divine origin of the
written or the Oral Torah. Instead the Oral tradition is the rightful
possession of any Jew who claims this tradition as the means by which she
expresses her loving testimony to God. In this way Rosenzweig's theology
of the Word of God negates the distinction between *Gesetz* and *Gebot* that
constituted the basis of the modern Jewish division between liberal and
orthodox Jews. Modernity decreed that liberal Jews rejected the specificity

of rabbinic and *halakhic* texts in favor of the universality of the Bible and its moral commands in contrast to the orthodox Jews, singularly committed to the divine authorship of the Torah, understood as both Written and Oral. If, however, Rosenzweig's theology of the Word of God identifies particular Jewish texts and life as expressions of theological testimony, the difference between liberal and orthodox Jews disappears. So-called liberal Jews actively and justifiably participate in the particularities of Jewish life no less than their orthodox counterparts. One may easily celebrate Jewish particularity without falling prey to Jewish dogmatism or fanaticism.[101]

Rosenzweig's hermeneutics of desire and repentance are also of great benefit to Christian hermeneutics. If, as we have discussed above, Rosenzweig's dialectical theology of the Word permits Christians to critique, retrieve and feel commanded to testify to the Word of God in the scripture, Rosenzweig's hermeneutics of desire and repentance lends theological meaning to the testimonial language of the communities of witness. As a result, theologians like Elizabeth Schüssler Fiorenza, who seek to grant theological significance to the testimony of contemporary church communities, may now understand such testimony as the rightful and obedient response to the God who lovingly reveals God's love in the text. Rosenzweig's theology of the Word of God, coupled with his hermeneutics of desire and repentance, presents a basis for a praxis-oriented Christian theology that falls prey neither to contemporary subjectivism nor to theological dogmatism.

Together with his philosophy of language, Rosenzweig's theology of the Word of God offers a revolutionary model for postmodern Jewish and Christian life. By asserting an alliance between philosophy and theology, Rosenzweig on the one hand has offered a valid apologetics of revealed religion, an apologetics that opens the door to future exchanges between revealed religion and philosophical studies broadly meant to include cultural studies, anthropology, literary studies and more. On the other hand, Rosenzweig's radical re-interpretation of the Word of God offers a new basis for a vital, non-dogmatic, praxis-oriented retrieval of classical sacred scriptures and liturgical worship.

## Notes

1  Franz Rosenzweig, *The Star of Redemption* (trans. William W. Hallo; New York: Holt, Rinehart and Winston, 1971), p. 94. Franz Rosenzweig, *Der Stern der Erlösung* (Frankfurt: Suhrkamp Verlag, 1988), p. 104.

2 Rosenzweig, *Star,* p. 95/105.

3 Rosenzweig, *Star*, p. 95/106.

4 My reading of Rosenzweig's notion of miracle differs from that offered by Leora Batnitzky in her *Idolatry and Representation* (Princeton: Princeton University Press, 1999). Batnitzky holds that miracles are narrative 'signs' that point to the reality of a self-interpreting tradition. But for Rosenzweig miracles are not just narrative signs but they are signs of God. Consequently, Rosenzweig is not concerned with a crisis in human meaning, but a crisis in theological meaning. *The Star of Redemption* seeks to demonstrate how Judaism and Christianity publicize the miracle of God. *The Star* presents a theology of witness that has hermeneutical ramifications but cannot be reduced to the hermeneutical practice of any human culture. At the heart of Rosenzweig's effort to speak to the theological crisis of his day is his turn to covenantal theology. See Chapter 6 of this work for a more extensive comparison between Batnitzky's cultural–linguistic reading of *The Star* and the covenantal reading offered here.

5 Rosenzweig, *Star*, p. 100/111.

6 Rosenzweig, *Star*, p. 103/114.

7 Rosenzweig, *Star*, p. 103/114.

8 Rosenzweig, *Star*, p. 107/119.

9 Rosenzweig, *Star*, pp. 107–08/119–20.

10 St. Thomas Aquinas says, 'The invisible things of Him are clearly seen, being understood by the things that are made (Romans I. 20). But this would not be unless the existence of God could be demonstrated through the things that are made.' 'Summa Theologica Part I', in *Philosophy in the Middle Ages* (eds Arthur Hyman and James J. Walsh; Indianapolis: Hackett Publishing Company, 1983), p. 525.

11 For Heidegger's discussion of *Dasein* see Martin Heidegger, *Being in Time* (trans. John Macquarrie & Edward Robinson; San Francisco: Harper, 1962).

12 Rosenzweig, *Star*, p. 121/134.

13 Rosenzweig, *Star*, p. 121/134.

14 This may sound similar to Tillich's notion of correlation wherein the problem of existence meets with its correlative answer in Being. Nonetheless, there is a marked difference between the two models. Rosenzweig's analysis of creation does give rise to the question of existence; however, Rosenzweig's notion of revelation does not provide the answer of Being. As we have already seen, revelation does not provide propositional or ontological information concerning the nature of existence. For Tillich's discussion see Paul Tillich, *Systematic Theology* (vol. 1, *Reason and Revelation, Being and God*; Chicago: The University of Chicago Press, 1951).

15 Rosenzweig, *Star*, pp. 120–21/133–34.

16 Rosenzweig, *Star*, pp. 135/149–50.

17 Rosenzweig, *Star*, p. 146/162.

18 Rosenzweig's critique of idealism shares much in common with the critique of modern philosophy issued by Catherine Pickstock and John Milbank. Rosenzweig, Pickstock and Milbank all agree that modern philosophy's static schematization of reality dissolves into an ontological nihilism. Speaking of the nihilism at the root of idealism Rosenzweig says, 'Idealism had been unable to comprehend phenomena as "spontaneous", for that would have meant denying the omnipotence of the logos, and so it never did it justice. It had to falsify the bubbling plenitude into a dead chaos of givens. That All as one-and-universal can be held together only by a reasoning which possesses active, spontaneous force. But if vitality is thereby ascribed to reasoning, it must willy-nilly be denied to life – life denied its liveliness.' Rosenzweig, *Star*, p. 47/50. Similarly, in the introduction to their edited volume, *Radical Orthodoxy*, Pickstock and Milbank accuse modern philosophy of falling into an anti-theological nihilism. Speaking of modern philosophy they say, '[A]lthough it might seem that to treat of diverse worldly phenomena such as language, knowledge, the body, aesthetic experience, political community, friendship, etc., apart from God is to safeguard their worldliness, in fact . . . it is to make even this worldliness dissolve . . . First, without an appeal to eternal stability, one has to define a purely immanent security . . . [T]he latter [modern philosophy] abolishes these phenomena in favour of an immanent static schema or *mathesis* . . . [I]t is immanence that is dualistic and tends to remove the mysterious diversity of matter in assuming that appearances do not exceed themselves.' See Milbank, Pickstock, Ward (eds), *Radical Orthodoxy: A New Theology* (New York: Routledge, 1999), p. 3.

19 Stéphane Mosès, *System and Revelation: The Philosophy of Franz Rosenzweig* (trans. Catherine Tihanyi; Detroit: Wayne State University Press, 1982), p. 87.

20 For this particular understanding of *Dasein's* relation to its world prior to revelation, my analysis is largely indebted to that provided by Stéphane Mosès in his book *System and Revelation*.

21 Rosenzweig, *Star*, p. 128/142.

22 'Readiness-to-hand is the way in which entities as they are "in themselves" are defined ontologico-categorially.' Heidegger, *Being in Time*, p. 101. For Heidegger's discussion of the relation between concern and readiness to hand or equipment, see Heidegger, *Being in Time*, pp. 91–145.

23 Rosenzweig, *Star*, p. 131/145.

24 Rosenzweig, *Star*, p. 222/248.

25 Robert Gibbs, *Correlations in Rosenzweig and Levinas* (Princeton: Princeton University Press, 1992), p. 241.

26 Rosenzweig, *Star*, p. 241/268.

27 Rosenzweig, *Star*, p. 240/268.

28 Rosenzweig, *Star*, pp. 302–03/336.

29  Rosenzweig, *Star*, p. 303/336.

30  Rosenzweig, *Star*, p. 292/324.

31  Rosenzweig, *Star*, p. 241/268.

32  That Catherine Pickstock begins her *After Writing: On the Liturgical Consummation of Philosophy* with a quote from *The Star* that speaks to this potential critique of the state, demonstrates a point of similarity between her view of the state and Rosenzweig's. Pickstock believes, like Rosenzweig, that devoid of a God-*Gestalt*, the type which for Rosenzweig is represented in the Jewish and Christian liturgical years and for Pickstock in the liturgical life of the church, the state, left to its own devices, necessarily deteriorates into a self-serving instrument of human self-interest. Pickstock therefore says, 'These unholy cities which claim clarity and knowledge as their secure foundations, conceal a nihilistic aspect which is the inevitable outcome of a separation of ontology from theology.' Catherine Pickstock, *After Writing: On the Liturgical Consummation of Philosophy* (Oxford: Blackwell, 1998), p. 3.

33  For a similar critique of the Constantinian church and its effects on the modern nation state, see Scott Bader Saye, *Church and Israel After Christendom: A Politics of Election* (Boulder: Westview Press, 1999).

34  Despite this critique Rosenzweig maintains faith in the modern nation state, particularly the modern nation state as it participates in what he, following Schelling, referred to as the Johannine period. As such, the modern nation state absorbs the best of Christian values while negating any particular church dogma. In a 1915 letter to Eugene Rosenstock-Huessy, Rosenzweig says, 'For nationalism expresses not merely the peoples' belief that they come *from* God . . . but that they go *to* God.' Eugene Rosenstock-Huessy, (ed.), *Judaism Despite Christianity: The Letters on Christianity and Judaism between Eugene Rosenstock-Huessy and Franz Rosenzweig* (New York: Schocken Books, 1971), p. 131.

35  Rosenzweig, *Star*, p. 286/318.

36  Rosenzweig, *Star*, p. 108/120.

37  For a more extensive discussion concerning the relationship between Rosenzweig's New Thinking and cultural studies see my 2001 AAR paper, 'Challenging Assumptions: Rosenzweig's Concept of Original Sin'.

38  Rosenzweig, *Star*, p. 386/429.

39  Rosenzweig, *Star*, p. 386/429.

40  Rosenzweig, *Star*, p. 390/434.

41  Rosenzweig, *Star*, p. 393/437.

42  Rosenzweig, *Star*, p. 389/432.

43  Rosenzweig, *Star*, pp. 391–92/435–36.

44  Rosenzweig, *Star*, pp. 151/167–68.

45  This view is best represented by Yudit Greenberg's kabbalistically informed reading of *The Star of Redemption*. In Yudit Greenberg, 'The Hermeneutic Turn

in Franz Rosenzweig's Theory of Revelation', in Stephen Kepnes (ed.), *Interpreting Judaism in a Postmodern Age* (New York: New York University Press, 1996), Greenberg argues that for Rosenzweig revelation is an event wherein God speaks and engages human listening and response. According to Greenberg this dialogue generates a proximity between God, human beings and their language.

46 Franz Rosenzweig, 'Revelation and Law', in *On Jewish Learning* (trans. N.N. Glatzer; New York: Schocken Books, 1965), p. 118.

47 Despite Rosenzweig's own peculiar and pejorative reading of Islam, there is no reason why the claims he makes regarding religious language could not be applied to Islam as well as to Judaism and Christianity.

48 Rosenzweig, *Star*, p. 176/196.

49 Rosenzweig, *Star*, p. 179/200.

50 Rosenzweig, *Star*, p. 179/199.

51 Rosenzweig, *Star*, p. 180/200.

52 Rosenzweig, *Star*, p. 180/200.

53 Rosenzweig, *Star*, p. 204/228.

54 Franz Rosenzweig, 'The Builders: Concerning Jewish Law,' in *On Jewish Learning*, p. 75.

55 Rosenzweig, 'The Builders', p. 76.

56 Susan Handelman explores the concept of the Torah's self-divestment in Susan Handelman, 'The Torah of Criticism and the Criticism of Torah: Recuperating the Pedagogical Moment', in Steven Kepnes (ed.), *Interpreting Judaism*. Here she raises the compelling suggestion that, like the psychoanalyst who 'becomes the student of the patient's knowledge', Torah too can be appreciated as a 'non-authoritative knowledge not in possession of itself'. Handelman, 'The Torah of Criticism', p. 224. However, Handelman does not pursue this notion of the Torah's self-divestment to its logical dialectical conclusion. Instead, her essay lapses into a call for the dialogical model. The Torah, she says, divests itself so far as it is 'polyphonous, filled with multiple meanings, and the task of Israel is to continue Sinai, to re-enact the revelation by uncovering those meanings'. Handelman, 'The Torah of Criticism', p. 230. But the interpretability of the Torah is not the same as its self-divestment.

57 Rosenzweig, *Star*, p. 319/354.

58 Rosenzweig, *Star*, p. 319/355.

59 Rosenzweig, *Star*, p. 321/356.

60 Rosenzweig, *Star*, p. 321/357.

61 Rosenzweig, *Star*, p. 365/405.

62 Rosenzweig, *Star*, p. 345/382.

63 Rosenzweig, *Star*, p. 366/407.

64 Rosenzweig, *Star*, p. 341/378.

65 '[H]ow can it be that the text that resides at the very core of Judaism, the Pentateuch itself, is susceptible to textual criticism that reveals it to be both internally uneven and apparently inconsistent with observed Jewish law?' David Weiss Halivni, *Revelation Restored: Divine Writ and Critical Responses* (Boulder: Westview, 1997), p. 1.

66 Elisabeth Schüssler Fiorenza, *Bread Not Stone: The Challenge of Feminist Biblical Interpretation* (Boston: Beacon Press, 1984), pp. 13–15.

67 Fiorenza, *Bread Not Stone*, p. 3

68 Fiorenza, *Bread Not Stone*, p. 13.

69 Fiorenza, *Bread Not Stone*, p. 40.

70 See Elizabeth Schüssler Fiorenza, 'Feminist Spirituality, Christian Identity and Catholic Vision', *Womanspirit Rising* (ed. Carol P. Christ; San Francisco: Harper, 1992), p. 146.

71 In contemporary parlance we may say that Rosenzweig introduces a form of scriptural pragmatics. Like proponents of scriptural pragmatism including Peter Ochs, Robert Gibbs and John Milbank, Rosenzweig's scriptural hermeneutics highlights both the interpretability and perpetual meaningfulness of scriptural texts. However, Rosenzweig's scriptural pragmatism is the pragmatism of theological desire, an element not explicitly addressed in either Ochs' rabbinic pragmatism or Gibbs' phenomenology of intersubjective responsibility. See Ochs, *Pierce, Pragmatism and the Logic of Scripture* (Cambridge: Cambridge University Press, 1998) and Robert Gibbs, *Why Ethics: Signs of Responsibility* (Princeton: Princeton University Press, 2000). All four modes of scriptural pragmatism contribute to and develop the return to the text movement inaugurated in large part by the work of George Lindbeck. Most significantly all four forms of scriptural pragmatism recognize scriptural texts as practices of verification which presuppose both the fallibility of their claims as well as the philosophical plausibility and need for these claims. In this way, each corrects a fatal flaw in Lindbeck's cultural-linguistic program, namely, its insulation from exterior doubt and what amounts to its inability to actively engage with the non-believing community outside the church. A thorough comparison between these modes of scriptural pragmatism and their relation to Lindbeck's cultural-linguistic approach is beyond the scope of this work. Peter Ochs has discussed the comparison between his own rabbinic pragmatism and Lindbeck's cultural-linguistic approach in 'Scriptural Logic: Diagrams for Postcritical Metaphysics', *Rethinking Metaphysics* (eds Gregory Jones and Stephen Fowl; Oxford: Blackwell, 1995). For a comparison between Rosenzweig's scriptural pragmatism and John Milbank's hermeneutics see my 'The Meaning of Theological Desire: A Jewish Response to John Milbank's Ontology of Peace', American Academy of Religion, 2002. For a careful analysis of Lindbeck's work as a form of scriptural pragmatism see C.C. Pecknold, *Transforming Post-Liberal Theology* (London: T&T Clark, 2005).

72  Rosenzweig, *Star*, p. 201/225.

73  Rosenzweig, *Star*, p. 202/226.

74  Rosenzweig, *Star*, p. 183/204.

75  Rosenzweig, *Star*, p. 203/227.

76  Rosenzweig, *Star*, pp. 203–04/227–28.

77  Rosenzweig, *Star*, p. 231/258.

78  Rosenzweig, *Star*, pp. 251–52/280.

79  Rosenzweig, *Star*, p. 233/260.

80  Rosenzweig, *Star*, p. 252/280.

81  Rosenzweig, *Star*, p. 234/261.

82  Rosenzweig, *Star*, p. 238/265.

83  Robert Gibbs provides a similar analysis of Rosenzweig's theology of history in his *Correlations in Rosenzweig and Levinas*. There Gibbs says, '[W]e can see what relationship occurs between history and grammatical thinking by considering again the importance of temporality in the analysis of speech in Part II of *The Star of Redemption*. The truth of experience relies upon the distension between past, present and future, which is expressed in speech by different moods as well as tenses ... The very task of the historian is conformed to the task of narration ... But the task of redemption becomes excluded from history, because redemption is not narrated but is instead a matter for communal cohortation.' Gibbs, *Correlations*, pp. 116–17.

84  Rosenzweig, *Star*, p. 290/322.

85  Rosenzweig, *Star*, p. 291/323.

86  Here my discussion differs from Robert Gibbs' analysis of social practice in his *Correlations*. There Gibbs highlights the sociological element of Rosenzweig's thought and rightly understands Rosenzweig's discussion of social practice as linguistic expression. However, Gibbs fails to articulate the connection between this linguistic form and the election event of the commanding God. From Gibbs' perspective it would appear that cultural and social practices, the likes of the Jewish and Christian rituals, theoretically available to any society, suffice to provide the antidote to the language and lifestyle of 'use' typical of the Heideggerian self or the right and might of the state. However, for Rosenzweig, language becomes redemptive only when it aids us in witnessing to the God who elects us into a relationship of love.

87  Rosenzweig, *Star*, pp. 295–96/328–29.

88  Rosenzweig, *Star*, p. 313/347.

89  Rosenzweig, *Star*, p. 313/347.

90  Rosenzweig, *Star*, p. 314/348.

91  Rosenzweig, *Star*, p. 325/360.

92  Rosenzweig, *Star*, pp. 325/360–61.

93  Rosenzweig, *Star*, p. 353/392.

94  Mosès, *System and Revelation*, p. 251.

95   Rosenzweig, *Star*, pp. 340/377–78.
96   Rosenzweig, *Star*, pp. 371–72/413–14.
97   Rosenzweig, *Star*, pp. 373/415–16.
98   Rosenzweig, *Star*, pp. 373–74/416.
99   Franz Rosenzweig, 'Renaissance of Jewish Learning', *On Jewish Learning*, p. 69.
100  Rosenzweig, 'Renaissance of Jewish Learning', *On Jewish Learning*, p. 69.
101  For a discussion regarding how this kind of model can be applied to a feminist agenda like that presented by Judith Plaskow, see my 'Exegesis, Redemption and the Maculate Torah', in *Textual Reasonings* (eds Peter Ochs and Nancy Levene; London: SCM Press, 2002).

# Chapter 4

# Barth's *Epistle to the Romans* and the Theology of Practical Witness

Our discussion of Cohen's theology of acknowledgment and Rosenzweig's theology of election through testimony of action now complete, the second part of the essay will demonstrate the family resemblance between Cohen, Rosenzweig and Karl Barth with respect to the theology of election through testimony. That Rosenzweig and Barth both participated in the Patmos group, a study group of Jewish and Christian theologians who critiqued the liberalism of the prior generation, has been well documented.[1] However, there has been no extended analysis of theological resemblance between the two thinkers. The import of the comparison exceeds the bounds of intellectual history. Not only is Rosenzweig's New Thinking best viewed within the context of Barth's dialectical theology but Barth's doctrine of election is deepened when read next to Rosenzweig's phenomenology of testimony. Beyond this, Rosenzweig and Barth arguably represent the two greatest twentieth-century theologians of their respective traditions and are sought out as critical guides for contemporary Jewish and Christian communities. This comparison will illustrate how the theology of testimony in both thinkers offers a viable model for overcoming the damaging antagonisms between modern reason and biblical faith. Ultimately the comparison between Barth and Rosenzweig will bring Judaism and Christianity closer by illuminating their parallel sources and religious, communal and political commitments.

## A. Introduction

In what follows I will argue that, for Barth, the essence of theological knowledge is rooted in the practical acknowledgment or testimony of the obedient and faithful individual who is seized by the event and commandment of divine revelation, and that this knowledge, as described in the *Epistle to the Romans* (2nd edition) and the *Church Dogmatics*, is structurally the same kind of knowledge as that advanced by Rosenzweig in *The Star of Redemption*. The immediate point of this chapter is to articulate the model as it first appears in *Romans* II.

Prior to launching into a direct analysis of *Romans* II, I will introduce the architecture of the comparison between Rosenzweig's theology and Barth's theology as found in *Romans* II. For Rosenzweig and Barth, revelation is the event where God enacts his love to establish (or re-establish, in the case of Barth) a loving relationship with humankind. Additionally, for both Rosenzweig and Barth, revelation is the event when God establishes or re-establishes the righteousness or morality of human beings who have formerly been captured in sin. Both Barth and Rosenzweig recognize that God's love is wholly other from the individual to whom it is directed. Consequently both theologians maintain that, as exterior to all that human beings know about their world, God's love assumes the form of a commandment. In revelation the wholly other God demonstrates his wholly other ways to humankind so that humankind will hear and testify to God's love, God's goodness and God's transcendence.

Additionally, for Rosenzweig and Barth, revelation provides the basis for the moral life. Revelation commands human beings to love, praise and recognize God as he whose will is to be done. Revelation establishes love of God as the essence of the good. More specifically, revelation awakens humanity to an ethic of acknowledgment or testimony.

Finally, loving witness to God provides the basis for theological knowledge in Barth and Rosenzweig. Both thinkers hold that witness provides practical knowledge of the transcendent God. Re-visiting Cohen's model of ethical acknowledgment, both Barth and Rosenzweig establish a model of acknowledgment but resituate this model in an election context. In this way Barth and Rosenzweig offer a corrective to Cohen's model of correlation such that our morality is nothing other than the response to the commanding God, a demonstration of his moral primacy, a testimony to God's goodness and love and not a self-legislated act. Only a morality that depends upon or acts *after* the independently enacted goodness of the transcendent God can provide the basis for a theology of testimony. Cohen's commitment to an autonomous human ethics prevents him from asserting this kind of divine command ethic and prevents him from successfully articulating a theology of acknowledgment.

Moral action that depends upon God's primary moral activity or righteousness maintains a cognitive reference to the transcendent God. While for Kant knowledge of God is implicated in the autonomous work of the moral self whose rationality of action requires such an implication, for Barth and Rosenzweig knowledge of God is implicated in the acting after or testifying to God's own primary act of love or righteousness. Demonstrating or testifying to God's love presupposes an acknowledgment of God's own unique act. Knowledge of the transcendent and wholly other God is implicit not only because the individual's testimony derives from the divine commandment, but also because practical testimony means acting after God's own uniquely transcendent love. The transcendent God whose righteous and loving act we seek to glorify or proclaim is implicit in the testimony of action.

Rosenzweig's and Barth's theologies of testimony offer a secure basis for theological knowledge without falling prey to the pitfalls of a pre-critical natural theology or nineteenth-century subjectivism. Their theologies avoid these pitfalls because they maintain the asymmetrical nature between God and humankind and advance a knowledge afforded only through practical testimony. The theology of practical testimony affords knowledge of a real and transcendent God because the practical response depends upon a real encounter with a wholly other God who commands unprecedented acts of moral goodness. Moreover, the theology of testimony does not succumb to the logocentricism of natural theology because, even when we achieve knowledge of the transcendent and loving God, our knowledge never affords us information about God's being. The theology of testimony affords a practical knowledge only for those who obey a commanding and loving God.

Finally, both Rosenzweig and Barth radically transform what it means to speak about the Word of God. For Rosenzweig, religious language or the Word of God is the guardian of the human experience of divine command and testimony. For Barth, as we will see below, the Word of God is also a guardian of the event of divine election and human testimony, albeit a guardian with greater theological significance than in Rosenzweig's account. Central, however, to both theologians' work is the claim that religious language and/or religious institutions cannot make claims to a theological knowledge that extends beyond the knowledge achieved through election. The theology of testimony therefore offers both theologians a basis for a meaningful and non-dogmatic religious life.

## B. *Epistle to the Romans* and the Theology of Witness

Considered a tour de force in the 1920s and 1930s, Karl Barth's *Romans* II is a powerful testament to his revolutionary theological genius. Often appreciated for its provocative presentation of dialectical theology, Barth's *Romans* II is nonetheless often dismissed as overly sermonesque and anecdotal in character. Additionally, *Romans* II has often been accused of promoting a kind of theological agnosticism, doing more to demolish advances in theology than produce them.[2] In what follows I will argue against this charge of theological agnosticism in *Romans* II by demonstrating its contribution to what I have been calling a theology of witness or testimony. Furthermore, I will argue that this theology of witness continues throughout Barth's later work up to and including his *Church Dogmatics*. While this analysis of the relation between *Romans* II and the *Church Dogmatics* will take up a number of themes presented in the works of such well-known Barth scholars as Bruce McCormack and Michael Beintker, it will chart new territory by focusing on this concept of witness as it permeates Barth's later works.[3] This analysis will thereby establish the basis of a productive comparison between Barth's work and that of Franz Rosenzweig as discussed above.

## C. Revelation as the Act of God's Righteousness

### a. *The World Prior To Revelation: The Absence of God in Our World*

For Cohen, Rosenzweig and Barth, human beings achieve knowledge of God primarily through God's revelation. God's revelation does not offer information about God's being but only about his ways or righteousness or love. Consequently, all three thinkers maintain that without revelation the world is morally deficient. It is impossible to consider what, according to Cohen, the world prior to revelation would look like since Cohen identifies revelation with the creation of human reason. However, Rosenzweig's New Thinker philosopher-theologian did analyze the world prior to revelation and gleaned important information regarding revelation from this analysis.

The New Thinker discovered that the world prior to revelation was the incomplete world defined by human self-interest and its quest for eternity. Consequently, for Rosenzweig, revelation is the event wherein God reveals his will so that, in fulfilling God's commandment to follow his will, human beings help God in the task of completing the world.

122

For Barth, the world without revelation is the sinful world that human beings have willfully chosen for themselves and through which they deservedly incur the wrath of God. 'Originally one with the creator',[4] pre-Fall humanity knew God within the context of the righteous relationship between the creator and the creature. 'The natural order then, as such, was holy, because holiness is its characteristic mark.'[5] Conversely, in the event of the Fall, human beings willfully chose to service themselves and severed their relationship to God. This breach in the relationship produced a breach in the knowledge of God that naturally followed from the relationship of service. With sin, human beings lost the capacity to recognize the righteous God. Not a mere Kantian limitation of theoretical reason, the condition of not-knowing God prior to revelation is the condition of moral impairment or sin. 'The world was originally one with the Creator, and men were one with God . . . [but out of sin] we make of the eternal and ultimate presupposition of the Creator a "thing in itself" above and in the midst of other things.'[6] Consequently, the possibility of re-visiting knowledge of God depends upon the possibility of re-entering a relationship of service to God which in turn requires a change in our sinful status.

For Barth, therefore, our knowledge of God and our moral condition are inextricable. Sin ensures that our knowledge, actions and efforts at worship are irretrievably tainted and incapable of directing themselves to and/or acquiring any recognition of the God of righteousness. Incommensurate with our world, the true God is the 'unknown God' beyond our world, knowledge and morality.

Arrogantly, in our efforts to secure ourselves against the forces of a meaningless world, we often, Barth says, assert knowledge of God as Being, First Cause or Reason. But the metaphysical God is the no-God, merely the reflection of our sin and our quest to assert ourselves as the end and purpose of our world. 'We are not concerned with God, but with our own requirements, to which God must adjust Himself . . . And so, when we set God upon the throne of the world, we mean by God ourselves . . .'[7] 'If God is to us no longer the Unknown, what has become of the glory we owe Him?'[8]

As sinful, there is nothing human beings can do to acquire knowledge of the unknown God. Living in sin and unable to know or service God in his righteousness, human beings inevitably incur the wrath of the God. 'The wrath of God is the judgment under which we stand in so far as we do not love the Judge; it is the "no" which meets us when we do not affirm it . . . Indeed, it is the fact most characteristic of our life.'[9]

## b. *Impresses of Revelation*

This having been said, human beings may, prior to the revelation in Christ, arrive at some recognition of their sin. While the cross and resurrection of Jesus as the Christ will uniquely reveal both God's wrath and righteousness, history has all along, Barth says, provided opportunities for human beings to recognize the infinite qualitative difference between themselves and God – their sin and God's judgment. History, says Barth, provides signposts that, like the cross, point to the absence of God in our world. By themselves such signposts do not point to the righteousness of God that in the revelation of Christ will complement and complete this expression of wrath. Nonetheless, if properly appreciated they can inspire one to begin a path of repentance, to recognize the *Krisis* of their sin and judgment. 'The utter godlessness of the course of history does not alter the fact that it is marked everywhere by peculiar impressions of revelation, by opportunities and open doors, which, when seen from God's side, can summon men to recollection and knowledge.'[10]

Of course, knowledge of God requires a return to righteousness that human beings cannot bring about for themselves. 'There is no human righteousness that can escape the wrath of God.'[11] We know God only by an act of God's grace through which God lovingly displays his righteousness and commands us to obedience, despite and because of the fact that, as sinners, we deserve only his wrath and judgment. Revelation is that act of grace. 'Whence then, comes the righteousness of men? And the answer is, it comes by the revelation of God ... by divine proximity and election through which men now here, now there, are enabled to have faith in God and to obey Him in awe and in humility (ii.14). But what proceeds from God is in our eyes a miracle ...'[12]

## c. *Revelation as Election*

For Barth, as for Rosenzweig, revelation is the event that restores the human relationship to God by revealing divine righteousness in the form of a divine command. Revelation is the event of divine election.

To understand Barth's concept of revelation it is necessary to analyze its form and its content. The form of the revelation or what Barth calls the medium of the revelation can be summed up in the words 'Jesus Christ'. The content of the revelation is the grace of God's righteous action and command to human beings. At issue in the immediate discussion is the content of the revelation and not the form. While the immediate conversation will make reference to the cross and the resurrection, we will only later discuss these forms as the means of God's revelation.

While, as we have seen, Barth avers that history has provided human beings with other occasions for recognizing the fundamental wrath of God and the utter questionability of all human history, he also maintains that only the event of Jesus' passion and resurrection portrays the full meaning of this wrath in the context of the justification of sin by the righteous God. While former impresses of revelation have pointed to the absence of God in our sinful world, only Jesus Christ, through the passion and the resurrection, provides the parable that points to a complete revelation of God's reality – his 'Yes' and not strictly his 'No'. 'Jesus Christ our Lord . . . In this name two worlds meet and go apart, two planes intersect, the one known and the other unknown.'[13] Unique as an event that transpires *in* time but is not, according to Barth, *of* time, the revelation is the historical event that puts an end to history. Jesus Christ is the 'Messiah, is the End of History . . .'[14]

### d. *The Cross and the Divine Judgment*

Like the former impresses of revelation, Jesus' death awakens humanity to the *Krisis* of its world. To know God is to be righteous and to stand in the proper relationship of service to God. However, the ability to recognize God's wholly other righteousness requires a recognition of God's absence in the current world. Like Rosenzweig's dialogue which awakened the elected self to its former sin, Jesus' death on the cross confronts human beings with their own moral deficiency. 'The revelation which is in Jesus . . . becomes a scandal . . . In Jesus the communication of God becomes a rebuff, with the exposure of a vast chasm, with the clear revelation of a great stumbling block.'[15]

Jesus' death on the cross depicts God's righteous judgment of universal human sin. Barth's notion of sin extends beyond that experienced by the self in Rosenzweig's *Star*. Scrupulously critiqued and aware of its sin, Rosenzweig's self remains confident that it may restructure its world to meet the purpose of the Other who loves. For Barth sin asserts a more powerful and disintegrating effect. What is for Rosenzweig an incomplete world awaiting its fulfillment through the soul's animation and obedience to the purpose of God is for Barth a world irretrievably condemned by sin to judgment. Sin has corrupted the self and its world and Jesus' death on the cross issues an awareness and critique of the self *and* its world. 'What is there, then, in Christ Jesus? There is that which horrifies: the dissolution of

125

history in history, the destruction of the structure of events within their known structure . . . [T]he Son of man proclaims the death of the son of man.'[16]

### e. *Resurrection and the Divine Command*

Announcing judgment, the *Krisis* through Jesus' death on the cross echoes and continues the announcements made by prior revelations. However, as God's effort to re-establish the proper relationship between himself and humanity, revelation must initiate humanity's renewed righteousness. Revelation provides an opportunity for this transformation through the resurrection of Christ and the power of obedience it expresses.

By restoring Jesus' life, the resurrection of Jesus on the cross demonstrates God's loving righteousness and helps humanity recall this righteousness. However, people mired in sin cannot act obediently before the righteous God. Only God can renew their ability to respond obediently to the righteous God. According to Barth's account, God restores the human ability to obedience by issuing a command that the sinner cannot disobey, a command uniquely expressed through the convergence between God's judgment and God's forgiveness.

In the event of the cross, God reveals his wrath to humanity. Faced with the death of Jesus on the cross, humanity confronts the punishment of death and the dissolution of its sinful world. However, judgment not only awakens persons to the reality of sin, it also awakens them to the reality of divine power. God's judgment dissolves all that we know of the world and ourselves and demonstrates God's authority over human existence. The judgment is a testimony to divine sovereignty and human powerlessness.

Subsequent to the *Krisis* of the cross, the resurrection permits the defeated individual to re-encounter God, now as forgiving and loving. The convergence of these two events alerts persons to their own powerlessness and to God's sovereignty as the loving source of existence. Faced with the awareness of their own sin and therefore dismissive of the authority of their own claims and faced with the reality of divine grace and forgiveness, persons are compelled to acknowledge the reality of God. As Bruce McCormack says, '[T]he Self-revelation of God is not only revelation; it is also command.'[17] In his loving grace God commands humanity to acknowledge his exclusive and loving sovereignty by making it impossible for us to recognize sovereignty in anything else, particularly in ourselves. Under the grace of the cross our ability to sin has been destroyed. There remains nothing for us save acknowledgment and obedience to the righteous God through whom alone we may have life.

> Grace is the power of obedience . . . It is the indicative which has the significance of the absolute, the categorical imperative. And it is the imperative, the call, the command, the demand which one cannot not obey . . . [18]

## D. The Subjective Reality of Revelation

### a. *From Commandment to Fulfillment: Faith as Obedience*

Having detailed Barth's theology of revelation through divine command we must now discuss the subjective reality of revelation, the human response to election. This analysis of the subjective reality of revelation will illuminate how and what kind of theological knowledge revelation affords.

In the above chapters we analyzed Rosenzweig's understanding of the human response to God's commandment and examined its import for a theology of election through witness. Structurally, Barth's analysis of the individual's response to the revelation of God's love and command is very similar to the Rosenzweigian model. Like Rosenzweig, Barth sees revelation as the event of God's judgment, love and commandment to the sinful human being who must testify to the God who loves through this command.

Rosenzweig and Barth part company on the issue of where and when covenantal life with God is possible. While Rosenzweig holds that human beings cannot acquire a *direct* awareness of God's reality through their experience within the created order, Rosenzweig also holds that the created order is the sign or prophecy of God and therefore of covenantal life. The world we live in is the world where covenant is possible. It is the world that waits for God's further revelation. Consequently, while the created world is not synonymous with the redeemed world, it is the place where the redeemed world is possible. The kingdom of God is not the negation but the completion of the world as we know it. More specifically, even though the beloved who receives divine love meets with an unprecedented form of love, she does have recourse to what I earlier called the language of love or desire as the means of testifying to her experience of this love. Clearly she cannot testify to God's love in a way that identically repeats the character of this love. Nonetheless, as created by God she may testify to her reception of this love in the form of desire. In this manner the beloved can testify to God's love in her world – she may relate to God covenantally through obedient testimony. Rosenzweig espouses a qualified, realized eschatology. On the one hand, revelation invites believers into a covenantal life here and now. Believers can love God in return. On the other hand, a 'not yet' is inscribed over covenantal life here and now. So long as human beings continue to regard the world as their own and as the battleground between the forces of nature and the forces of self-preservation or culture, human beings will remain subject to the forces of time and will not dwell in covenantal eternity with God. This tension manifests itself in the character of human testimony to God as repentance and desire. Rosenzweig's hermeneutics of religious texts and religious life reflects this tempered realized eschatology. Sacred texts and religious rituals are, for Rosenzweig, authentic and immediate expressions of covenantal life with God as lived here and now in this not-yet of redemption.

Like Rosenzweig, Barth espouses a qualified, realized eschatology as well, though for different reasons. In *Romans* II, Barth argues that Jesus' passion and resurrection has invited all humankind into covenantal life with God. God's revelation restores humankind to their relationship with God by revealing God's righteousness through a divine command they cannot not obey. In this sense, God's revelation signals God's eternal redemption of humankind and the kingdom of God is now.

> I know that my redeemer liveth (Job xix.25). In such knowledge men love God, not before or after, but in the 'Moment' which is no moment in a series and which is the meaning of every moment . . . The eternal meaning occurs . . . when instead of seeing in a glass darkly, we see face to face . . . and we know even as we are known . . . . Love proclaims that the new man stands before God . . . [19]

Nonetheless, like Rosenzweig's, Barth's realized eschatology is qualified by his recognition of the current divide between the human and divine orders. However, Barth and Rosenzweig offer different accounts of the condition and meaning of our current world. If, for Rosenzweig, we currently dwell in the created, not yet fulfilled world, for Barth we currently dwell in the sinful world whose existence negates the possibility and reality of God's redemption. Consequently, the redemption afforded in revelation does not pertain to or have any positive effect on our current world. Covenantal life negates all that we know here and now. Neither human beings nor their world provide a possible site for God's order. To participate in God's order, human beings must take on the new man and dwell with God in the new world. Despite her apprehension of God's redemption, the believer dwells in the world of the unbelievers who have not recognized God's eternal redemption. If redemption is now, but not here, how can a believer live covenantally in the current world?

According to Barth, the believer responds through faith. While in Rosenzweig's account divine election invites individuals to righteousness, in Barth's account *God* actively restores the individual to righteousness. 'Justification is the act of God by which men are not left as they are but wholly transformed.'[20] Whereas Rosenzweig's self actively embraces its own new path, Barth's individual stands before the grace of God who turns her to this new path. Moreover, God's gracious election restores her ability to love God as her redeemer only in God's new world. Currently, the believer's actions are restricted by the conditions of the sinful order and she cannot employ any means of her own to positively testify to God's love. Barth's indebtedness to the notion of sin means that she cannot, like Rosenzweig's believer, express her desire for divine love, for this assumes that she positively experiences God's love in her current condition. Barth's believer may only testify to her own inability to do this work – she may only testify to her own negation and, in this negation, indirectly reference God. This is what Barth refers to as faith. 'Only faith survives: faith which is not a work, not even a negative work; not an achievement, not even the achievement of humility . . . Faith is the ground, the new order . . . [W]here boasting ends the true righteousness of God begins.'[21]

As the expression of the individual's recognition that *I* am not righteous before you, God, faith is synonymous with repentance. An action that is a no-action but an action that defers to God's act of righteousness, repentance is the only way for the individual to respond to the commanding God.[22] '[T]hrough Jesus . . . we know the mercy of God to be the end of all things and the new beginning, and we know what this means for us – it means that we must be led unto repentance.'[23]

Barth calls repentance the 'primary form of ethical activity'.[24] Both Rosenzweig and Barth hold that revelation provides the basis for human morality. For Rosenzweig, revelation spawns an ethic of the love of God enacted through the testimony or publication of the miracle of God's love. For Barth, revelation restores human morality by allowing believers to recognize the God who loves us and has granted us existence.

> What is it possible for us to do in order that the sacrifice by which men are overcome and God is glorified, may shine forth in our actions? . . . We can exhort them – and above all we can exhort ourselves – to repentance. Repentance is the

'primary' ethical action upon which all 'secondary' ethical conduct depends . . . [and] it is the act of re-thinking . . . which, because it dissolves both itself and every act is identical with the veritable worship of God.[25]

Like Rosenzweig, Barth maintains that election gives rise to an ethic of love or praise of God – an ethic of witness. Bruce McCormack echoes this point when he says,

> In *Romans* II . . . Barth provides a critical correction to idealistic ethics in that he makes the unintuitable Christ the standard by which human ethical activity is to be judged . . . , rather than Kant's universal law of reason. What emerges is an ethic of witness – witness to the divine command contained in God's Self-Revelation in Jesus Christ.[26]

Unlike Cohen's rational self, who seeks to act after the holiness of the revealing God but cannot locate the reality of God's loving act and ultimately enacts a self-generated moral good, Rosenzweig and Barth recognize the electing God whose real act of love provides the impetus and basis for a morality of testimony. McCormack says, for Barth, 'Ethics must concern itself first and foremost with what God has done in Christ . . . The criterion of the truth of this ethic is solely its witness to the reconciling work of God in Jesus Christ.'[27]

### b. *Theological Implications of the Ethic of Witness*

Like Rosenzweig, Barth maintains that practical testimony affords theological knowledge. Negating the value of her own actions, Barth's repentant individual directly testifies that her actions are sinful and indirectly testifies that God's acts alone are righteous. 'Repentance is the renewing of your mind, that ye may *prove* [emphasis mine] what is the will of God, even what is good and acceptable and perfect.'[28] As the act whereby we sacrifice our view of the world in favor of God's reality, repentance is a 'demonstration demanded by God for His glory'.[29] The primary ethical action, repentance, says Barth, engenders what he refers to as secondary ethical actions or 'demonstrations' – concrete actions that point to the primary reality of God's act of loving righteousness. Below we will discuss the nature and possibility of these concrete actions or demonstrations. Here it is sufficient to point out that such demonstrations, be they of peace or love or prayer, testify to (albeit indirectly) and therefore imply the reality of the loving God. Just as Barth tells us the May Day demonstration is not the

Labor Movement itself but a demonstration which implies the reality of the Labor Movement, ethical demonstrations implicitly acknowledge the act of God's righteousness to which they testify. While for Kant moral action implicates a God who binds morality and happiness together, the practical act of testimony is more suggestive, for it implicates a God who is uniquely righteous and commands us to testify to our recognition of his free act of love. Revelation restores us to the practical knowledge of God's will that we lost with the Fall. 'Grace is the power of obedience; it is theory and practice . . . Grace is the knowledge of the will of God.'[30]

## E. *Nach-Denken* and the Ethic of Witness

I want to conclude this examination of the place of testimony in Barth's *Romans* II by detailing Barth's consistent commitment to this theology in his *Romans* II and post-*Romans* II work. Not only has Barth's *Romans* II been indicted on charges of theological skepticism, charges here overturned by the model of ethical witness, but there has also been a trend among Barth scholars to posit a difference between the so-called dialectical theology of *Romans* II and Barth's later work. Conversely I maintain that *Romans* II establishes a model of theology as testimony that Barth never abandons in his subsequent work. Consequently I assert that there is no radical break in the theological character of Barth's work after *Romans* II.

Throughout the history of Barth studies many scholars have advanced theories concerning the evolution of Barth's intellectual corpus. The most well-known theory has been presented by Hans Urs von Balthasar in his book, *Karl Barth: Darstellung und Deutung seiner Theologie.* Here von Balthasar argues that Barth's theological career can be marked by two decisive turning points, the first identified in *Romans* II and the second found in his famous rereading of Anselm's ontological proof, *Fides Quaerens Intellectum.*[31] In his now acclaimed book, *Karl Barth's Critically Realistic Dialectical Theology*, Bruce McCormack challenges this argument, claiming instead that, although there are differences between the theological position of *Romans* II and that of the *Church Dogmatics*, one can recognize a common dialectical theology throughout these works. More specifically, McCormack argues one can identify a particular type of dialectical theology rooted in what he calls 'Realdialektik'.[32]

According to McCormack, while Barth presents a more muscular and positively developed view of theology in the *Church Dogmatics* than in *Romans* II, both put forth a common dialectic of veiling and unveiling.

What McCormack means is that, for Barth, theology is always tensed by the dialectical relation between human knowledge and divine knowledge. The dialectical character of theological knowledge arises from the reality of human sin. Any knowledge human beings profess to have *about* God is not knowledge *of* God. Nonetheless, according to both *Romans* II and the *Church Dogmatics*, human beings *do* acquire some theological knowledge. This theological knowledge is an impossible possibility, uniquely provided by God. The knowledge we have of God is never the knowledge *we have* of God but only the knowledge *God* has provided for us. According to McCormack, and I agree with him, all theological knowledge from *Romans* II to the *Church Dogmatics* is dialectical, for all theological knowledge depends on a divine act of grace whereby God knows himself and offers the faithful the opportunity to witness to or think-after this act. '[For Barth,] Knowledge of God consists for human beings in a following-after and a thinking-after the movement of God in His Self-revelation. Hence, it can only be dialectical.'[33] Consequently, McCormack argues that while Barth's work in *Fides Quarens Intellectum* appears to present a more objective view of God, even this so-called objective knowledge remains qualified by the implicit *Realdialektik* present throughout Barth's later works. Von Balthasar is wrong to see the *Fides Quarens Intellectum* as a significant turning point in Barth's work.[34]

My reading of the structure and theological implications of the practical act of witness is consistent with what McCormack calls the dialectical theology of veiling and unveiling. The difference between McCormack's position and mine is one of emphasis. In tracing the dialectical strain in Barth's later work, McCormack highlights the reality of God's revelatory act of unveiling or grace. My reading of a theology of witness derives from the same fundamental event. Nonetheless, Barth's dialectical theology of veiling and unveiling stands within the context of a theology of witness that includes the believer's practical obedience to the commandment issued forth in the event of veiling and unveiling. I agree that the later Barth roots theology in the primary and fundamental act of God's veiling or unveiling. However, this act is inextricable from the context of divine election and commandment whereby God not only acts to unveil his reality, but acts more specifically to display his righteousness and actively restore our own. What is for McCormack a particular epistemological dynamic is for me an event of election and commandment which elicits the practical and moral witness of the faithful adherent who, in her acting-after or testimony to this event, accesses the practical theological knowledge hereby made available by God's act of grace.

Consequently, while I believe that McCormack correctly recognizes Barth's concept of *Nach-denken* as described in his *Fides Quaerens Intellectum* as a continuation and not a departure from the dialectical theology of *Romans* II, it is important to further identify the similarity between the concept of testimony in *Romans* II and that of *Nach-denken* in the work on Anselm and its further use in the *Church Dogmatics*.

According to Barth's *Die christliche Dogmatik im Entwurf*, the concept of *Nach-denken* suggests that all human 'intelligere' or understanding about God is absolutely dependent on 'a prior act of God'.[35] Theological knowledge is never generated by human consciousness, but is always the 'thinking after' this prior act. In this sense, '[k]nowledge here means fundamentally *acknowledgment* [emphasis mine]. Thinking means thinking-after.'[36]

Of course Barth refers to the concept of *Nach-denken* in his work on Anselm as well. In both cases Barth's use of the concept of *Nach-denken* substantiates McCormack's insight that, even in his reading of Anselm, Barth maintains a dialectical theology rooted in the *Realdialektik* of the relation between the sinful human and the righteous God. The concept of *Nach-denken* is a re-articulation of the dialectical relation between God and human beings whose knowledge of God is always inadequate to the divine reality. The *Realdialektik* necessarily leaves the possibility of all theological knowledge in the hands of divine grace. However, there is also a similarity between the concept of *Nach-denken* or 'acknowledgment' here described and the concepts of 'demonstration' or 'witness' in *Romans* II. It is none other than the prior *act* of God's revelation and grace that an individual thinks-after. Thinking-after is faith and, specifically, the faith that expresses itself in practical obedience or witness to this grace.[37]

While explicit mention of the divine election and commandment context of *Nach-denken* is missing from Barth's *Fides Quarens Intellectum*,[38] this is unquestionably the context of this concept in the *Church Dogmatics* as I will show below.[39] The concept of *Nach-denken*, as it appears in this context in the *Church Dogmatics*, is the continuation of the concept of practical witness or testimony through repentance described above in *Romans* II.

This dominant theological strain in Barth's post-*Romans* II work echoes the theme of testimony in Rosenzweig's *The Star of Redemption*. Consequently, both Rosenzweig and Barth advance non-logocentric, critical and non-subjectivistic models for theological work rooted in practical acknowledgment of the divine act of love and righteousness. In *Romans* II and, as we will see, in the *Church Dogmatics*, this theological knowledge is critical and non-logocentric because it is a strictly practical acknowledgment of a God outside of human consciousness. Individuals may testify to God but God's reality is never fully present to their thinking. Furthermore, the practical acknowledgment afforded Barth's faithful is always dialectically related to the God through whose grace alone it is possible.[40] As we will discuss below, readers have often interpreted the *Church Dogmatics* as an example of Barth's renewed theological positivism. Alternatively I will argue that references to God's objectivity in the *Church Dogmatics* have less to do with a renewed positivism and more to do with Barth's re-examination of the nature and extent of God's own divine act of grace or election, more specifically Barth's extended account of Christology.

## Notes

1 For a discussion of Rosenzweig's and Barth's participation in the Patmos group see David N. Myers, *Resisting History: Historicism and Its Discontents in German-Jewish Thought* (Princeton: Princeton University Press, 2003), pp. 95–98 and Graham Ward, *Barth, Derrida and the Language of Theology* (Cambridge: Cambridge University Press, 1995), pp. 63–78.

2 Most well known for his charge of skepticism regarding *Romans* II is Paul Althaus who accused Barth of forwarding a theology of a content-less God whose path had been already established by the likes of Nietzsche and Overbeck. See Paul Althaus, 'Theologie und Geschichte: Zur Auseinanderetzung mit der dialektischen Theologie', *Zeitschrift für systematische Theologia*, I (1923/4), 746. Graham Ward makes a similar claim in his *Barth, Derrida and the Language of Theology* where he says, 'Ultimately, it is the sheer agnosticism of Barth's position as it is developed in the writing of the second edition of *Romans* and its exposition in dialectical theology which distinguishes Barth from the philosophers of dialogue.' Ward, *Barth, Derrida*, p. 92.

3 While Paul D. Matheny's *Dogmatics and Ethics: The Theological Realism and Ethics of Karl Barth's Church Dogmatics* (Frankfurt am Main: New York: P. Lang, 1990) makes a similar argument concerning the relation between ethics and dogmatics in the *Church Dogmatics*, his discussion does not include an analysis of *Romans* II.

4 Karl Barth, *Epistle to the Romans* (trans. Edwyn C. Hoskyns; Oxford: Oxford University Press, 2nd edn, 1968), p. 247.

5 Barth, *Romans* II, p. 247.

6 Barth, *Romans* II, p. 247.

7 Barth, *Romans* II, p. 44

8  Barth, *Romans* II, p. 48.

9  Barth, *Romans* II, p. 42.

10  Barth, *Romans* II, p. 80.

11  Barth, *Romans* II, p. 56.

12  Barth, Romans II, p. 63.

13  Barth, *Romans* II, p. 29.

14  Barth, *Romans* II, p. 29.

15  Barth, *Romans* II, p. 98.

16  Barth, *Romans II*, p. 103.

17  Bruce McCormack, *Karl Barth's Critically Realistic Dialectical Theology* (Oxford: Oxford University Press, 1997), p. 277.

18  Barth, *Romans* II, p. 207.

19  Barth, *Romans* II, pp. 319–20.

20  Barth, *Romans* II, p. 191.

21  Barth, *Romans* II, p. 110.

22  G.C. Berkouwer observes similarly and says, '[For Barth] the proclamation of the crisis . . . is the testimony concerning the exclusion of human righteousness, and in this exclusion it points to God's incomprehensible forgiveness as "the fundamental change underlying the relation between God and man".' Berkower, G.C., *The Triumph of Grace in the Theology of Karl Barth* (Grand Rapids: Eerdmans, 1956), p. 33.

23  Barth, *Romans* II, p. 106.

24  Barth, *Romans* II, p. 432.

25  Barth, *Romans* II, pp. 436–37.

26  McCormack, *Karl Barth's Critically Realistic Dialectical Theology*, p. 275.

27  McCormack, *Karl Barth's Critically Realistic Dialectical Theology*, p. 276.

28  Barth, *Romans* II, p. 436.

29  Barth, *Romans* II, p. 431.

30  Barth, *Romans* II, p. 207.

31  Although von Balthasar does recognize that 'the real concern of Barth's early years was the same as that of his mature work . . .' Hans Urs von Balthasar, *The Theology of Karl Barth* (trans. John Drury; New York: Holt, Rinehart and Winston, 1971), p. 46, and according to von Balthasar the real concern of Barth's work is the effort to articulate the truth of God's pure act of revelation, nonetheless von Balthasar asserts that Barth's thinking underwent a radical change from dialectical theological to a theology rooted in the *analogia fidei*. As we will see, von Balthasar fails to recognize that even after *Romans* II theology remains dialectical for Barth simply because the human–divine relationship is itself always dialectical. Von Balthasar's insistence on this change in Barth's thought is motivated by his effort to show the correlation between Barth's theology and Catholic natural theology.

32  For McCormack's distinctions concerning the meaning of dialectic in Barth's *Romans* II and elsewhere see his *Karl Barth's Critically Realistic Dialectical Theology*.

33  McCormack, *Karl Barth's Critically Realistic Dialectical Theology*, p. 270.

34  Graham Ward also makes this point in *Barth, Derrida and the Language of Theology* when he says, 'Anselm did not teach Barth anything about theological method...he supplemented Barth's epistemological dialectic (worked out thoroughly in the second edition of *Romans*) with an ontological dialectic. [Therefore]...there is no ontological participation or correspondence which is other than by faith.' Ward, *Barth, Derrida* pp. 101–02.

35  Barth, *Die christliche Dogmatik im Entwurf*, from McCormack, *Karl Barth's Critically Realistic Dialectical Theology*, p. 425.

36  Barth, *Die christliche Dogmatik im Entwurf*, from McCormack, *Karl Barth's Critically Realistic Dialectical Theology*, p. 425.

37  That the concept of *Nach-denken* as Barth describes it in the text on Anselm reflects both McCormack's *Realdialektik* as well as my concept of testimony or acknowledgment in obedience is evident in passages like the following: 'The knowledge, the *Intellectus*, with which Anselm is concerned is the *Intellectus Fidei*. That means that it can consist of positive meditation on the object of faith. It cannot establish this object of faith as such but rather has to understand it in its very incomprehensibility...And it would not be what it is or achieve what it does achieve if it were not the knowledge of faith-obedience. In the end, the fact that it reaches its goal is grace, both with regard to the perception of the goal and the human effort to reach it.' Karl Barth, *Anselm: Fides Quaerens Intellectum* (trans. Ian W. Robertson; London: SCM Press, 1960), p. 40.

38  Of course it is clear in the *Fides Quaerens Intellectum* that knowledge happens in the context of or presupposes the revelation of Christ. While there are many such references to this in the text, noteworthy is Barth's discussion of the *aliquid quo nihil cogitari possi* as nothing other than one of the 'name[s]' of God...selected from among the various revealed Names of God ...' Barth, *Fides Quaerens Intellectum*, p. 75.

39  See Chapter 5.

40  This is not to say that the theology in *The Star* is not dialectical, but its dialectical nature has to do with the fact that practical acknowledgment is always apprehended as meaningful through language, and language can never express the content of the divine reality but only dialectically point to it by identifying its absence within its own expression.

136

# Chapter 5

# Beyond Revelation: The Life of the Children of God

The dialectical theology of repentance in *The Epistle to the Romans* transformed the theological landscape of Barth's time. More than a simple inversion of modernity's humanism, Barth's *Romans* II undermines the apologetic divide between faith and reason by exposing how God's revelation through Christ funds a reasoning practice or theological critique performed in the very act of worship as repentance. However, for all of its power, *Romans* II leaves believers wondering about the possibility of a positive praise of God. If *Romans* II relocates reasoning within the life of worship as repentance, can it provide a more positive account of that worshipping life? What is the relation between repentance and the sacramental life of believers within the church community?

Like Rosenzweig's *The Star of Redemption*, Barth's *Epistle to the Romans* II presents a theology of election and testimony. As we have established above, however, *Romans* II limits the form of testimony to repentance for believers in the current reality. For Rosenzweig, however, testimonial response to the commanding God includes the testimony of repentance and the testimony of desire. According to Rosenzweig, revelation awakens the beloved to an experience of God's absence as well as God's love, experienced by the recipient as desire. The beloved's desirous testimony is replete with theological meaning. By testifying to her desire the beloved pragmatically proclaims the reality of the creator, revealer and redeemer God. Moreover, these theological proclamations have social consequences as well, for by testifying to the God of the past, the believer becomes joined with others who share the same theological history, and by testifying to God's redemption, the believer participates in shaping the redeemed community here and now. The beloved's desirous testimony provides the basis for a positive covenantal life with an electing God in the present. Theologically speaking, testimony is only limited to repentance if the beloved cannot in any way positively experience or express the event of divine love. In view of the theological import of the testimony of desire we must examine whether Barth's theology affords a parallel form of testimony. At stake is the ability of Barth's theology to provide a basis for a positive covenantal life of believers. In what follows I will argue that although both *Romans* II and the *Church Dogmatics* maintain a theology of practical witness, they offer different portraits of the form of the divine act of revelation. Only the form of revelation advanced in the *Church Dogmatics* provides the necessary conditions for positive theological work in the time/place prior to the kingdom of God without sacrificing the dialectical character of the Word of God and the church life that emerges from it.

## A. Positive Testimony and the Word of God in *Romans* II

For Rosenzweig the Word of God expresses believers' experience of divine command and their testimony to God. The Word of God is always human language that dialectically tenses towards a divine reality that it cannot directly represent. Religious language is the guardian of the believers' life of election and testimony and does not overreach into dogmatism or meaninglessness.

Similarly for Barth the Word of God only assumes meaning when understood within the context of what God has done to re-establish the practical relationship between himself and humankind. Moreover, like Rosenzweig, Barth asserts the dialectical character of the Word of God.

There are, however, differences between the two theologians' interpretations of the Word of God. The central difference between them concerns their assessment of sin. According to Barth, sin prevents humankind from receiving and/or testifying to God's love. If humankind is to be restored by God into covenantal relationship, God must not only reveal his love to humankind (as is the case for Rosenzweig), but must also provide them with means to express this love. Barth does not share Rosenzweig's assessment of the creaturely status of humankind but holds that all persons are mired in sin and blind to an irruption of the divine in their world. While Rosenzweig's God does not speak and does not have to speak (given the language of love shared by God and humankind), Barth's God does not have recourse to this language of love and must use Word or language to mediate his revelation to persons who dwell within the unredeemed world. The Word of God assumes a theological significance for Barth that it does not have for Rosenzweig. For Barth, the Word of God is a necessary feature of God's electing love and commandment. Therefore, to discern if Barth's theology offers a parallel to Rosenzweig's life of covenantal testimony in this world is to discern how the Word of God mediates revelation to humankind and to what extent that mediation affords believers a way to positively testify to God here and now in the unredeemed world.

## a. Romans *II*

The central claim that runs through all of Barth's work is the notion that, through Christ, God has destroyed the barrier of human sin and invited humankind into the new world of eternal life with the loving God. Revelation is inextricably tied to redemption since it provides humankind with access to eternal life. As discussed above, this does not mean that revelation makes redemption available to humankind here in this world. Revelation destroys the current world and refers to an eschatological reality. The mediating power of God's Word does not transform this world into the kingdom of God. Even Barth's most ecclesiastically focused writings do not identify the church with the kingdom of God. However, Barth's later work does recognize the church as an 'order of praise' permitting believers to see their lives as preparatory for their citizenship in the kingdom of God. First, however, let us examine the portrait of the church in the earlier *Romans* II.

In *Romans* II the electing God makes himself free for humankind by veiling himself in the creaturely reality of Jesus on the cross and then unveiling himself to humankind by the negation of that creaturely reality. Committed to a time–eternity dialectic whereby all creaturely reality remains sinful, Barth cannot identify the God in *Romans* II with the God of the incarnation whose Word assumes the fleshly reality of Jesus. God relates to Jesus or the Word as a workman to his tool. In his creaturely reality Jesus is the medium in whose negation the transcendent reality of God is disclosed. '[B]y his death He declares the impossible possibility of our redemption ...'[1] Nonetheless, 'the Kingdom of God has its beginning on the other side of the Cross ... for it is in the perspective of death that the unseen things of God are made manifest'.[2]

Barth's analysis of the dialectical expression of God's transcendence parallels Rosenzweig's analysis of the role of dialogue in revelation. Nonetheless, while Rosenzweig holds that language can assume a positive function within the bounds of its own limitations, Barth holds that the

139

dialectical status of language (or creaturely signs) derives strictly from its finitude and sinfulness. Revelation assumes no positive, objective form but only awakens humanity to the *Krisis* in its world and the promise for an unseen world beyond presented exclusively through the negation of the current reality. The Word of God does not allow believers to positively testify to God's reality in this world because it does not permit them to apprehend God's reality in terms they can express through language or institutions.

If, however, church life is rooted in Jesus' positive testimony to God's redemption transmitted to the apostles who transmit it to the community of believers, Barth's account of the Word of God does not provide a basis for the church. Jesus' Word offers a strictly negative testimony to divine reality and affords no basis for the Catholic Church's claim to be the body of Christ in this world nor for the qualified claim that the church can positively proclaim the eschatological future of God's redemption.

## b. *The Church of Esau and the Church of Jacob*

Barth's discussion of the Church of Esau and the Church of Jacob plays out the ecclesiastical implications of his dialectical theology of the Word. There is, Barth tells us, 'an eternal opposition between the Gospel and the Church'.[3] The church that rises up in response to the revelation of Christ is necessarily sinful and inevitably drawn to acts of 'titanism' that seek to concretize, control and humanize a strictly divine possibility.

> The Church does not wish to be a stranger in the world. It does not wait for the City which is built upon a foundation. It cannot stay itself in the position of Christianity before the Resurrection, in the Passion of the rejected Christ. The Church is in great haste; it is hungry and thirsty for the concrete joys of the marriage feast.[4]

The Church of Esau translates the obedience of repentance into a 'form of human righteousness'[5] and exhorts its members to adhere to this form.

Can the revelation of Christ affect this church? If justification of the world means its dissolution, the answer would be a clear and resounding 'No'. Nonetheless, Barth argues that God's claim for our self-abandonment may be sustained within the world so that in this world we may at least 'make room for His work'[6] and engage in secondary ethical activities 'which seem so transparent that the light of the coming day is almost visible in them'.[7]

Despite his actualistic view of revelation, Barth maintains that revelatory moments leave 'signs' in the wake of their emergence that provide 'copies' or 'impresses' of the revelation within the historical and concrete world that we know. Is there, he asks, any 'relation between occurrences and experiences and the eternal content of all occurrence ... May it not be that the perception of God as the Judge involves the denial of all connection and relation between here and there?'[8] 'The utter godlessness of the course of history does not alter the fact that it is marked everywhere by peculiar impressions of revelation, by opportunities and open doors, which ... can summon men to recollection and to knowledge.'[9] Like bomb craters, impresses mark the site where the revelation was and is no longer. Even before the revelation of Christ, God's revelation of the law left an impress that alerted Jews to divine judgment. Only the revelation in Christ, however, reveals God's wrath and the invisible light of the kingdom of God.

Like other impresses of revelation, the Church of Esau can serve as a parable for the kingdom of God by announcing itself as the dialectical site of divine absence. Like other impresses of revelation, the Church of Esau loses its parabolic significance when it claims to possess revelation. Impresses of revelation cannot point beyond themselves to God's reality but can only 'make room for the miracle' of divine grace. Still, members of the Church of Esau may regard this church in its tribulation and *Krisis* as the site of the absence of God – a place where they may wait for the divine miracle that redeems the church into a site of revelation.

> The Church, every Church, is dethroned – but *perhaps* [emphasis mine] also justified. Yes, justified, if the dethronement and judgment inherent in this relationship be veritably the Word of God, if the veil of time be rent asunder in the eternal 'Moment' of revelation ...[10]

The Church of Esau waits to be and invites the presence of what Barth calls the Church of Jacob and can remind its members of the revelation of Christ and the command to obedience and repentance while they live here in this world.

## c. *The Negative Demonstrations*

In view of the above analysis Barth can now assert that even though ethical or loving action is possible with God alone, human beings can perform what he calls secondary ethical demonstrations. Secondary ethical demonstrations make room for the miracle and may be valuable as witness to God's glory if

God so decides. We may therefore live as the elected children of God in this world if: 1) we position ourselves and wait to accept God's miracle and 2) if God extends his miracle over our actions.

> How can the gravity and power of ethics, the gravity and power of the great disturbance, lie in . . . [concrete] acts and deeds? Nevertheless there are actions from which the light of sacrifice shines, actions where men are offered up, not in order that a new human achievement . . . may be brought to view, but that the peculiarity of God, His particular will and power and might, may be disclosed, and that he may be known as – Lord.[11]

Secondary concrete ethical demonstrations are possible because the Church of Esau may wait in its *Krisis* for the promise of the Church of Jacob and provide a reminder of the revelation which calls sinners to act as if the miracle will come, though it not be present at any given specific moment. Secondary ethical demonstrations can be negative or positive. Negative demonstrations are concrete and specific actions of protest against human forms of certainty and claims of objective rightness. For example, '[A]venge not yourselves, beloved, but give place unto the wrath of God.'[12] Do not, the church may exhort its members, execute judgment on another for all individuals stand judged by God alone. '[D]escend from every warlike high place.'[13] Do not act on and embrace human ideologies that claim their own path to rightness.

Barth's account of these negative possibilities culminates in his description of the 'Great Negative Possibility', the exhortation to refuse to participate in revolutionary enterprises. This act assumes parabolic potential because it undermines revolutionary attempts to assert strictly human forms of worldly critique. While members of the church ought not to lend arms to the powers that be, they should not participate in revolutionary efforts either.

> What man has the right to propound and represent the 'New'? The moment it becomes a human proposition, must it not be numbered among the things that are? . . . Far more than the conservative, the revolutionary is overcome of evil, because with his 'No' he stands so strangely near to God.[14]

What can the reformed revolutionary do? He can turn back 'to the original root of "not-doing" . . . There is here no word of approval of the existing order; but there is endless disapproval of every enemy of it.'[15]

### d. *The Theological Implications of the Negative Demonstrations*

What are the theological implications of this ethical life? As we can recall, *Romans* II advances only a negative ethic of witness or repentance. Active love of God is only possible in the eschatological future and only for the 'new man'. 'Who then are those that love God? Rightly understood, there are no Christians: there is only the eternal opportunity of becoming Christians – an opportunity at once both accessible and inaccessible to all men.'[16] Repentance provides practical knowledge of the transcendent and loving God but only by testifying to its own inadequacy. Revelation promises a hope for the positive reality of God's kingdom.

> By hope we are saved . . . Could we wish anything else than that this saving hope should always be declared at the Cross, should always set a boundary against everything in our world . . . ? Were we to know more of God than the groans of the creation and our own groaning; were we to know Jesus Christ otherwise than as crucified . . . then there would be no salvation.[17]

Negative demonstrations therefore do not necessarily assume any theological import. Only God decides if they achieve parabolic status and function as witness. Even if they are taken up by God as obedience, they cannot afford theological knowledge beyond that afforded by repentance. The theological import of negative demonstrations is limited by the revelation in Christ and does not extend beyond the practical recognition of our sin accompanied by the hope of God's kingdom. 'The theme of theology is men – men in their final distress and hope, men as they stand in the presence of God. Scientific theology is repentance.'[18]

### e. *The Analogue of Election*

In the section entitled 'The Great Positive Possibility', Barth makes the following claim: 'Love beholds in every concrete neighbor only the parable of him who is to be loved; but nevertheless it does really see, it really does see in every temporal "Thou" the eternal, contrasted "Thou".'[19] Here Barth suggests that when we love the neighbor we glorify or testify to God and gain the theological knowledge afforded by practical witness. Also called the 'analogue of election', love of the neighbor uniquely enables sinners to positively testify to the promise of God's kingdom by their demonstration of love to an other. 'When and where are we to discover the impossible possibility of fulfilling the law? An unparalleled occasion must correspond with the unparalleled significance of the action of love.'[20] '[T]he kingdom of God cometh. Love, and all that proceeds from love, demonstrates . . . this coming.'[21] In what follows I will question Barth's analysis of the significance of the love of the neighbor within the context of the Christology presented in *Romans* II. Ultimately, I will argue that although *Romans* II does not advance a theological agnosticism, it cannot extend beyond a theology of repentance.

### f. *Love of the Neighbor and the* The Star of Redemption

Prior to investigating the analogue of election in *Romans* II and its relationship to theological knowledge, it is important to recall the role of the analogue of election in *The Star of Redemption*. Rosenzweig's love of the neighbor does provide a positive testimony to God. We may fulfill the commandment to love God through loving the neighbor and achieve the knowledge implicit in the practical witness of acting-after God's commandment.

How, according to Rosenzweig, can I glorify God when I love the neighbor? An individual, we may recall, is prompted to love the neighbor when she testifies to God's love through her desire for more of God's love in her world and in her future. The believer expresses her desire for this love by pragmatically asserting the truth of this reality, namely, that God loves the world beyond her and, in particular, the neighbor immediately next to her. The believer, therefore, allows the neighbor to act as a sign of God's redeeming love. In this way the neighbor prompts the believer to act as she acts before the loving God, i.e. lovingly and selflessly. This love of the neighbor rests on two conditions. First, the beloved must be able to testify to God's love by testifying to her experience of this love. Second, she must be able to imagine the neighbor as another possible recipient of God's love. She must be able to recognize the neighbor as a sign or a representation of God's redemption. While the individual who testifies to God as redeemer through the love of the neighbor must act on faith because she currently dwells in the not-yet redeemed world, she *can* act on this faith. The individual can act on her faith in God as redeemer because she can increasingly see her world as the *sign* of God's reality – as a prophecy that anticipates its own completion. There is a positive, albeit dialectical, relationship for Rosenzweig between the world we live in and God's reality. Our world is the incomplete world that we help transform into God's reality by fulfilling God's commandment to love.[22] By loving the neighbor we inscribe God's reality into our world and simultaneously transform our world into God's reality. Theology is performed in the labor of redemption.

### g. Romans *II and the Analogue of Election*

Barth's portrait of the love of the neighbor in *Romans* II is strikingly similar to Rosenzweig's in *The Star* and both assert that love of the neighbor offers an analogue of election. For Barth, the love of the neighbor is an example of a positive possibility of ethical demonstration. In contrast to negative demonstrations that critique the existing world, positive demonstrations testify to the positive reality of God's kingdom.

> It is not permitted us to excuse ourselves for the absence of love by saying that since we live in the shadowy region of evil, we can only bear witness to the Coming Word by not doing. Even in the world of shadows love must come into active prominence . . . [B]y love we do the 'new' by which the old is overthrown.[23]

The love of the neighbor is the sum of all the positive possibilities which include hope, hospitality and rejoicing.

As we have established, however, love of the neighbor can function as the analogue of election only if two conditions obtain. First, the believer must be able to overcome her sin and act in a loving way. Second, the believer must be able to recognize or imagine the neighbor as a referent of the kingdom of God (in Barth's case, as a referent of the promise of the kingdom of God).

Barth's believer cannot accommodate the first condition of the love of the neighbor since Barth's believer is afflicted by sin here and now and cannot love. However, the question at hand is not whether Barth's believer may love the neighbor and thereby positively testify to God's redemption here and now. The question for Barth is whether the believer may love the neighbor as a sign of the *promise* of the kingdom of God. Despite Barth's claims to the contrary, the answer is No. According to *Romans* II, no creaturely reality, including Jesus on the cross, can positively represent God's reality. This must be true for the neighbor as well. Barth's own assertion that the church cannot assume this parabolic status contradicts his claims regarding the analogue of election.

Nonetheless, in his discussion of the Great Positive Possibility, Barth vacillates between claiming that the neighbor offers a sign of the promise of God's kingdom and claiming that the neighbor offers a sign of God, Godself, and therefore may serve as a conduit through which God's commandment to love is represented.

> [W]hile considering the relation between man and God, we have at crucial moments, encountered the extremely enigmatic conception of love [and] . . . we

have always encountered it lying beyond the possibility, the conceivable possibility of any concrete or analysable experience of the relation between man and God.[24]

Barth says we may 'really see in every temporal "Thou" the eternal, contrasted "Thou"'[25] and hereby feel claimed by God to positively testify to our love of him through our love of this other. Barth wants to claim that in encountering the other we may encounter God, his commandment and grace, and we may positively testify to his glory here and now and fulfill his commandment. 'He that loveth the other hath fulfilled the law, does the truth and is therefore proceeding along the more excellent way.'[26]

So presented, the analogue of election promises enormous theological significance. Positive testimony to God's glory here and now should afford positive knowledge of God and his kingdom. 'Love of men is in itself trivial and temporal: as the parable of the Wholly Other, it is, however, of supreme significance; for it is both the emissary of the Other and the occasion by which it is apprehended ...'[27] Through the analogue of election Barth attempts to extend the ethic of witness beyond the theology of repentance.

Still, Barth's phenomenology of revelation cannot justify the analogue of election. The neighbor cannot assume a positive parabolic meaning and cannot provide the occasion for the sinner to fulfill the commandment to love God here and now. Like *The Star of Redemption*, Barth's *Romans* II advances a view of theology as practical witness or testimony to the electing God. However, practical testimony in *Romans* II is limited to repentant action through negative ethical demonstrations. Barth's efforts to arrive at a theology rooted in the analogue of election will only succeed with the more developed Christology of the *Church Dogmatics*.

## B. The Word of God and Election in the *Church Dogmatics*

Barth's post-*Romans* II theological work retains the structure of the theology of testimony advanced in *Romans* II. What sets the *Church Dogmatics* apart from *Romans* II is the *Dogmatics'* more developed Christology and threefold form of the Word of God. We cannot underestimate the significance of this Christological shift so far as it grounds the life of the children of God here and now prior to the kingdom of God in a way that the theology of repentance in *Romans* II could not.[28] In what follows I will develop this argument by diagramming the theology of testimony and extended Christology of the *Church Dogmatics*.

## a. *The Word of God as the Criterion of Dogmatics*

Despite common readings that highlight the differences between Barth's *Romans* II and his *Church Dogmatics*, both texts present the same theology of testimony. The *Church Dogmatics* begins with the claim that dogmatics is grounded in the Word of God proclaimed in the church. Dogmatics does not require a basis in the philosophical prolegomena of modern theology or the doctrinal creeds of the Catholic Church, both of which inaccurately assume that God's reality may be located in human anthropology or church doctrine.

> [T]he place from which the way of dogmatic knowledge is to be seen and understood can be neither a prior anthropological possibility nor a subsequent ecclesiastical reality, but only the present moment of the speaking and hearing of Jesus Christ Himself.[29]

Proclamation alone allows the 'Free Lord of Existence' to reveal himself because it is God's own act of speaking graciously expressed through human words in the church. 'Proclamation is human speech in and by which God Himself speaks like a king through the mouth of his herald and by which God Himself speaks ...'[30]

## b. *The Word of God and a Theology of Presence?*

Barth's emphasis on the Word of God raises significant questions concerning the relation between the *Church Dogmatics* and *Romans* II as well as the relation between the *Dogmatics* and *The Star of Redemption*. A dogmatics predicated on the reality of God's speaking and our listening would seem to invite charges of a renewed logocentrism whereby knowledge of God transpires through the presence of the divine through speech, a presence clearly challenged by Barth's former emphasis on revelation as *Krisis*. Barth interpreters who over-emphasize the turn in Barth's theology from *Romans* II to the *Church Dogmatics* misread Barth's Word of God theology as a neo-orthodox return to a theology of presence.[31] If this reading is correct, then a chasm is created between the *Dogmatics* and Barth's earlier work in *Romans* II as well as between the *Dogmatics* and *The Star of Redemption*. A careful reading of Barth's theology of the Word as described in the *Dogmatics* will undermine this thesis.

Bruce McCormack's *Karl Barth's Critically Realistic Dialectical Theology* offers a formidable challenge to neo-orthodox readings of the later Barth by redefining and consequently relocating the dialectical character in Barth's

*Church Dogmatics.*[32] However, an argument against a neo-orthodox reading of Barth's *Dogmatics* must consider not only the *Realdialektik* character of our knowledge of God's Word as Barth presents it in the *Dogmatics*, but even more significantly the fact that, as Word, God's reality is not a *presence* which transferred through speech may be possessed by human thinking and language but an *act* or an *event* to which human beings may respond through a corresponding act of witness.[33] While the *Dogmatics* expands upon the capacity of human language to both bear and witness to God's revelation, this capacity derives from Barth's doctrine of the threefold form of the Word and not from a reversion back to a more characteristically natural theology position. A proper reading of the *Dogmatics* requires an analysis of God's Word as God's act of free and loving election.

### c. Nach-Denken *in the* Dogmatics

In the previous chapter I discussed Barth's understanding of the knowledge of God in his *Anselm: Fides Quaerens Intellectum*. There I argued that, although this text espouses a theological objectivism unlike that described in *Romans* II, it does not constitute a return to a theology of presence but must be understood within the framework of Barth's concept of *Nach-denken*. We know God only after God's prior act of revelation and gain a knowledge that cannot be extricated from a practical act of obedient testimony.

In the *Dogmatics*, Barth revisits the concept of *Nach-denken*. An analysis of its use in the *Dogmatics* will dislodge misconceptions concerning Barth's later dogmatic enterprise. As before, Barth's discussion on the objective reality of Jesus begins with an inquiry into the possibility of theological knowledge.[34] Once again Barth dismisses the idea that theological knowledge requires prolegomena since prolegomena do not focus on the reality of God itself. Instead one must begin with the reality of the revelation and the subsequent knowledge hereby afforded. At this point in the prior discussion Barth introduces the concept of the Word of God as the criterion of dogmatic knowledge. In this later discussion Barth turns instead to a discussion of the *Nach-denken*. While the concept of the Word of God is implicit in this discussion, Barth's focus here on the concept of *Nach-denken* dispels concerns that his dogmatics is rooted in a logocentric conception of the Word of God. Here, Barth's focus is on the Word as a divine *act* which prompts faith and obedience.

> His revelation is...an *act* [italics mine] of his freedom...[T]hat is why the language of the prophets and apostles about God's revelation is not a free,

selective and decisive treatment of well-founded convictions, but – which is something different – witness . . . Their thought and language follow the fact of God's revelation.[35]

The section entitled 'The Nature of the Word' makes this connection between the Word of God and God's act explicit. 'As mere Word it is act . . . God's speaking, and therefore the Word of God in all its forms, is in fact the act of God.'[36] But what kind of act is this and what is the meaning of this act? The Word of God is an act that makes a claim on those who hear it. Like the cross in *Romans* II, the Word of God is God's grace as God's commandment. 'Gospel and Law as the concrete content of God's Word imply always a seizure of man.'[37] While Barth does not provide a detailed analysis of the doctrine of election until volume II.II.,[38] his discussion here anticipates this doctrine. This discussion of the Word of God also anticipates the theology of testimony in election or what in volume II.II. Barth refers to as the alliance between theology and the ethical life. Barth argues that if God's Word is commanding act, then knowledge of God can only be the practical and obedient acknowledgment of this act. 'If a man knew nothing of this power that both sustains and stimulates, both protects and punishes . . . if he merely heard about it without it as a power, he would only give evidence that he knew nothing of the Word of God.'[39]

Barth acknowledges that since our knowledge of things in the world is rooted in experience it makes sense to think that knowledge of God arises from an experience of the Word. Still, he argues, an experience of God's Word is not an experience in the Kantian sense wherein we receive and categorize information. Original sin precludes the possibility of this kind of religious experience. God alone determines our experience of his prior acting and our knowledge of God is our after-knowing or witness to God's determination of our experience and knowledge of his Word. Moreover, by determining our experience, God acts as Lord and commander and our acknowledgment is our obedience to God or, as I will discuss later, our ethical life. In his discussion of the knowability of God[40] Barth explicitly connects acknowledgment or witness and practical life or obedience.

> As we turn back again to the Bible we remember that what is there described as the knowledge of God stands in contrast to all other human cognition in that it always in fact coincides with some action of God. God is known, not simply because He is God in Himself, but because He reveals Himself as such . . . Biblical knowledge of God is always based on encounters of man with

God; encounters in which God exercises in one way or another His lordship over man, and in which He is acknowledged as sovereign Lord and therefore known as God.[41]

In a later section entitled 'The Fulfillment of the Knowledge of God', Barth reiterates this point.

Knowledge of God is obedience to God...It is an act of human decision corresponding to the act of divine decision; corresponding to the act of the divine being as the living Lord; corresponding to the act of grace in which faith is grounded and continually grounded again in God. In this act God posits Himself as our object and ourselves as those who know Him. But the fact that He does so means that our knowing God can consist only in our following this act, in ourselves becoming a correspondence of this act, in ourselves and our whole existence and therefore our considering and conceiving becoming the human act corresponding to the divine act...and only – as this act of obedience, is the knowledge of God knowledge of faith and therefore real knowledge of God.[42]

Later I will examine how even the use of human language in the context of this obedience depends upon God's election. While I will argue that Barth's understanding of acknowledgment as love in the *Dogmatics* differs from his understanding of repentance in *Romans* II, this analysis will not negate my more fundamental claim that both texts maintain a theology rooted in the obedient acknowledgment and testimony to the loving and commanding God.

### d. *The Word of God or Jesus Christ and the Doctrine of Election*

Thus far I have argued against the claim that Barth's theology of the Word of God marks a return to a theology of presence. I have suggested that the dynamic play between God and humankind through the Word of God is the event of divine election. I will now provide a more detailed analysis of the doctrine of election in the *Church Dogmatics*. Just as in *Romans* II, the *Church Dogmatics* portrays revelation as the righteous God's free and loving election of humankind back into a relationship of righteousness and as the exclusive context for theological knowledge.

In volume II.II. of the *Dogmatics* Barth asserts that the Word of God is God's enacted decision to establish a covenant with humankind.

Jesus Christ is indeed God in His movement towards man...in His movement towards the people represented in the one man Jesus of Nazareth, in His covenant

150

with this people . . . Jesus Christ is the decision of God in favour of this attitude or relation.[43]

To say Jesus Christ is to speak of the divine election of grace for 'the doctrine of the divine election of grace is the sum of the Gospel. It is the content of the good news which is Jesus Christ.'[44] According to Barth, God's revelation is the enactment in history of God's primal and eternal decision in his tri-unity as Father, Son and Holy Spirit to open himself to fellowship with humankind and open humankind to fellowship with himself by God's own self-determination in Jesus Christ.

> In the beginning it was the choice of the Father Himself to establish this covenant with man by giving up His Son for him, that He Himself might become man in the fulfillment of his grace. In the beginning it was the choice of the Son to be obedient to grace, and therefore to offer up Himself and to become man in order that this covenant might be made a reality. In the beginning it was the resolve of the Holy Spirit that the unity of God, of Father and Son should not be disturbed or rent by this covenant with man, but that it should be made the more glorious, the deity of God, the divinity of his love and freedom, being confirmed and demonstrated by this offering of the Father and this self-offering of the Son . . . As the subject and object of this choice, Jesus Christ was at the beginning.[45]

As God's eternal self-determination to enter into covenant with humankind, Jesus Christ is both God's election of humankind, his enacted commitment to stand in relationship to humankind as well as God's active establishment of the elected human being who stands in fellowship with God.

As electing God, Jesus Christ is God's loving decision to take on the necessary rejection of the world in order to participate in fellowship with humankind. Election means 'God's hazarding of His Godhead . . . a certain compromising of Himself . . . that God should give Himself to [human beings] as His own possession'.[46]

As elected human being, Jesus Christ is God's loving decision to enable humanity to participate in and 'attest [to] the overflowing glory of the Creator'.[47] He is God's 'Yes' to humankind as a covenantal partner. God has chosen him to suffer and maintain obedience so that all humanity may be freed from sin and live as children of God through him.

> In the One in whom they are elected, that is to say, in the death which the Son of God has died for them, they themselves have died as sinners. And that means their radical sanctification, separation and purification for participation in a true creaturely independence, and more than that for the divine Sonship of the creature which is the grace for which from all eternity they are elected in the election of the man Jesus.[48]

Jesus Christ is God's eternal decision 'to divert to man the portion which rightly belongs to Himself', namely, the ability to participate in and testify to the glory and blessedness of God. 'God has elected and ordained man to bear the image of this glory.'[49]

### e. *Election and Ethical Life*

According to Barth, the doctrine of election is not strictly the doctrine of God's eternal decision in favor of our participation in and practical knowledge of his reality but also the basis for ethical life. Like Rosenzweig, Barth holds that God expresses his love to human beings in the form of a commandment. God's law or the good is based in God's love.[50] 'The one Word of God which is the revelation and work of His grace is also Law.'[51] As election, revelation discloses God's love for us in the form of an imperative to do the good or love God, for the loving God seeks our responsible participation in covenant. Consequently, knowledge of the God whose revelation is election through commandment can only mean fulfillment of this commandment through gracious obedience or praise and love of God.[52] Theological work is ethical life in the context of God's gracious election.

Barth establishes this connection between God's grace in Jesus Christ and God's law in Chapter VIII, 'The Command of God'. Here we find the clearest explication of Barth's allegiance to a theology of practical testimony in the context of election. The chapter begins by identifying God's Word in Jesus Christ or God's grace of election with the concept of God's law or God's determination of the 'good'. Next, Barth argues that the doctrine of election is not limited to God's act of love and grace in Jesus Christ but also includes the development of human responsibility within this context. Human participation in God's predestined election through Jesus Christ presupposes human responsibility and the freedom to act responsibly as a partner with God. Consequently, God's grace must include God's law for, by adhering to this law, humanity can responsibly live in covenant with the loving God. 'The one Word of God is both Gospel and Law ... That is, it is a prior decision concerning man's self-determination. It is the claiming of his freedom. It regulates and judges the use that is made of this freedom.'[53] In predestining humankind to partnership, God predestines humankind to a life of righteousness through his Word in Jesus Christ.

On what grounds is God's command ethically authoritative? As in *Romans* II, God's Word is ethically authoritative because it is the Word of our judgment and our salvation and, as our salvation, it is the Word that we cannot not obey. The power of God's command derives from the power of the cross to judge us as sinners and also liberate us as new people.

> The grace of this God is this. When he took our flesh in Jesus Christ, God Himself undertook in our place to subject Himself to the judgment and punishment that must be executed if we are to be raised up to Him. He Himself renounced and confessed our self will and godlessness . . . In the midst of death we have in Him no future but that of resurrection and eternal life. The grace of this God decides and has already decided concerning our human existence. What does it mean to be a man now that this decision has been reached by the grace of God? It obviously means to be one who stands and walks and lives and dies within the fact that God is gracious to him .[54]

What is the content of the divine commandment? If God's Word is God's command and if God's command is the basis for human ethical life, what constitutes the good – 'what ought men to do?' The content of human ethical life is the practical witness to God's primary revelatory act. If God seeks to re-establish a relationship of love or righteousness with humankind, the content of the divine claim can be nothing other than the imperative to love God – to stand in conformity with his grace. By commanding humankind to love God, God guarantees that humanity can and will stand in a responsible covenantal relationship with him. Human beings love God only when they witness to God's prior love for them. Unlike Cohen, Barth and Rosenzweig understand the difference between the command to be holy like God and the command to testify to God's holiness. Only the latter secures the difference between the transcendent God and the finite creature.

> The correspondence which alone can be considered in this connection cannot and will not mean abolition of 'the infinite qualitative difference' between God and man. It is a question of responsibility and therefore of a correspondence in which God and man are in clear and flexible antithesis . . . Whatever the action

> demanded of us may be, it will be our action . . . It will have to attest and confirm the great acts of God.[55]

To love God is to 'accept God's action as right',[56] 'to attest to it, but attest in definite deeds'.[57] The ethical life of the believer is *Nach-denken*.

Lastly, if revelation as the Word of God is the event of God's election and if God's election constitutes the context for our ethical life, it follows that knowledge of the God of revelation happens strictly within the context of one's participation in election or praise of God. More than speech, God's Word is God's act of loving command. Dogmatics, therefore, is ethics.

> We merely deceive ourselves if we try to be only hearers of this Word, and not doers because we are hearers. As real hearers we are indeed taken prisoner by this Word . . . Because it is the Word of the Lord, to hear the Word of God is to obey the Word of God . . . This Word, this Law lays claim to us, and in so doing, it lays claim to our freedom.[58]

## C. The Word of God and the Church in the *Church Dogmatics*

By establishing the common election motif that runs through *Romans* II and the *Church Dogmatics*, I have challenged the view that Barth's *Church Dogmatics* constitutes a radical turn from the dialectical theology of *Romans* II. This is not to say, however, that there are not significant differences between the theology of the Word in the *Church Dogmatics* and the theology of *Krisis* in *Romans* II.

The fundamental difference between *Romans* II and the *Church Dogmatics* concerns what McCormack calls the event of God's veiling and unveiling. In both cases, human knowledge of God depends upon God's own act of self-revelation or unveiling whereby he graciously provides the conditions for our apprehension of his righteousness. The God described in *Romans* II provides no visible means through which believers may concretely anticipate the reality of God's kingdom. In contrast, the *Dogmatics* includes the incarnation as part of God's gracious act through Jesus Christ. By the time he had written the *Göttingen Dogmatics*, Barth had reclaimed a post-Reformation appreciation for the doctrine of the incarnation.[59] This more developed Christology provides the basis for the claim in the *Church Dogmatics* that persons can participate in God's election prior to the kingdom of God.

## a. *The Incarnation and the The Objective Reality of Revelation*

According to the *Dogmatics*, God's self-determination in Jesus Christ is the objective reality of revelation. To understand this we must understand God's reality as the Logos or Word. According to the *Dogmatics,* one aspect of God's eternal life is his self-testimony in the second person of his being as Son or Word. As eternal Son or Logos, the second person of the trinity 'is the eternal Word of the Father who speaks from all eternity ... the Word in which God thinks Himself or expresses Himself by Himself'.[60] 'The Logos is He who proclaims God.'[61] In revelation, God's Word or self-proclamation becomes incarnate. Through this event God's Word becomes visible to human beings enabling them to know the promise of their own participation in the proclamation and praise of God.

How does this take place in the event of revelation? As we recall, Jesus Christ is God's election of humankind. He is the electing God and the elected human being. While the electing God in *Romans* II actively condescends into the realm of human sin by revealing himself through a creaturely medium (from which he remains separate), only the God of the *Church Dogmatics becomes* flesh or incarnates himself *into* a creaturely reality. 'The Son or Word of God ... was made flesh.'[62] Through the incarnation God proclaims or testifies to himself through the creaturely reality of the man Jesus. Jesus' creaturely reality becomes the site of positive testimony to God.

God's incarnation not only transforms the character of God's condescension to humankind, it also effects God's determination of Jesus as elected human being insofar as Jesus' creaturely reality remains the positive site of God's proclamation even after the negation of the flesh in the crucifixion. If, however, Jesus' creaturely reality continues as the site of positive proclamation even after the crucifixion, humankind gains visible access to a portrait of the promise of the kingdom of God, a portrait of the elected human being who positively loves and participates in the glory of God. This differs from the view presented in *Romans* II that Jesus' reality offers only an invisible hope of an unimaginable kingdom.

The reality of the man Jesus constitutes the first and only time God commissions a creaturely reality as the site for his own self-proclamation. As the logos incarnate, the man Jesus 'is taken up into unity with God'.[63] Nonetheless, God's decision to commission the man Jesus as the site of the Word foreshadows the redemption of all creaturely reality. 'The man Jesus is the first to rise out of the series of creatures ... [T]he fact that He does so is a promise for the rest of God's creation.'[64]

155

## b. *Veiling and Unveiling in the Objective Revelation*

How does God's incarnation in the man Jesus anticipate the redemption of the man Jesus if, as Barth claims, the incarnation is a veiling of God's reality? In *Romans* II and the *Church Dogmatics*, Barth suggests that no matter how God uses creaturely forms of revelation (i.e. whether God remains separate from the form or whether God incarnates himself into the form), he strictly 'veils' himself in these forms so that his reality is simultaneously disclosed and hidden. In *Romans* II, God discloses his righteous transcendence through a creaturely reality, in whose negation alone his transcendence and wholly other God's reality can be acknowledged. But how can the language of veiling and unveiling make sense in view of the theology of the Word made flesh, which anticipates the redemption of creaturely reality and the positive attestation of God in this creaturely reality? If God veils himself in the negation of creaturely reality, how can that same creaturely reality function as the positive site of the proclamation of God?

To answer this we must understand the act of divine veiling and unveiling within the anhypostatic-enhypostatic Christology of the *Church Dogmatics*. By anhypostatic-enhypostatic Christology Barth means that Jesus Christ's humanity exists only in the divine person of the Word, not without it. According to Barth, God's incarnation is the event of God's positive participation in creaturely reality. However, to say that God participates in creaturely reality or that God's Word becomes flesh is not to say that creaturely reality becomes ontologically identical with God's reality. God's Word is present in a creaturely form only insofar as God actively 'commissions' this reality to function as an instrument of God's own self-witness. By himself, the man Jesus is not identifiable with, but in fact other than, God. He becomes a positive testimony to God only when God commissions this creaturely reality as the site of his self-proclamation through a gracious act that remains hidden yet negatively suggested. As man, Jesus positively witnesses to God's reality but only because *God* is man and not because God is *man*.

> When the creature in its objectivity becomes the representative of the objectivity of God Himself, it hides it. When God makes Himself visible for us through it, He accepts the fact that He will remain invisible as the One He is in Himself and as He knows Himself.[65]

'Not of and by itself, but of and by God's appointment and grace, the creature can be the temple, instrument and sign of God Himself.'[66]

Barth's anhypostatic-enhypostatic Christology gives him a new lens for interpreting the event of Jesus Christ's crucifixion. While the crucifixion of the man Jesus marks the negation of Adamic man or sinful being, it does not imply the death of creaturely reality as it does in *Romans* II. Judgment prepares creaturely reality for its proper function as proclamation of the glory of God.

> The suffering borne on the Cross of Golgotha by the son of man in unity with the Son of God, who is as such a sacrifice for the sins of the world, is a stage on the road . . . to the glory of the resurrection, ascension and session. But it is not the Son of God who is glorified . . . He does not experience glorifying, but rather in the power of His deity, He realizes and accomplishes it. The glorification is of the Son of David. His is the justification, His the salvation from death, His the exaltation to fellowship with God . . . It is evident that by an act of renunciation God diverts to man the portion which rightly belongs to Himself . . . He has given away what is His . . . He has given away . . . all the prerogatives of His Godhead. He has given them to the man Jesus and in Him to the creature.[67]

'[B]ecause the human nature of Christ was also creature, and did not cease to be so, it can be a witness to God in its creatureliness, when and where the disposition and grace of God permit it.'[68] As God's extended act of grace, the revelation that includes the incarnation of the Logos culminates in the exaltation of Jesus the man who can love and proclaim God fully. 'By the Word of God becoming Adam the continuity of . . . the Adamic existence is broken and the continuity of a new Adamic existence is opened up.'[69] The objective reality of revelation is the event of God's Word spoken in the flesh of the man Jesus in a particular moment in history perceptible by humankind who dwell in the sinful world. The incarnation of the Word is the form of God's election.[70]

This reinterpretation of divine veiling and unveiling does not compromise the dialectical character of Barth's theology. Rather, in Bruce McCormack's terms, it provides Barth with a new way to understand the dialectical character of the God–human relationship within the context of a positive expression of God's reality. Neither, however, does this extended view of revelation challenge the theology of command and election introduced in *Romans* II but only supplements it with a more extensive Christological account.

### c. *From the Objective Reality of the Word to the Subjective Reality of the Word*

The objective reality of God's revelation in Jesus Christ paves the way for the positive life of the children of God here and now. Both *Romans* II and the *Church Dogmatics* assert that it is impossible for humanity to fulfill the commandment to love God prior to the eschaton. In the *Church Dogmatics* Barth makes this point when he says that 'every expression of our love to God, however well intended, is inexorably exposed to the law of the corruption and transitoriness of this world and of our old nature'.[71] Does this mean, as it did in *Romans* II, that all subjective response to revelation here and now is necessarily limited to the negative testimony of repentance, or is it possible for human beings to testify positively to God despite the reality of sin?

Unlike the recipient of revelation in *Romans* II, the recipient of revelation in the *Church Dogmatics* can repeat or proclaim the promise of revelation through love of the neighbor. The *Church Dogmatics* does not dismiss the necessity of repentant action. The Holy Spirit ensures that sinners experience judgment and realize that they cannot effect righteous behavior themselves. Nonetheless, the God of the *Church Dogmatics* seeks human partnership in the communication of his Word and grants them the means to proclaim the coming of the kingdom and fulfill God's commandment to love him in a form appropriate to the time of waiting. God makes himself objective in the creaturely world through Jesus Christ. And while only Jesus' creaturely reality is currently redeemed, through him all persons can recognize the promise of their own future redemption. Human beings may not yet testify to God as Jesus does, but they can acknowledge God's reality here and now. The objective revelation offers the Word in a concrete form that recipients can attest to and repeat.

> God gives Himself to be known ... in an objectivity different from His own, in a creaturely objectivity ... [Moreover,] [b]ecause the eternal Word Himself became flesh ... we know the same revelation of God wherever it is attested in expectation and recollection. For in the light of the attestation of God which occurred through the man Jesus, we find the attestation of God, wherever it is the attestation of that occurrence.[72]

Moreover, and of equal importance, God's objective representation through Jesus Christ lays the groundwork for the love of the neighbor. Not only can persons perceive a visible representation of the kingdom of God in the man Jesus, but they can also recognize a repetition of the promise of revelation in another person and, in loving the neighbor, enact obedience and practical testimony to God in this world. Like Rosenzweig, Barth can now rightfully assert that we love and know God when we love the neighbor.

How does this work? In both *The Star* and the *Dogmatics*, the love of the neighbor allows persons to verify their faith in and anticipate the 'not yet' reality of God's order. According to Rosenzweig, we act 'as if ' or confirm our belief in God's redeeming presence as one who loves all humankind and in this way we participate in God's redemption of humankind. Barth's believer only proclaims the reality of the promise to come. Nonetheless, Barth's believer helps to 'build the order of praise' and, in so doing, gains an opportunity to fulfill God's commandment to love him prior to the reality of the kingdom of God.[73]

But how, given Barth's doctrine of sin, can the neighbor offer a material representation of the kingdom of God so that in seeing her I am summoned to praise the redeemer God? In Jesus Christ, God presents a material vision of the kingdom of God enabling individual believers to recognize and *imagine* the redemption promised to all humankind. If I can imagine the redemption of all persons through Jesus, I can imagine all persons as bearers of this promise.[74]

> Because in this One human existence became once for all and uniquely a testimony to the fact that God has assumed it, there can and must be a praise of God by other men ... [M]an himself now becomes a sign ... He can and must summon to a genuine praise of God, and in that way render to the children of God that necessary service.[75]

As bearers of the promise of divine redemption, all human beings may, like Jesus, become our 'benefactors' or 'neighbors' and summon us to praise and thank the God who will bring about this future redemption.

There are, therefore, two occasions of witness according to the *Church Dogmatics*. On the one hand, witness means the love or praise of God. On the other hand, in the time prior to the kingdom, witness means testimony in the love of the neighbor. When I love my neighbor, I testify to my love for the God who will redeem me. To love the neighbor is to behave morally toward her in the only way possible, to speak to her of the help of God. 'By my assistance, I can only set up a sign of that assistance. But even in this limited sense I can and should and must act for him ... If my witness is a witness to the name of Jesus Christ, it is not just a word, but as a word it is the most concrete act.'[76] Love of the neighbor is the social and ethical expression of theological testimony here and now. While Barth's Christian does not, like Rosenzweig's believer, build the kingdom of God through her testimony, she does build an order of praise or sacrament for the coming kingdom.

> [I]n and with his election and calling . . . the ongoing of the reconciling work of the living God in the world is included and takes place. The election of each individual involves . . . an opening up and enlargement of the closed circle of the election of Jesus Christ and His community in relation to the world – or an invasion of the dark kingdom . . . a real crossing of frontiers, to the gain of the kingdom of God as the kingdom of grace . . . In this way the truth is repeated and confirmed.[77]

### d. *Beyond the Revelation – The Word of God and the Word of Man*

The ability to see the other person as a bearer of the promise of the kingdom gives rise to two other forms of the Word of God, Holy Scripture and Church Proclamation. These forms derive from the particular dynamic above described between the objective and subjective realities of the revelation.

According to Barth, church life is based in the testimony of the apostles. The first to recognize a material representation of the kingdom in Jesus himself, the apostles testified to or repeated this promise in the form of the Holy Scripture or the second form of the Word of God. Through their testimony in the Holy Scripture, the apostles became the first community of neighbors commissioned by the grace of God to represent the revelation and summon others to analogous proclamation in the third form of the Word of God, Church Proclamation. With Church Proclamation, the revelation of the Word continues through time.

> Who and what a neighbor is, we can best realize from those who founded the Church, the biblical prophets and apostles. What they do is the purest form of that work of divine mercy which is assumed by the children of God. They bear witness to Jesus Christ. In that way they order the praise of the children of God; they make it possible as a real praise of the real God. But the same thing happens wherever the Church is the Church . . . In the Church we flee to Jesus Christ proclaimed, that is, to our neighbor, who offers us the service of proclaiming Jesus Christ.[78]

160

The human repetition of God's Word is possible only when commissioned by God. The same grace at work in the anhypostatic-enhypostatic Christology is present in the *analogia fidei* or analogy of faith. Just as God's Word chose to become the man Jesus but the man Jesus could not take on the character of God's Word, so human beings may not choose to bear the repetition of God's Word. Proclamation of God's promise is possible only through faith. 'No proclamation is real proclamation to the degree that...it does not rest on the commission which we cannot in any way take to ourselves...which we can only have in the act of receiving...'[79]

Dependent as it is upon God's prior act of grace, proclamation transpires within the context of divine veiling and unveiling and assumes the same dialectical quality characteristic of the relation between the man Jesus and God's Word as *Logos*. In both instances, God has freely chosen to communicate his self-proclamation through a creaturely form that nonetheless veils the very act of grace necessary for it to serve this function. Religious language or Church Proclamation is always dialectical and subject to critique. As human, it is inherently flawed.

Finally, like the anhypostatic-enhypostatic Christology, the *analogia fidei* must be recognized within the context of divine election. By granting persons the ability to testify to their love of God and offer this witness to others through Church Proclamation, God enables human beings to fulfill the commandment to love him in the present. '[W]e learn from biblical witness to revelation that Jesus Christ has given His Church not only the commandment of faith, and love and hope...but also the commission of proclamation.'[80]

Of course, for Barth, divine election is an eternal decision of the Triune God. God's Word and loving self-communication and relation transpire within God's own triune self.[81] Geoffrey Bromiley highlights the connection between God's love toward us through Jesus and God's love toward Godself through the Son who becomes incarnate in Jesus. 'Jesus enables sinners to hear God's Word by reconciling them to God...but God is this second mode of being as the Son, not just for us, but already in himself.'[82] Similarly, the love and grace God expresses through Holy Scripture and Church Proclamation derives from God's own self-communication as Holy Spirit.[83] Bromiley says,

> The Holy Spirit is not just the Holy Spirit in revelation to and in us...He is this because he is antecedently the Holy Spirit in himself...the eternal Lord, distinct

161

from the Father and the Son and yet related to them as their common factor or fellowship. He is God as the act of Love.[84]

If, therefore, God's self-communication is God's self love and testimony, so all additional forms of God's speaking are also God's love and testimony, here expressed to humankind. Neither Holy Scripture nor Church Proclamation in preaching and sacrament can be separated from the context of the believer's loving witness to the commanding and loving God. As God's Word, love or testimony before the neighbor is the fulfillment of the commandment to love God here and now. Through this witness, believers may anticipate the promise of participation in God's eternal life of self-glorification and praise.

Lastly, the possibility of positive church life affords the possibility of more extensive theological knowledge. Knowledge of God derives from ethical testimony in the context of God's election. For Rosenzweig and Barth, theology is the life of the children of God or the witness to the God who loves us in his freedom. For Barth, dogmatics is the witness of Christ proclaimed through the neighbor that vigilantly tests the Word of God spoken in the church. Dogmatics is the ethical life that transpires within the church community.

> The function of dogmatics is to be a demonstration and proof, a sign and witness of the presence and validity of the Word of God . . . Dogmatics cannot desire to be anything but a witness to this transcendent point of view, just as preaching itself and Holy Scripture . . . can only be a witness to it. The dogmatician too has the Word of God only in virtue of the freedom and sovereignty of the Word itself and therefore in the hiddenness of his faith and obedience which are the gift of the Word. In dogmatics, too, the Word of God can become visible only as the divine is reflected in human being and action.[85]

'Knowledge of God is obedience to God'[86] as it is practiced within the sacramental anticipation of the church.

## D. Conclusion

The above analysis of the *Church Dogmatics* deepens the comparison between Barth's theology and Rosenzweig's. If *Romans* II advanced a theology of testimony that bore marked similarities to the theology of testimony in *The Star of Redemption*, the *Church Dogmatics* incorporates the theology of testimony into an ecclesiastical and sacramental context that permits the possibility of positive covenantal life here and now in a way that resembles the covenantal life described in *The Star*. Through their independent efforts Barth and Rosenzweig succeed in establishing the basis for a theology that falls prey neither to modern humanism nor to neo-orthodox positivism. By situating knowledge of God within the context of election, Barth and Rosenzweig guard theology from apologetics and humanism. By appreciating the relationship between the Word of God and divine election, Barth and Rosenzweig limit their theological pretensions to the practical encounter between a commanding God and an obedient believer. Finally, by insisting upon the inextricable relationship between the Word of God and divine election, both Barth and Rosenzweig present dialectical conceptions of the Word of God that nonetheless permit believers to engage in positive proclamation here and now.

There are differences between Rosenzweig's and Barth's theologies of the Word of God. As we have discussed, Rosenzweig maintains that religious language is a human instrument used to lend expression to the desire for God who is not fully present. As a guardian of human desire, however, language moves toward the silence of the redemptive fulfillment of this desire. For Barth, the divine Word is eternal and inseparable from the event of divine election.[87] This difference does not, however, overshadow the powerful overlap in their theologies of testimony, theologies that permit both theologians to advance models for meaningful and non-dogmatic covenantal communities.

## Notes

1 Karl Barth, *The Epistle to the Romans* (trans. Edwyn C. Hoskyns; Oxford: Oxford University Press, 6th edn, 1968), p. 105.
2 Barth, *Romans* II, pp. 159–60.
3 Barth, *Romans* II, p. 334.
4 Barth, *Romans* II, p. 368.
5 Barth, *Romans* II, p. 440.
6 Barth, *Romans* II, p. 437.
7 Barth, *Romans* II, p. 435.
8 Barth, *Romans* II, p. 78.
9 Barth, *Romans* II, p. 80.
10 Barth, *Romans* II, p. 396.
11 Barth, *Romans* II, p. 435.
12 Barth, *Romans* II, p. 471.

13  Barth, *Romans* II, p. 471.
14  Barth, *Romans* II, p. 480.
15  Barth, *Romans* II, p. 481.
16  Barth, *Romans* II, p. 321.
17  Barth, *Romans* II, p. 314.
18  Barth, *Romans* II, p. 531.
19  Barth, *Romans* II, p. 495.
20  Barth, *Romans* II, p. 497.
21  Barth, *Romans* II, p. 501.
22  According to Kendall Soulen, the metaphysical difference I am referring to in Barth and Rosenzweig reflects the more common difference between the Jewish and Christian canonical narratives. Soulen argues that Judaism maintains a creation–consummation model while Christianity has historically attached itself to a sin–redemption model. Soulen argues that Christianity can and ought to recognize its narrative of sin and redemption within the context of the creation–consummation model. By so doing it will recognize its God as the God of Israel and identify its covenant with God's covenant with the Jewish people. For Soulen's argument see his *The God of Israel and Christian Theology* (Minneapolis: Fortress Press, 1996).
23  Barth, *Romans* II, pp. 492–93.
24  Barth, *Romans* II, p. 493.
25  Barth, *Romans* II, p. 495.
26  Barth, *Romans* II, p. 494.
27  Barth, *Romans* II, p. 452.
28  By arguing that Barth's *Dogmatics* presents a portrait of ethical life of the children of God here in this created order, I will challenge an argument presented by Alexander Altmann in his essay entitled 'A Discussion with Dialectical Theology' in Alexander Altmann, *The Meaning of Jewish Existence: Theological Essays, 1930–1939* (ed. Alfred L. Ivry; Hanover: Brandeis University Press, 1991), Ch. 9. Here Altmann asserts that the fundamental difference between a Jewish theology of decision and a Christian theology of decision, like that found in Karl Barth's *Dogmatics*, consists in the fact that since it does not embrace a doctrine of original sin, only Jewish election 'sustains the authentic event of revelation by preserving the knowledge of creation'. Altmann, *Meaning*, p. 80. Altman argues that the theology of decision presented in the *Dogmatics* necessitates a turning 'away from the world'. Conversely, I will argue that Barth's theology of the threefold form of the Word of God as explicated in the *Dogmatics* differs from the time–eternity dialectic revealed in the *Krisis* of the cross in *Romans* II and allows for the possibility of sustaining revelation here in this world, prior to the kingdom of God.
29  Karl Barth, *Church Dogmatics*, I.I. (eds G.W. Bromiley, T.F. Torrance; trans. G.W. Bromiley; Edinburgh: T&T Clark, 1957), p. 41.

30  Barth, *Church Dogmatics,* vol. I.I., p. 52.

31  One proponent of the view that Barth's *Dogmatics* presents an undialectical Word of God is Eberhard Jungel. See Eberhard Jungel, 'Von der Dialektik zur Analogie: Die Schule Kierkegaards in der Einspruch Petersons', in idem *Barth-Studien* (Zurich and Cologne: Benzierger Verlag, and Gütersloh: Gütersloher Verlagshaus Gerd Mohn, 1982), pp. 127–79.

32  In *Barth, Derrida and the Language of Theology,* Graham Ward also challenges this common reading, arguing instead for the continued dialectic at work in the theology of the Word described in the *Dogmatics.* See Ward, *Barth, Derrida,* pp. 147–70.

33  McCormack makes this point when he says, 'The analogy of faith refers most fundamentally to a relation of correspondence between an act of God and an act of a human subject; the act of divine Self-revelation and the human act of faith in which that revelation is acknowledged . . . The analogy of faith is to be understood "actualistically" . . . strictly as an event. The relation of correspondence which is established in the revelation-event does not become a predicate of the human subject.' Bruce McCormack, *Karl Barth's Critically Realistic Dialectical Theology* (Oxford: Oxford University Press, 1995), p. 17. Nonetheless, McCormack does not appreciate the connection between God's act and our corresponding act in the analogy of faith and God's election and our corresponding testimony and obedience.

34  Karl Barth, *Church Dogmatics,* vol. I.II. (trans. G.T. Thomson and Harold Knight; eds; G.W. Bromiley, T.F. Torrance; Edinburgh: T&T Clark, 1994).

35  Barth, *Church Dogmatics*, vol. II.I., p. 7.

36  Barth, *Church Dogmatics*, vol. I.I., pp. 144–45.

37  Barth, *Church Dogmatics*, vol. I.I., p. 150.

38  For an insightful account of the events that prompted Barth's interest in election see McCormacks' *Karl Barth's Critically Realistic Dialectical Theology,* Ch. 4.

39  Barth, *Church Dogmatics*, vol. I.I., p. 150.

40  Barth, *Church Dogmatics*, vol. II.I.

41  Barth, *Church Dogmatics*, vol. II.I., p. 23.

42  Barth, *Church Dogmatics*, vol. II.I., p. 26.

43  Barth, *Church Dogmatics*, vol. II.II., p. 7.

44  Barth, *Church Dogmatics*, vol. II.II., p. 10.

45  Barth, *Church Dogmatics*, vol. II.II., p. 101.

46  Barth, *Church Dogmatics*, vol. II.II., p. 162.

47  Barth, *Church Dogmatics*, vol. II.II., p. 169.

48  Barth, *Church Dogmatics*, vol. II.II., p. 124.

49  Barth, *Church Dogmatics*, vol. II.II., p. 173.

50  It is worthwhile to compare Barth's appreciation for the love–law character of election with Jon D. Levenson's reading of the Sinai covenant. See Jon D.

Levenson, *Sinai and Zion: An Entry in the Jewish Bible* (San Francisco: Harper & Row, 1985) where he says, 'Covenant love is mutual . . . On God's side lies an obligation to fulfill the oath he swore to the Patriarchs . . . Israel, for her part, is to realize her love in the form of observance of her master's stipulations, the *mitzvot*, for they are the words of the language of love . . . It is not a question of law *or* love, but law conceived in love, love expressed in law. The love of God moves Israel to embrace the norms of Sinai.' Levenson, *Sinai and Zion,* p. 77. Barth's appreciation for the love–law character of election draws his theology close to the Jewish conception of covenant.

51 Barth, *Church Dogmatics*, vol. II.II., p. 511.

52 David Novak has noted the import of Barth's appreciation for the love–law character of covenant for Jewish–Christian theological exchange. According to Novak, Barth's emphasis on grace and law illuminates the fact that 'Christianity did not substitute for the Law of Judaism a spontaneous, unstructured faith. Christianity, as well as Judaism, affirms the role of both logos and ethos in the life of faith.' David Novak, *Jewish–Christian Dialogue: A Jewish Justification* (New York: Oxford University Press, 1989), p. 88.

53 Barth, *Church Dogmatics*, vol. II.II., p. 152.

54 Barth, *Church Dogmatics*, vol. II.II., p. 558.

55 Barth, *Church Dogmatics*, vol. II.II., p. 580.

56 Barth, *Church Dogmatics*, vol. II.II., p. 580.

57 Barth, *Church Dogmatics*, vol. II.II., p. 579.

58 Barth, *Church Dogmatics*, vol. I.II., p. 305.

59 For a fuller discussion of this point see McCormack's *Karl Barth's Critically Realistic Dialectical Theology*, Ch. 8, pp. 328ff.

60 Barth, *Church Dogmatics*, vol. I.I., p. 436.

61 Barth, *Church Dogmatics*, vol. II.I., p. 132.

62 Barth, *Church Dogmatics*, vol. I.II., p. 133.

63 Barth, *Church Dogmatics*, vol. II.I., p. 54.

64 Barth, *Church Dogmatics*, vol. II.I., p. 54.

65 Barth, *Church Dogmatics*, vol. II.I., p. 54.

66 Barth, *Church Dogmatics*, vol. II.I., p. 54.

67 Barth, *Church Dogmatics*, vol. II.II, p. 173.

68 Barth, *Church Dogmatics*, vol. II.I., p. 54.

69 Barth, *Church Dogmatics*, vol. I.II., p. 157.

70 G.C. Berkouwer makes a similar point regarding the relation between Barth's *Romerbrief* and his later works including the *Church Dogmatics* when he argues that the common thread that runs from the *Romerbrief* through the *Dogmatics* is the triumph of God's grace. While *Romans* speaks in the language of crisis and the *Dogmatics* in the language of Christology, both designate *expressions* of God's grace. 'When the prevalence of the Yes over the No, or rather, the merciful dealing of God in crisis and in judgment, is not fully recognized and understood

it might be thought that Barth has . . . exchanged a pessimistic for an optimistic, a desperation-theology for a theology of triumph. That which is later more clearly unfolded in Barth's dogmatic writings is, notwithstanding all manner of variations and surprises, an underscoring of this *grace-accent* . . . a more emphatic and persistent pointing to the decisive grace and love of God which could already in the *Romerbrief* be discerned as standing in intimate connection with the crisis motif.' G.C. Berkower, *The Triumph of Grace in the Theology of Karl Barth* (Grand Rapids: Eerdmans, 1956), p. 37. Despite his recognition of the theme of God's active grace in *Romans* II and the *Dogmatics*, Berkouwer does not identify this grace as command and therefore Berkouwer cannot appreciate the full breadth of the similarity between *Romans* II and the *Dogmatics*.

71 Barth, *Church Dogmatics*, vol. I.II., p. 414.

72 Barth, *Church Dogmatics*, vol. II.I., pp. 52, 54.

73 In a conversation with the Jewish theologian Michael Wyschogrod, Barth once claimed that 'we Christians have both the promise and fulfillment'. See Michael Wyschogrod, 'A Jewish Perspective on Karl Barth', from *How Karl Barth Changed My Mind* (ed. Donald K. McKim; Grand Rapids: Eerdmans, 1986), p. 161. Barth continued to remark to Wyschogrod, 'You Jews have the promise but not the fulfillment.' Wyschogrod, 'A Jewish Perspective on Karl Barth', p. 161. The above analysis of the difference between Rosenzweig and Barth concerning the life of election here and now challenges Barth's quick dismissal of Judaism and even his confident assertion regarding Christianity's full access to the reality of the kingdom.

74 It is on this point where my reading of Barth most differs from von Balthasar's. According to von Balthasar, God's incarnation in Christ redeems the created here and now. Interpreting the *Dogmatics* he says, 'Because the Word, as Redeemer, becomes man in time, all creation is thereby good and justified . . . It is only logical that natural law should now emerge with new and stronger meaning.' Von Balthasar, *Theology of Karl Barth*, pp. 101, 105. However, Barth is not arguing that the incarnation redeems creaturely reality now, but only in the eschatological future. Christ's incarnation does allow human beings to recognize the *promise* of their future creaturely redemption and the neighbor as a sign of this future redemption, but the neighbor remains only a *sign* of this *promise* and not its fulfillment here and now. Loving the neighbor and participating in the life of the church is the way we love God presently but it is not identical with participation in the kingdom of God. Creaturely reality is only fully redeemed with the kingdom of God. Here again is the fundamental difference between Barth's theology and the Catholic view of the church.

75 Barth, *Church Dogmatics*, vol. I.II., p. 424.

76 Barth, *Church Dogmatics*, vol. I.II., pp. 444–45.

77 Barth, *Church Dogmatics*, vol. II.II., pp. 417–18.

78 Barth, *Church Dogmatics*, vol. I.II., p. 422.

79  Barth, *Church Dogmatics*, vol. I.I., p. 90.

80  Barth, *Church Dogmatics*, vol. I.I., p. 57.

81  In *Barth, Derrida and the Language of Theology* Graham Ward correctly points out that the mediated activity of verbal testimony of the Word enacted in church life derives from what is an immediate act of self-testimony in the triune God itself. He notes that the trinitarian God participates in a type of self-communication through the immediacy of the Word, 'a hermeneutic activity, that of the Trinity, in which God speaks ... and where there is an equation of word with object and the communication is direct, God speaks and interprets God by God (Jesus Christ) through God (the Holy Spirit) to God.' Ward, *Barth, Derrida*, p. 16. Ward references this feature of the triune God in order to highlight what he takes to be the essentially hermeneutical character of the divine life for Barth and our corresponding life of faith. Nonetheless, Ward fails to appreciate the context of divine election within which this hermeneutical life transpires. There are significant theological ramifications to Ward's oversight of the election motif in Barth's work. While Ward's work is an effort to applaud Barth's theology of language as an example of a postmodern theology of the Word, his analysis does not do justice to the content of Barth's theology. If the limitations of linguistic knowledge are recognized in the context of a theology of election as practical witness, it is possible to understand not only a 'theological reading of *différance*', but rather the commanding and electing God who we know in practical witness – the objectively loving, real and active God, the God of the scriptures. Ward's failure to highlight the election component in Barth's theology will keep him from recognizing the ethical contribution to Barth's theology and what derives from this ethical component, Barth's value for social criticism. Ward alludes to the theological significance of righteousness as testimony when comparing Barth and Levinas and says that 'Barth's theology of the Word and Levinas's philosophy of Saying ... both present an an-archeology of logocentrism; both argue for an ethics or righteousness beyond and yet constitutive of meaning.' Ward, *Barth, Derrida*, p. 170. Still, Ward does not pursue this line of inquiry nor root it in Barth's doctrine of election.

82  Geoffrey Bromiley, *Introduction to the Theology of Karl Barth* (Edinburgh: T&T Clark, 1979), p. 19.

83  Eugene Rogers emphasizes the witness of the Holy Spirit within God's triune reality in 'Supplementing Barth on Jews and Gender: Identifying God by Anagogy and the Spirit', *Modern Theology* (1988), pp. 43–69. Rogers argues that a fuller appreciation of God's triune witness of the Holy Spirit invites a new appreciation for the life of the consummate community of believers within the church. Appreciating Barth's emphasis on the witness of the Holy Spirit can, according to Rogers, reveal a more ecumenical and gender-sensitive aspect to Barth's theology.

84  Bromiley, *Introduction to the Theology of Karl Barth*, p. 20.

85  Barth, *Church Dogmatics*, vol. I.II., p. 814.

86  Barth, *Church Dogmatics*, vol. II.I., p. 26.

87  There are a number of ramifications to this difference in their theologies of the Word of God. Rosenzweig's resistance to theological origin of religious language makes him vulnerable to charges of religious relativism and indeterminacy. If religious language is an expression of theological desire, religious traditions cannot present their world-views as absolute or exclusive truth. Second and perhaps more problematic is the charge of indeterminacy. Are there no standards for the particular expression of desire? Can testimony to the creator, revealer and redeemer God look like anything the believer desires or are there better and worse ways of articulating the transcendent God who loves? For a detailed analysis of this question see Martin Kavka and Randi Rashkover, 'A Jewish Divine Command Ethics', *Journal of Religious Ethics* (2004), pp. 387–414. Kavka and I argue that Rosenzweig's indeterminacy may be remedied by a Maimonedian negative theology. Clearly, Barth's theology of the Word keeps him invulnerable to either of the above charges. Still, Barth's theology of the Word is vulnerable to charges of intolerance for other traditions. An in-depth discussion of this comparison remains, however, beyond the scope of the present work.

# Chapter 6

# The Politics of Praise

Thus far the primary goal of the book has been to demonstrate how a theology of testimony can ground meaningful and non-dogmatic expressions of Judaism and Christianity. In this respect, a theology of testimony nourishes and sustains the vitality of these two religious traditions by energizing their spiritual, ethical and social significance. To live as a Jew or a Christian is to live within a covenantal community of believers who together testify to the God who loves. If a theology of testimony supports and generates covenantal communities, we must still examine whether it can play any role in developing and/or healing the relationship between our covenantal communities and our larger human family. In this chapter I will argue that a theology of testimony can ground a 'politics of praise' through which Judaism and Christianity can contribute productively to the political environment without succumbing to either Constantinianism or secular invisibility. More specifically, according to Rosenzweig and Barth, the key to Judaism and Christianity's productive participation in the political arena rests in their ability to engage in a covenantal life of testimony or praise of God. As politically directed, covenantal testimony assumes two distinct voices: the prophetic call of proclamation and critique, and the cry for justice. Both voices presuppose the non-apologetic 'reasoning after revelation' structure present in Rosenzweig's and Barth's theology of testimony. Only the community that speaks with both voices balances between divine ethics and human justice.

## A. Glorification of the Name and the Prophetic Community

The greatest casualty of the centuries-old battle between church and state in Western history has been the loss of the prophetic voice within Judaism and

171

Christianity. This loss dates back to the birth of the dangerous liaison between church and state in Constantinianism when church and state collapsed their differences and opted to battle one another for increased power. Conversely, the voice of the prophet always emerges from outside. While, on the one hand, Constantinianism's marginalization of the Jews might on the surface appear to have handed Jews a perfect platform for prophetic critique, the disempowerment of the Jews was so extreme as to guarantee that any prophetic critique they might offer would fall on deaf ears. On the other hand, by politicizing Christianity, Constantinianism dealt an equally devastating blow to Christian propheticism leaving Christianity no place outside of the political from which to issue its vigorous and critical proclamation.

Sadly, modernity's triumph over Constantinianism has not marked the resurrection of the prophetic voice. Stanley Hauerwas makes this point when, echoing themes in John Yoder's work, he says, '[W]ith the Enlightenment the link between church and state was broken, but the moral identification of Christians with the state remained strong.'[1] Christians, Hauerwas argues, are caught in the bad habit of Constantinianism. While the separation between church and state could arguably afford religion an opportunity to reclaim its prophetic voice, few Jewish and Christian communities have taken up this challenge. Again, Hauerwas argues similarly and says, 'Christians lose exactly the skills necessary to see how deeply they have been compromised by the assumption that their task is to rule ...'[2] Many contemporary theologians have bemoaned John Locke's identification of church and synagogue as 'voluntary associations' on the grounds that, as Scott Bader-Saye puts it, 'the church was given the dubious honor of a protected place within the culture. But such protection has turned out to be equally a containment. Christianity is protected as a private belief system but is contained insofar as these beliefs cannot challenge the public realm; that is, they cannot translate into actions that are in conflict with the interests of the nation state.'[3]

Still, the separation between church and state may yet prove to be a fertile breeding ground for the resurrection of the prophetic voice. In fact, I maintain that a theology of testimony, like that found in Rosenzweig's and Barth's theology, carves out a practical game-plan for reasserting the prophetic voice of covenantal communities within this context of the separation of church and state. Readers may ask, if the goal is to re-establish the prophetic voice in order to once again sound the proclamation of the divine name within the larger, extra-covenantal community, why not advocate the dissolution of the church–state divide altogether and opt instead for an alternative constellation of the political/social and religious communities? John Milbank's work has advocated some such transformation on the grounds that the church–state divide is nothing more than an artificial designation determined by those who refuse to recognize their own theological indebtedness as well as the artificial character of their own model. For him, models for society are narratives written and lived in social practices. Overcoming the church–state divide is as simple as performing a new narrative. Unfortunately, Milbank's Christian reality remains blind to the realities of our political world and guilty of utopianism.[4] It is not enough to simply act as if the kingdom of God is now. Believers must simultaneously act as if the kingdom of God is now and also confront and tackle the reality of the unredeemed world.[5] The covenantal community must frankly acknowledge the character of the church–state divide that informs contemporary Western society.[6]

If, however, Judaism and Christianity must accept the current church–state constellation, neither community must sentence itself to the silence its legally privatized position appears to guarantee. In other words, while today's political theology must be realistic, it must not become Niebuhrian. Reinhold Niebuhr's *Moral Man and Immoral Society* is a testament to the tragic divide between the moral standards of religious individuals and the moral standards of groups, particularly national, racial and international groups. According to Niebuhr's analysis, while religious individuals may, by virtue of their direct encounter with individual others, gain an appreciation for the reality of another and empathetically consider the other's interests, groups lack this type of intimacy and are incapable of authentic empathetic recognition. Instead, groups act in their own interests and at best work to restrict abuses of power that may result in but cannot assert any higher moral standard.

> What is lacking among moralists, is an understanding of the brutal character of the behavior of all human collectives, and the power of self-interest and collective egoism in all inter-group relations. Failure to recognize the stubborn resistance of group egoism to all moral and inclusive social objectives inevitably involves them in unrealistic and confused political thought ...[7]

Despite Niebuhr's passionate love for the religious life and its ability to nourish the lives of those within covenantal communities, Niebuhr is far too quick to admit the defeat of the prophetic voice within the world of realpolitik.

Barth's and Rosenzweig's theology of testimony navigates between these two extreme positions by calling for Judaism and Christianity to bravely acknowledge the realities of the political world and, as private communities, issue forth a bold and indefatigable voice of proclamation and critique.

### a. *Rosenzweig: Judaism, Christianity and the Prophetic Community*

Despite differences in their external form both Judaism and Christianity in Rosenzweig's account assume the role of prophetic communities who, by virtue of their glorification of the divine name, necessarily posit an ongoing critique of all forms of human ideology, and in particular the state, in its self-understanding as a structural representation of the human moral order.

As we have seen, for Rosenzweig, to be a Jew or a Christian is to live together in the community of those who testify to the loving God. Furthermore, we have seen that for Rosenzweig testimony is always dialectical in character. If revelation is an event that discloses God's wholly transcendent love, then human testimony to this love is necessarily inadequate. Consequently, believers testify to God by testifying to their own inability to directly refer to God. In other words, glorification of the divine name is always concomitant with a critique of human experience and human expression. Proclamation of the divine name cannot be self-interested or self-valorizing without ceasing to be testimony about God in God's transcendent otherness. Divine witness offers a theological basis for *Ideologiekritik*. My account of Rosenzweig's theology of the Word of God has demonstrated how, for Rosenzweig, Judaism and Christianity lend expression to testimony without forfeiting its dialectical character. Both Judaism and Christianity maintain the finite and maculate character of their revelatory texts. Furthermore, while both traditions lend expression to believers' positive loving testimony to God, their articulation of this testimony is always limited by the character of human desire and is further tempered by the repentant testimony expressed through the liturgical cycle. Religion's dialectical character distinguishes it from all other forms of human culture, forms of culture that are necessarily called into question by the proclamation of the divine name.

Politics is among the forms of culture challenged in the proclamation of divine witness. While Rosenzweig recognizes differences in the relationship between Christianity and the state and Judaism and the state, both traditions, he argues, must stand prophetically outside of the state and issue an overarching critique of the character of realpolitik.

We may examine Rosenzweig's support for the prophetic role of Jewish covenantal community in the context of his rejection of the alliance between Judaism and the modern liberal nation state. In the eighteenth and nineteenth centuries Jewish philosophy argued in favor of a marriage between Judaism and liberalism. In *Jerusalem*, Moses Mendelssohn argues that the church and the state share the same goals and, while religion focuses on perfecting men's convictions but only the state secures proper action, the marriage is a union of separate but equal partners. 'State and church have for their object the promotion, by means of public measures, of human felicity in this life and in the future life . . . [T]he state can compel actions . . . divine religion commands actions only as tokens of convictions . . .'[8] Mendelssohn implies that Judaism is the state's ideal religion because it most efficiently secures the monotheistic convictions necessary to promote the moral life demanded by the state.

> Although the divine book that we received through Moses is, strictly speaking, meant to be a book of laws containing ordinances, rules of life and prescriptions, it also includes, as is well known, an inexhaustible treasure of rational truths and religious doctrines which is so intimately connected with the laws that they form but one entity. All laws refer to, or are based upon eternal truths of reason, or remind us of them, and rouse us to ponder them.[9]

Judaism loses nothing in this alliance with the state. The fully observed *halakhic* life offers the greatest opportunity for promoting monotheism.

Rosenzweig's covenantal theology of testimony motors his critique of this liberal Jewish tradition, sometimes referred to as ethical monotheism which, even in its most critical form (arguably that of Hermann Cohen), sees Judaism as an accomplice to the hopes and goals of the modern nation state. Recent interpreters of Rosenzweig have sought to position Rosenzweig within the tradition of ethical monotheism. The most noteworthy of these efforts is Leora Batnitzky's *Idolatry and Representation*. Batnitzky argues that *The Star* is primarily concerned with the 'crisis of meaning'[10] in the modern world. According to this reading, modern theology's emphasis on present experience destroys human meaning because meaning requires time. Consequently she holds that Rosenzweig's call for the recovery of miracles is like Romanticism's call to recover the value of the past. Miracles, Batnitkzy reads Rosenzweig to say, are essentially signs that acquire their meaning by referencing something else that will be true in the future. In Batnitzky's reading, miracles are narrative elements that presuppose an ongoing script that can be read forward from its signs, or backwards from its future. Either way, miracles suggest the reality of self-interpreting traditions. 'It is in the telling and ongoing creation of the story that the meaning of miracles is found.'[11]

However, self-interpreting traditions not only speak to the crisis in meaning, but they also guard against idolatry. If, as Batnitzky claims, Rosenzweig appreciates Mendelssohn's belief in the Jewish tradition as right worship, he adds to it by arguing that the Jewish tradition is also a self-interpreting story that perpetuates an ever-fluid expression of meaning. According to Batnitzky, Rosenzweig believes that proper worship of God is equal to proper participation in one's own finite, self-witnessing hermeneutical tradition. In contrast, Batnitzky says, to the

> 'Nietzschian point-of-view philosopher [who] worships himself because he does not understand his own finitude properly... Rosenzweig maintains that to be compelled by a tradition is to be compelled by a past, for which the individual qua individual cannot fully account. It is to be more than an individual ...'[12]

According to this reading, the revelation event described in Part II of *The Star* is the particular miracle that inspires the Jewish script and capacity for self-interpretation. God's call is the claim issued by one's own tradition, and the human's response is a particular Jew's willingness to witness to and share in the perpetual interpretation of the tradition. Rosenzweig's divine command ethics turns into the imperative to become a card-waving member of the Jewish people.

Batnitzky's hermeneutical reading of Rosenzweig colors her analysis of what Rosenzweig means by Judaism's Messianic politics. According to Batnitzky, Rosenzweig's Judaism shares much in common with the ethical monotheist tradition. Batnitzky claims that, like Cohen, Rosenzweig's Judaism is that monotheistic model that helps the nations of the world move nearer to their own fulfillment as models of monotheism.

> Rosenzweig's thought parallels most closely the ethically monotheistic philosophy of Hermann Cohen... But Rosenzweig expands Cohen's ethical monotheist argument into an argument about the present's relation to the past... While Rosenzweig follows Cohen's ethically monotheistic vision in

176

arguing that the Jewish people contribute uniquely to world culture, he transforms Cohen's argument by turning the argument about the Jewish mission to the nations into a general hermeneutic theory.[13]

Judaism is the necessary accomplice to the goal and fulfillment of the nations. From this reading, Rosenzweig's Judaism is just as implicated in the *Deutschtum–Judentum* alliance as Mendelssohn's or Cohen's.

I believe that Rosenzweig would see this Judaism as fanatical. A worldview is fanatical, according to Rosenzweig, when it posits itself as the bearer of eternity. Consequently, the fanatic claims to know what the Messianic goal is and precisely how to achieve it. Conversely, Rosenzweig's Jew lives within a covenantal community whose Torah and Torah life are dialectical expressions of testimony to a commanding God. As such, Torah and Torah life are always tensed by their effort to articulate a reality of divine revelation that exceeds human expression and temporality. Jewish texts that posit claims regarding the redeemer God express longing rather than certainty. Moreover, proclamations regarding redemption are further tempered by the liturgical cycle that consummates yearly in the repentant self-critique of Yom Kippur. As a dialectical tradition of testimony Judaism cannot lay claim to the defined goals of a secular tradition. As earlier discussed, secular traditions, unlike religious traditions, do assert defined visions of their ultimate expectations. The goal of all secular cultures is self-preservation expressed through culture. Judaism longs instead for a future that it cannot represent with absolute certainty. From a Rosenzweigian perspective Judaism cannot ally itself with the goals of a secular nation state. But if, as Batnitzky's account claims, Judaism is pivotal in helping the nations achieve their final goal as bearers of monotheism, it would appear that it understands itself as the proper tool for achieving the proper goal. A Judaism implicated in any version of liberalism's dreams would be fanatical from a Rosenzweigian perspective simply on the grounds that secular liberalism defines its utopia.

Judaism pursues instead what Rosenzweig refers to as Messianic politics – a politics directed toward a Messianic era that cannot be directly expressed or pursued but longingly and faithfully proclaimed in the context of the loving and repentant testimony to God. Rosenzweig's Judaism does have a unique role with respect to its relation to the rest of the world. Judaism's task is to live covenantally outside the current of the secular arena. But Judaism's testimony is not only for itself. Rather, it is the fire whose light burns and radiates its proclamation of God and its scorn for idolatry far beyond its own community borders. Judaism's prophetic separation from the secular world constitutes its greatest political contribution. Jews are politically active in their political inactivity. As the community who glorifies the name of God, they must remove themselves from the sphere of realpolitik, the arena where nations assert their particular aims against one another. 'The only genuine pacifist, the Jew remains remote from the chronology of the rest of the world.'[14] Judaism, Rosenzweig says, provides 'the wordless evidence which gives the lie to the worldly and all-too-worldly sham eternity of the historical moments of the nations, moments expressed in the destiny of their states'.[15] Of course this does not mean that Judaism may pride itself on possessing the truth either. Judaism's prophetic critique extends back to itself. 'This people has a land of its own only in that it has a holy land...God tells it, this land is mine.'[16] Of their language Rosenzweig says, '[N]othing is more essentially Jewish in the deepest sense than a profound distrust of the power of the word and fervent belief in the power of silence.'[17] Finally, their law too points away from itself, negatively referring to the God who is praised. 'The Jewish people does not count years according to a system of its own. For neither the memory of its history nor the years of office of its law givers can become a measure of time...for the people...has no time of its own.'[18] The Jew maintains no particular goal for his own people – no particular political dream.

Rooted in an event of revelation which exceeds its own testimony and temporalization, Judaism, according to Rosenzweig, cannot implicate itself in the liberal Jewish alliance between church and state but must commit itself to prophetic proclamation. Batnitzky's claim to the contrary derives from her neglect of Rosenzweig's theology of revelation. If, according to Batnitzky, revelation is the particular miracle that inspires the Jewish script and capacity of self-interpretation, then Jewish narrative becomes the self-referential interpretation of the Jewish tradition over time. From such a perspective Judaism becomes another, albeit a highly creative and reflective, generator of human self-understanding. No wonder Batnizky maintains that this particular culture can ally itself with other cultures. In Batnizky's account, Judaism maintains no unique theological commitment separating it from all other human sources of meaning. The primary flaw in Batnizky's reading of *The Star* concerns her interpretation of Rosenzweig's concept of miracle. Batnitzky holds that miracles are narrative signs that point to the reality of a self-interpreting tradition. But for Rosenzweig, miracles are not simply narrative signs, but signs of God. Consequently, they point to the possibility of divine revelation and not simply to the restoration of self-interpreting communities. Although Batnitzky realizes that the Jewish narrative in *The Star* is a narrative of the Jewish community's practices, the fact that she privileges Part III over Part II means that she cuts God out of the equation. Her reading of Rosenzweig is Cohenian in the sense that, for her, revelation is no more than the precondition for community life.

According to Rosenzweig's account, Christianity must also assume a prophetic role within the world community. As earlier discussed, Christianity's expression of revelation and testimony differs from Judaism's. Christians experience and respond to divine love as individuals. Consequently, Christians do not have a ready-made community with whom to testify. The Christian community is a product of outreach. Christian life is necessarily involved with secular reality and, historically speaking, this involvement has often led to Christianity's inability to distinguish between persuasion and domination. Throughout its history the church's actions have often more resembled the coercive measures of the unhealthy state than the prophetic community. Nonetheless, as our examination of Christianity's liturgical year revealed, Rosenzweig appreciates the Christian Word as an expression of theological desire and the Christian liturgical cycle as repentant testimony. Rosenzweig recognizes that Christianity has had to traverse a two-thousand-year history to reach its true expression in what he calls the Johannine church and in this, its most developed phase, the church frees itself from its exercise of domination and assumes its rightful position in relation to the world.

Like Judaism, Christianity cannot ally itself with the aims of the secular nation. Despite the superficial differences in their religious expressions, Christianity and Judaism are both covenantal communities of testimony. Unlike Judaism, Christianity's testimony reaches out to individuals beyond the pale of the church community of any given time. This does not, however, alter Christianity's prophetic role. It simply makes it more difficult to achieve. Still, one must not make the same error regarding the meaning of Christianity that Christianity herself has made for centuries – that is, one must not misconstrue Christianity's proclamation to the unbeliever with Christianity's involvement in the world of realpolitik. In other words, Christianity's compassionate engagement with the nonbeliever does not compromise the prophetic power of her proclamation, its glory to God or its critique of the world of realpolitik. As the community or ecclesia of those who proclaim the divine name, the Johannine church looks nothing like the nation state. Unlike the nation state, the Johannine church has no 'visible form of its own'.[19] Like the Jewish community, she longs for a future she cannot fully represent. The Johannine church 'is not built . . . it can only grow . . . It is amorphous and necessarily unestablished.'[20] A communion of individuals who love and desire God, the church quietly dwells in the midst of the creaturely order, testifying to the birth of God's redemption. Its testimony to God separates it from the aspirations of the modern nation state just as much as it separates it from its former character carving out the space for its prophetic proclamation of God's love and its perhaps quiet, but nonetheless tireless, critique of the strictly secular.

## b. *Barth: Christianity and the Prophetic Community*

The dialectical character of a theology of witness mandates the restoration of the prophetic role in Barth's theology, just as in Rosenzweig's. Both theologians assert the radical Otherness of the revealing God whose revelatory love calls all human experience and knowledge into question. While Barth's theology of sin results in a more purist form of dialectical theology, both thinkers assert the concomitance of proclamation and critique.

While the development in Barth's Christology impacts upon the ability of the church to positively proclaim the promise of the kingdom of God, this development does not alter the prophetic character of the church's role within the political arena. Said in other terms, it is the dialectical character of Barth's theology that mandates its prophetic separation from the state. Consequently if, as I have argued, Barth's Christology does not compromise this dialectical character, it will not support a transformation of the church's relation to the secular state either. However, the development in Barth's Christology will impact on the vitality and extent of the church's prophetic witness for, while the church of *Romans* II may only issue a prophetic proclamation of repentant witness, the church of the *Dogmatics* can become the living community of believers who love the neighbor and dwell together in the promise of God's redemption. The difference between the two forms of prophetic proclamation can be best seen by recalling, on the one hand, Barth's notion of negative demonstrations, and considering, on the other hand, Barth's conception of the Confessing Church.

How can the church in *Krisis*, the church mired in sin, act prophetically? As we recall, according to *Romans* II, repentance is the primary form of ethical activity. The only form by which the church of *Krisis* may testify to the promise of God's redemption, repentant testimony can be politically relevant. While the church of *Krisis* cannot ally itself with any one form of human ideology, it can use its divine testimony to respond to the political environment. For example, what Barth calls the 'Great Negative Possibility', the exhortation to refuse to participate in revolutionary enterprise, is both repentant testimony to God, and political act. The Great Negative Possibility is repentant testimony so far as it boldly denies the validity of any human revolutionary action and indirectly proclaims God's sole redeeming and transforming power. On the other hand, the exhortation against participation in revolutionary activity applies this testimony to a concrete political situation. By applying its testimony to political events, the church's voice resonates politically but remains invulnerable to the spiritual corruption of the political environment.

Barth's *Church Dogmatics* deepens but does not depart from the theology of testimony advanced in *Romans* II. Consequently, Barth's political theology undergoes no marked change after *Romans* II. While Barth's developed Christology permits the church to positively proclaim the promise of the kingdom of God, this developed ecclesiology does not legitimize a renewed Constantinianism. On the contrary, Barth's more developed Christology only strengthens the church's ability to boldly proclaim its prophetic message. No longer restricted to repentant testimony, the church may now apply its witness of the coming kingdom to the political arena. The community of those who love the neighbor as the sign of God's promised redemption may now assume political meaning. Barth had the opportunity to see and develop this kind of church community in his own lifetime. One of the primary contributors to the Barmen Declaration issued in 1934, Barth helped create the only church in Germany willing to take a vocal stand against the Nazi regime. Boldly arguing against any German–Christian alliance, the Confessing Church asserted itself politically but in the only way appropriate to the church – through its confession to the belief in Jesus Christ as God's unique means to salvation.

> Jesus Christ, as He is attested to us in Holy Scripture, is the Word of God, whom we have to hear and whom we have to trust and obey in life and in death. We condemn the false doctrine that the Church can and must recognize as God's revelation other events and powers, forms and truths, apart from and alongside this one Word of God.[21]

This, according to Jeffrey Stout, represents Barth's marked advance over more anti-liberal minded theologians including Milbank and Hauerwas for, as Stout says, Barth's 'Barmen Declaration' demonstrates simultaneously the ability to maintain the integrity of its theological commitments without defaulting on its urgent obligation to join with others in the struggle for justice and peace. The Declaration says in no uncertain terms that theological commitments must determine the church's political stance... its 'No'! to Nazism was clear enough... but Barth was not content with mere refusal of the secular. He committed himself to a definite program of progressive politics consistent with orthodox doctrine.[22]

Moreover, ever vigilant in its prophetic tone, the Confessing Church could not and cannot inoculate itself from the criticism it extends to the state. The power of the church's message derives only from its confidence in God and God's order – an order the church may proclaim only with the grace and the power of God himself.

> If we really want to understand the genesis of Barmen, we shall be obliged to look finally neither to the Confessional Church nor to its opponents. For there is not much to be seen here. The Confessional Church was, so to speak, only the witness of a situation in which simultaneously there took place a remarkable revelation... It was only a witness... The emphasis of everything said previously lies in the fact that Jesus Christ has said something, and, what is more has said it about Himself: I myself am the way, the truth and the life. I myself am the door. The Church lives by the fact that it hears the voice of this 'I' and lays hold of the promise which, according to this voice is contained in this 'I' alone... it is not [able to act] on its own authority, or in the execution of its own security program, but on the basis of the necessity in which Jesus Christ Himself has said that no man comes to the Father but by Him.[23]

## B. The Call for Justice

The above discussion argues that Rosenzweig's and Barth's theology of witness permits the restoration of politically active prophetic communities of praise that successfully navigate between the Scylla and Charybdis of Constantinianism and secular invisibility. Can this argument withstand criticism? If Gillian Rose were alive today she would most likely beg to differ. Central to Rose's work was a virulent critique of postmodern theological ethics as utopian and antinomian. Rose's work launches this attack against a whole array of representatives of the contemporary theological tradition including Rosenzweig. Generally speaking, Rose attacks those systems of theological ethics that portray ethics as purified of the contingencies and power dynamics characteristic of systems of law.

Instead of recognizing and comprehending the opposition between 'nature' and 'freedom' as the tension of freedom 'and' unfreedom, and bearing that tension as agon of authorship, anxiety of beginning, equivocation and suspension of the ethical, these authorships invariably proceed to invent a 'passage', a path, from violence to the holy.[24]

Unfortunately, Rose maintained, postmodern theological ethics has renounced the labor of reason, positing instead a sundering of law and ethics, history and messianism. Speaking in particular about Rosenzweig, Rose argues,

The Star of Redemption opts for the Kingdom, the eternity of which will be the accomplishment of Judaism, while Christianity struggles with its 'not yet'. This is to overlook the connection between political and sacred history for both, and, especially for Judaism. For it ignores the formation of Talmud Torah – the changing relation between the three crowns of the prophet, priest and king, and the subsequent political success of the rabbis in inheriting the mantle of power – the right to interpret the relation between renewed commandment and imposed law as the fundamental political institution of Judaism.[25]

Of course Rose believed that postmodernism's mission to locate and celebrate a non-violent arena of pure ethics only resulted in its opposite, namely, the persistent presence of the forces of power devoid of the mediation of philosophical reflection. 'The investigation into the failures of modern regimes of law . . . is itself outlawed, because critical reflection lost its legitimacy when the self-validating ground fell away from reason.'[26] Power is mediated by the work of reason. To dismiss reason is to ensure the free and unregulated reign of forces of power.

Moreover, Rose maintained that not only do theologies of command ignore outside forces of power, but devoid of reason these self-same theologies become agents of injustice themselves. From Rose's perspective, theological ethics rooted in phenomenologies of a commanding Other are incapable of securing an authentic recognition of an other. 'This new ethics denies identity to the other as it denies identity to the actor, now passive beyond passivity.'[27] Why? According to Rose's account, command ethics determine that social relations among persons are always regulated strictly by the command issued by the authoritative Other. Applied to Rosenzweig's thought, my love for the neighbor is not a true recognition of the neighbor as she is. Rather, my love of the neighbor is a projection of my desire for God onto the neighbor. I see her only as I desire to see her – I project my own desired view onto her and disregard her in her own personhood. Said in Roseian terms, I attempt to bypass the encounter with an other whose otherness challenges my sovereign view of the world. My adherence to the command of the Other forces me to neglect the one who is not loved by God.[28] According to Rose, I fail to allow my own view of the world to be mediated by another and therefore do not participate in the process of reflection or reason – that is, the emergence of the universal or third that emerges in the encounter with another. Critiquing what she argues is Rosenzweig's sundering of self and soul which renders the soul incapable of mediation between itself and an other in *The Star of Redemption*, Rose says,

> Only if the other's being-for-self – the other's relation to their own boundary, becomes my being-for-self can there be a middle. Redemption would mean not that the other, the neighbour, is covered by love, is beloved, but that the bounded singularity of both one and the other fail towards the recognition of that sinful self- relation which denies the self-relation of the other in the relation to self... Revelation would be the incursion of the unwelcome news of the boundary and of the investment of reactive will to power in its denial, not the effacement of the boundary.[29]

But, according to Rose, this encounter with another is inevitable. My willful denial of it is an effort to negate the lawfulness of my human condition. My adherence to a divine command is therefore not simply irrational, but unlawful and unjust as well.

Is Rose correct? Does prophetic proclamation fulfill divine command at the expense of the need and reality of the other person? Are Rosenzweig's and Barth's believers not only guilty of the kind of blindness characteristic of Milbank's proclaiming Christian but, even worse, agents of injustice? Are divine command ethics and the pursuit of human justice necessarily at odds? Is there room within Barth's and Rosenzweig's accounts of the love of the neighbor for an encounter with the other who is not loved by God – what is an active engagement with the non-religious community?

Neither Rosenzweig's nor Barth's prophetic communities are guilty of Rose's charges for neither Rosenzweig's nor Barth's prophetic communities remain blind to the cry of justice from the one who is unloved by God. Let us review each theologian in turn.

## a. *Rosenzweig's Theology of Testimony and the Pursuit of Justice*

The central reason why Rosenzweig's expression of divine command ethics does not fall prey to this particular problem concerns the non-propositional character of Rosenzweig's divine command ethics. That is, the believer who testifies to God's love cannot testify with any degree of certainty regarding the content of her testimony. Said in Roseian terms, covenantal life with God in no way negates or ignores the lawfulness of the human condition as finite or subject to the mediation through another. On the contrary, Rosenzweig's believer never benefits from a divine speech or truth that transforms her status from the finite, social creature that she is. Her experience of God and her testimony to God are already mediated through her creaturely finitude. While Rosenzweig does not offer a social account of the believers' existential awareness, this is not to say that Rosenzweig's believer lacks this awareness. Consequently, Rosenzweig's believer experiences God's love dialectically. On the one hand, she is aware of divine love; on the other hand, she is aware of the absence of this love in the sense that, as finite, she does not 'have' this love. Consequently, theological desire prompts her to simultaneously proclaim, 'Where is God's love?' and, 'I believe it is here.' Theological proclamation is concomitant with theological doubt and therefore already rationally mediated through the encounter with the negative. The beloved experiences God's love in the context of the lawfulness of her human condition and therefore in the context of her own cry or desire for justice.

We must apply this analysis to the character of the believer's love for the neighbor. The believer's love of the neighbor is not an unyielding projection of her theological view onto another person. Rather, the believer's love of the neighbor is an expression of her dialectical and already mediated testimony. The believer's testimony is already tempered by law – her execution of the divine command already mediated by the cry for justice. She does not need the neighbor to introduce her to the unredeemed world – she has already been introduced to it through her own experience. One could argue even that the believer's recognition of the need of the other person exceeds the recognition of the unbeliever in Rose's account. Rose's account maintains the possibility of a third or mediated universal that may be said to finally and fully recognize the need of the other. In this respect, Rose's law-abiding individual may, theoretically, at some point rest secure in her acknowledgment of the needs of the other. Reason affords justice the possibility of closure and completion. Conversely, in Rosenzweig's account, the believer's theological doubt permits her to recognize the cry for justice

185

from the unbeliever but does not permit the believer to conclude her encounter with this other through a mediated third. Theological proclamation is always concurrent with theological doubt – the pragmatism that permits the believer to assert the other as a sign of God's redemption is always tensed by the epistemological precariousness of the believer's desire. In this respect, a believer may never feel that she has fully met the needs of the one who is unloved by God. The believer's theological commitment allows her to recognize that the unbeliever's cry for justice is more than a cry for mutual recognition, but a cry for the redeeming God. Rosenzweig's believer understands finitude as more than a cry for self-preservation but a cry for God's love – a sign or miracle. In Rosenzweig's analysis, to rest satisfied with a system of justice that pretends to achieve mutual recognition among persons is to behave sinfully, for sin is the failure to recognize this world as a sign of God's world. In this way, Rosenzweig's analysis of justice within the context of divine command resists the closure of law insofar as law means the universalization of standards and/or acts of justice.[30] Rosenzweig's analysis resists the final dominion of reason over issues of justice. Consequently, not only does Rosenzweig's theology of testimony recognize the cry for justice of another, it permits the believer to better appreciate the depth of this cry as one that cannot be fully met through human accommodation but requires the love of God which is deeper and more transformative than any strictly human acknowledgment. This is not to suggest that the other's needs may be fully met simply by pointing another in the direction of the loving God. It means that the turn to God is consistent with the ability to address the needs of the other through specific acts of justice and recognize the inexhaustible character of another's need. The turn to God is thereby consistent with the vigilant pursuit of just practices.

Consequently, from a Rosenzweigian perspective, neither Judaism nor Christianity neglects those who fall outside of their world-views. Theological doubt is an implicit element within Jewish and Christian religious experience itself and therefore Judaism and Christianity may confront instances of God's absence without departing from the context of their covenantal/prophetic lives. Moreover, insofar as Judaism and Christianity confront injustice within a covenantal context, both traditions offer a tireless account of the insufficiency of secular legal systems to meet the needs of those who cry out for justice. Contrary to Rose's analysis, it is precisely in their efforts to fulfill a divine command ethics that Judaism and Christianity become the tireless advocates of the oppressed.

186

## b. *Barth: Love of the Neighbor and Justice*

What happens when we apply Rose's critique to Barth's theology of command? Can Barth's Christian allow her proclamation to be challenged by the reflective encounter with the non-Christian such that she may recognize this person as she is and not strictly as a sign of the promise of the kingdom? Rosenzweig's immunity to the Roseian critique derived from the dialectical character of the believer's proclamation concerning the redemptive presence of God in the other. That is, Rosenzweig's believer lacked an absolute epistemological basis for her proclamation already leaving open a space to encounter another whose perspective negated her own. If, for Rosenzweig, testimony is epistemologically precarious, for Barth testimony is epistemologically impossible for, as we recall, theological witness, according to Barth, is not possible for any person save through what God has done through that person. Consequently, a believer's testimony for Barth is never analogous to Rose's self who asserts her position or perspective onto another and coerces the other into her own perspective. Barth's believer cannot lay claim to any perspective – the revelation through God has already mediated and even more so, judged and dismissed, the human self's perspective and, in this sense, has made abusive behavior impossible.[31] When Barth's believer recognizes the neighbor as a sign of God's future promise, she encounters an other who, as this provisional analogue of Christ, effects the same critique on the believer that the believer's initial encounter with Christ effects. A provisional bearer of Christ's revelation assumes the same expression of judgment over all human sin that Christ as crucified assumes. 'The neighbor shows me that I am a sinner. How can it be otherwise seeing he stands in Christ's stead, seeing he must always remind me of Him as the Crucified?'[32] In this way, Barth's neighbor performs the same function that Rose's other person performs – she challenges the sovereignty of the believer. Furthermore, insofar as my recognition of the neighbor as a sign of God's promise prompts me to a testimony which presupposes my self-negation, my recognition of the neighbor is not only not the unilateral and self-interested proclamation of my point of view, it is the call for the full attention to and care for the neighbor, a care that I know that I cannot myself provide but call on God to provide. Still, Barth says, by proclaiming the need for God's care for this other, I must

> set up a sign of that assistance . . . I can and should and must act for him . . . I
> cannot excuse myself by saying that I was required to do the impossible. If I give

> him this assistance, I still owe him the real help which he needs. I cannot therefore pride myself on my action ... But within this obligation I have fulfilled my responsibility to this extent: I have set up a sign of real help.[33]

Moreover, as was the case in Rosenzweig's theology of testimony, the mediation of Barth's believer exceeds the mediation of Rose's sovereign and lawful self, for while, theoretically speaking, in Rose's account an authentic system of justice may permit a self to rest satisfied that the needs of another have been met, neither Rosenzweig's nor Barth's believer may reach the same confidence. Rosenzweig's believer is ceaselessly challenged by her finite reception of God's revelation, and Barth's believer is ceaselessly challenged by the judgment effected on her by God's revelation. Barth's and Rosenzweig's believers recognize the reality of another person and launch stinging critiques of any human system of justice that claims to satisfy the needs of the oppressed.

Practically speaking, the upshot of this analysis is that prophetic proclamation of covenantal communities is inextricable from a proactive campaign in favor of those who cry out for justice.[34] Covenantal communities may not use their separation from the rules of realpolitik as an excuse to neglect the cause for justice. While Barth explicitly addresses the believer's responsibility to 'set up a sign of real assistance' and Rosenzweig only *suggests* an analogous enactment of justice, my analysis of Rosenzweig's thought demonstrates how similar practices are a necessary outgrowth of his theology of testimony. Covenantal communities must proclaim the glory of God and the critique and self-critique of the human. They must also call out in favor of those who have been forgotten, unrecognized by the secular and religious communities. As prophetic, and always dialectical, covenantal communities may not allow their advocacy for the oppressed to become ideological. Their advocacy for the other does not negate but emerges out of their testimony to God.

### c. *A Note About Law*

Thus far I have outlined how a theology of proclamation at once mandates the glorification of God and the pursuit of justice. Still, I have said little regarding the status of law within this theology of testimony. In the above discussion I maintained that Rosenzweig's and Barth's theologies of proclamation presuppose rather than preclude concern for the just treatment of a particular other. In this way, I argued, Rosenzweig's and Barth's theologies call the self-sufficiency of any legal system into question.

Law, of course, is the effort to universalize standards of justice to ensure symmetry of treatment for all. It is well noted that law and justice often stand at odds with one another. Still, the question here is not whether a theology of proclamation challenges the notion of law (that I have already argued) but whether this challenge precludes the possibility of conventional law altogether. Can a theology of proclamation permit the development and use of legal systems as vehicles for the standardization of practices of justice or do they resist such conventional formulations? In what follows I will argue that a theology of proclamation that generates a divine command ethics and a call for justice does not preclude the possibility of legal structure as long as such legal structures are always held in tension with the dialectical nature of proclamation and the cry for justice. Within this context, conventional law is possible only when it meets two conditions: it must serve as a form of testimony and, as such, law must be challenged by the claims of the particular other whose needs I am aware of in and through my proclamation.

The question concerning the status of conventional law within a theology of proclamation applies more to Jewish covenantal life than to Christian covenantal life and therefore my argument will examine the relation between *halakha* and proclamation. I do not want to suggest that a theology of testimony must express itself in legal terms. Insofar as a theology of testimony mandates a concern for the particular other within the context of a divine command ethics, it does not necessitate legal structure. Legal structures are necessary only so far as individuals have no immediate incentive or path for effecting just behavior. In secular contexts, legal structures can be second best efforts to mete out justice to the particular other. Within these contexts, legal structures are inevitably second best because the particular needs of an other are only met so far as they are universalizable – that is, so far as they may be formulated into standards and practices that all may carry out. As we have seen, theologies of proclamation suffer no such disability so far as a divine command ethics mandates concern for the particular other. While covenantal communities may encode practices that simultaneously address the needs of another and offer testimony, this dual ability of the just practice does not mean that the person protected by the just practice needs become a believer who accepts the community's world-view. Just practices are just practices whether they are also taken up as testimony or not and neither the recipient nor the practitioner needs participate in the wider community activity of testimony. Consequently, the question is not whether legal structure is necessary to

189

theologies of proclamation but whether legal structure is possible or acceptable within theologies of proclamation.

If legal structure is possible within a theology of testimony as a vehicle of proclamation, endlessly vulnerable to the claims of justice, then the Jewish rabbinic tradition offers a vibrant example of how such law develops and functions. I will begin the discussion with a general portrait of Jewish law within the wider Jewish exegetical tradition and will then provide an example.

Jewish theological desire propels rabbinic exegetical practice. Let us analyze the rabbinic exegetical tradition through the three categories of proclamation, the cry for justice and law. As discussed in Chapter 3, from a Rosenzweigian perspective rabbinic texts are the unique Jewish mode of pragmatic proclamation whereby Jews testify to the God of their past, present and future. As Torah, rabbinic texts are expressions of Jewish telling, Jewish memory, Jewish proclamation as Jewish hoping and Jewish longing.

As such, rabbinic exegesis preserves the connection between testimony and the pursuit of justice. Rabbinic exegesis is the proclamation of God's love through a perpetual series of questions and expressions of faith. The beloved who testifies obediently to God's love testifies to her desire for this love – a desire that proclaims both, 'God's love is here' and 'Where is God's love?' Rabbinic texts express the relentless cry for God's love – the pressing doubt that challenges my proclamation and cries out for justice. This doubt derives from the particular character of my own humanity and/or the particular character of another's humanity. Consequently, rabbinic texts permit concern for the justice of another person and for myself as well. More specifically, rabbinic texts are cauldrons of personal desire. Contemporary feminist thought has done much to highlight the expression of personal desire within the texts by focusing on the rabbis' desire to serve their own interests.[35] Of course, such accounts would be incomplete if they failed to appreciate that the rabbis' very ability to cry out on behalf of their own interests also permits them to cry out on behalf of the other's interests as well.[36] This is the unique feature of a theology of testimony. As the expression of my theological doubt, my desire permits me to recognize God's absence in the humanity of the other person as well. Consequently, rabbinic texts often take on the character of complex weaves of proclamation, self-interest and concern for the other.

Let us consider an example. It is interesting to note the form in which the pursuit of justice is expressed in rabbinic texts. Oftentimes rabbinic texts use narrative portrayals to express theological doubt. In her now classic text, *Engendering Judaism*, Rachel Adler tells us that narratives examine and lend voice to the individual overlooked by either law or stereotypes. In this way, narratives can promote the pursuit of justice. Adler's reading of *Berakhot* 51b demonstrates how rabbinic narratives press for justice against universalizing tendenices of stereotypes or law. *Berakhot* 51b tells the tale of a dinner at the house of R. Nahman and his wife Yalta. Also present at the meal is a guest named Ulla. The meal is finished and the moment comes for the guest Ulla to pass the cup of blessing to those collectively participating in the grace after meals. R. Nahman asks Ulla to pass the cup to his wife. Ulla, citing biblical texts that establish the male as the source of fertility, argues that if women's fertility is dependent on men, so her blessedness derives from men as well and refuses to pass the cup to Yalta. In response, Yalta goes down to the wine cellar and smashes four hundred jars of wine. Afterwards, R. Nahman repeats his request that Ulla pass her the cup. Ulla passes the cup but tells Yalta that he's passing her the equivalent of a plastic cup. He mocks her. She in turn mocks him saying, 'From travelers come tall tales and from ragpickers lice.'[37]

Adler tells us that this story occurs in the context of a Talmudic discussion concerning the laws of who participates in the grace after meals. Adler doesn't flesh out the meaning of the passage in this context. However, it's worth playing out some aspects of this more traditional reading. Interpreted in the context of the *halakhic* discussion concerning participation in grace after meals, the story helps form the apparently stable edifice of rabbinic positions (proclamations) regarding women and their participation in ritual activity. There are a number of assumptions at work in this *halakhic* reading. First, it assumes that it is normal for there to be a special conversation regarding women's participation. This suggests that women are not, somehow, the norm. Second, the story presupposes that men rightfully make the decisions regarding women's participation. Third, the story assumes that men's decision-making takes place in a conversation that excludes women (Yalta doesn't participate in the conversation – she goes away from the table to smash the wine jars). Read in this context, the rabbis appear confident in their views, what in our case is their use of law as an expression of testimony.

Contrary to this reading, Adler's interpretation focuses on Yalta. From the *halakhic* standpoint, Yalta is incidental. The main action happens between R. Nahman and Ulla as they play out the details of *halakha*. However, when we focus attention on Yalta, everything changes. Two men

191

debate the right a woman has to receive a ritually important glass of wine. They talk, they cite texts, they talk some more. All the while the woman removes herself from the drone of their exchange, goes down to the cellar and smashes four hundred wine jars. So much for the blessing over the cup – how are you going to make a blessing when there's no wine? The narrative's inclusion of Yalta's act challenges each of the assumptions above described and illuminates the particularity of a person neglected in those assumptions. First, by smashing the wine jars Yalta challenges the peripheral, non-normative status assigned her. She creates a situation where her position (not being able to participate in the ritual) shapes the situation for everyone since there's no more wine. Second, since her act determines the outcome of the situation, it challenges the assumption that men control legal decisions. Finally, her deed defies the paradigm of Torah conversation as the vehicle for legal determination.

In summary, Torah life as stories, law and practice constitutes the unique expression of Jewish covenantal testimony. Consequently, as expressed in Torah texts and as lived, *halakha* is one expression of the Jewish language of love for God. However, as an expression of testimony, law must be as tensed by the dialectical character of theological desire as any other form of proclamation. At its best, rabbinic law testifies to the glory of God and standardizes behaviors that simultaneously proclaim God and protect the one whose needs are neglected. Nonetheless, rabbinic law may be misused. On the one hand, rabbinic law may become dogmatic and fail to recognize its purpose as testimony. Of course, as we have discussed, Rosenzweig maintains that a proper recognition of the relation bewteen *Gesetz* and *Gebot* guards against this particular abuse.[38] Our current discussion has raised another possible problem, however. If testimony to God is, as I have argued, concomitant with recognition of the needs of another, does law's tendency to universalize and standardize behaviors make such recognition impossible? In other words, does law stand in the way of the pursuit of justice? The argument here is that rabbinic law does not stand in the way of the pursuit of justice so far as there is a mechanism at work which permits an active conversation between the needs of particular persons and the development and perpetuation of the laws that claim to protect them. Only law that has no immediate exposure or contact to the pursuit of justice risks injustice. But when law functions within the context of testimony it regularly encounters that rationally or narratively expressed doubt that challenges the sufficiency of the law's generalizations and illuminates the neglected other in all her particularity. As legal texts, rabbinic texts guard against this abuse so far as they weave together proclamation, doubt and legalization, and to study them is to participate in the dimensionality of the covenantal life.

## C. Where To From Here?

Religious life faces enormous challenges in our time. More specifically, Jewish and Christian communities in the United States and elsewhere are challenged to respond to the hazards of the contemporary international scene as well as face the range of social, moral and economic problems that plague individual nations. By way of conclusion I would like to offer suggestions for a way forward that emerges out of the path forged by Rosenzweig and Barth.

### a. *The Discernment of Need: Politics in the Chapel*

If, as I have tried to argue, the theology of testimony presented by Rosenzweig and Barth identifies the reasoning structure implicit within the biblical doctrine of revelation and if this reasoning structure permits both traditions to care vigilantly for the needs of their own members as well as those who are outside of the particular tradition, it becomes incumbent upon both traditions to incorporate this activity into their own hermeneutical and liturgical practices. Jews and Christians cannot be content to permit political parties to monopolize the language of policy and/or the language of need. Jews and Christians must confidently allow their language of testimony to govern their examination of social need. Churches and synagogues cannot shield themselves from political questions but neither should they limit themselves to the rhetoric and ideological platforms of conservative or liberal voices. The discernment of need and policy must arise from the reasoning practices that accompany the praise of God. Where, Cornel West asks in his *Democracy Matters: Winning the Fight Against Imperialism*, have the prophetic voices of Christianity and Judaism gone?[39] They are, I have argued, to be found in the study halls of the *beit midrash* and the scripture sessions of the churches. Propheticism becomes apologetics when it fails to originate from the proclamation and pursuit of justice commanded by the revelatory God.

There is, however, more theological work to be done here. On the one hand, Rosenzweig's insightful analyses of Jewish liturgical practice and the hermeneutics of desire must be followed up by detailed case-studies of how Jewish liturgical practice links to Jewish study and the discernment of needs. On the other hand, for all of its strengths, Barth's conception of witness remains ahistorical. For Barth, the church is the repetition of Christ's witness as elect and not a temporalization of this witness. While Barth's notion of witness is practical – that is, it participates in the move to a theology of doxological praxis – it is not pragmatic if by pragmatic we mean – problem-solving. If, as recent strains in post-liberal Jewish and Christian theology have suggested, the church shares in the form of Israel.[40] and if we assume that Israel performs pragmatically in its liturgical and hermeneutical practices, can we say that the church performs pragmatically as well? At stake is the church's ability to witness to God in a way that reacts to problems that emerge in time. Future theological work needs to examine the relationship between and the temporality of Jewish and Christian liturgical and hermeneutical practice.

### b. *The Discernment of Need: Jewish–Christian Relations*

Not only, however, does a theology of testimony awaken Jewish and Christian communities to the responsibility to integrate political questions into their liturgical lives, it also awakens Jewish and Christian communities to the significance of engaging in this work together. Jewish and Christian communities can work together to identify social need and devise policies for overcoming it. The claim that Jews and Christians can work together to identify human need is not new.[41] New, however, is the notion that Jewish and Christian articulation of need arises from their liturgical and hermeneutical practices of praise. Jews and Christians need not bracket off their liturgical practices when engaging in co-operative politics in favor of a shared language of political philosophy but may speak to one another out of the particularities of their own traditions.

Moreover, to the extent that both Judaism and Christianity can incorporate the needs of the non-member into liturgical and hermeneutical practices, Jews and Christians can benefit from inviting each other to their individual study tables as representatives of the human family whose needs each tradition must become practiced in identifying. While a detailed analysis of ground rules for this kind of Jewish and Christian scriptural study exceeds the bounds of this discussion, suffice it to say here that the presence of the other at one's study table tests the home tradition's ability to consider the needs of the world outside of its particular house.

More theoretical work needs to be done here as well. How can Jews and Christians present the policy proposals they develop from out of their reasoning practices to the public? What are the standards of reasoning within public discourse and to what extent are these standards flexible enough to permit religionists to advance their claims in the language of their own traditions? Beyond the scope of this book, this work promises to once and for all overturn the now obsolete Lockean model of church–state relations.[42] To the extent that it does, we may thank Rosenzweig and Barth for setting the stage for this much needed change.

## Notes

1 Stanley Hauerwas, 'A Christian Critique of America', *The Hauerwas Reader* (eds John Berkman and Michael Cartwright; Durham: Duke University Press, 2001), p. 476.

2 Hauerwas, 'A Christian Critique of America', *Hauerwas Reader*, p. 476.

3 Scott Bader-Saye, *Church and Israel After Christendom: A Politics of Election* (Boulder: Westview Press, 1999), p. 13.

4 Recently Jeffrey Stout has issued a similar critique of John Milbank's position. According to Stout, the problem with Milbank's position is not its commitment to theological presupposition but rather its naive refusal to recognize the ideological diversity present in our contemporary American or Western society. He says, '[O]ur society is religiously plural, and has remained so for several centuries... I fail to see how the sea change these theologians are calling for is going to happen. There is no point in trying to wish the social reality of religious diversity away, or in resenting this diversity as long as it lasts.' See Jeffrey Stout, *Democracy and Tradition* (Princeton: Princeton University Press, 2003), p. 100. Of course, Stout argues, recourse to atheological points of commonality is not unique to contemporary society but goes back to the early modern political debates among Christians who could not agree on theological matters but sought practical solutions to political problems. Pragmatically motivated, they shelved their theological positions and premised discourse on atheological grounds. Such theological shelving, however, is, according to Stout, only provisional and/or for pragmatic purposes and does not reflect the epistemological prioritization of the atheological over the theological.

5 In this respect, then, Stout's *Democracy and Tradition* is important so far as it suggests that contemporary American democracy might provide an environment for religionists to enter into pragmatically motivated conversations with non-religionists or religionists of varying traditions. Stout's argument is premised on the notion that a secular society need not be a society that single-mindedly embraces anti-religious beliefs or, in Max Weber's terms, is radically disenchanted. Rather, by a secular society Stout says he means a society that uses secular presuppositions as pragmatic bases for conversation but need not endow these bases with epistemological privilege. 'This is not because the discourse in

which they and their interlocutors are engaged commits everyone involved to relying solely on "secular reason" when thinking and conversing on political questions. Nor does it involve endorsement of the "secular state" as a realm entirely insulated from the effects of religious convictions, let alone removed from God's ultimate authority. It is simply a matter of what can be presupposed in a discussion with other people who happen to have different theological commitments and interpretive dispositions.' Stout, *Democracy and Tradition*, p. 97. The notion that our democratic society is less than evil in no way diminishes the prophetic role of the Jewish and Christian communities. Rather it makes such propheticism and what later I will describe as the work of justice easier to accomplish.

6  Moreover, Milbank's critique of Levinas does not apply to either Rosenzweig's or Barth's believer. In his essay, 'The Ethics of Self-Sacrifice', Milbank argues that Levinasian-type command ethics results in the nullification of the self who obeys. See John Milbank, 'The Ethics of Self-Sacrifice', *First Things*, 91 (1999), pp. 33–38. As such, Levinasian command ethics reinforces an ontology of violence and death which counts as the absolute opposite and inevitable negation of an ontology of peace, uniquely expressed within the Christian narrative and praxis. Such narrative and praxis celebrate the giftedness of the created order, the plenitude of creation in the self and the self in community with others. Milbank neglects to realize that this Christian narrative signals the death of the self as well – for Milbank's self is replete with fulfillment and has no unmet desire. In his efforts to overcome the antinomies presented by secular modernity, Milbank has negated the reality of the created order itself and the reality of the persons within it. Most importantly, Milbank has neglected the character of the creature who, as created but not yet privy to revelation, experiences a desire for God – a desire that remains even with divine revelation – a desire that grounds the call for justice – a desire that mediates between the world that needs God and the reality of God. One cannot launch this same accusation against other Radical Orthodox thinkers. Like Milbank, Graham Ward denounces modernity's exile of the sacred. Still, Ward's doctrine of creation permits recognition of the desirous nature of the human person without falling prey to secularism's dismissal of the sacred. Consequently, Ward's theology recognizes a transformative element in revelation that Milbank's de facto identification between revelation and creation cannot. Ward's work is, therefore, less vulnerable to charges of Platonism than Milbank's and offers a more authentic recuperation of Christian doctrine. For a more sustained comparison between Milbank's ontology of peace and a doctrine of theological desire like that found in Rosenzweig, see my 'The Meaning of Theological Desire: A Jewish Response to John Milbank's Ontology of Peace', 2002 AAR.

7  Reinhold Niebuhr, *Moral Man and Immoral Society: A Study in Ethics and Politics*, (New York: Charles Scribner's Sons, 1960), p. xx.

8 Moses Mendelssohn, *Jerusalem: Or On Religious Power and Judaism* (trans. Allan Arkush; Boston: Brandeis University Press, 1983), pp. 70–73.

9 Mendelssohn, *Jerusalem*, p. 99.

10 Leora Batnitzky, *Idolatry and Representation: The Philosophy of Franz Rosenzweig Reconsidered* (Princeton: Princeton University Press, 1999), p. 45.

11 Batnitzky, *Idolatry and Representation*, p. 43.

12 Batnitzky, *Idolatry and Representation*, p. 47.

13 Batnitzky, *Idolatry and Representation*, p. 32.

14 Franz Rosenzweig, *The Star of Redemption* (trans. William W. Hallo; New York: Holt, Rinehart and Winston, 1971), p. 331. Franz Rosenzweig, *Der Stern der Erlösung* (Frankfurt: Suhrkamp Verlag, 1988), p. 369.

15 Rosenzweig, *Star*, p. 335/372.

16 Rosenzweig, *Star*, p. 300/333.

17 Rosenzweig, *Star*, p. 302/335.

18 Rosenzweig, *Star*, pp. 304/337–38.

19 Rosenzweig, *Star*, p. 285/317.

20 Rosenzweig, *Star*, p. 285/317.

21 Karl Barth, *Church Dogmatics: The Doctrine of God*, vol. II.I. (trans.T.H.L. Parker et al.; Edinburgh: T&T Clark, 1992), p. 172.

22 Start, *Democracy and Tradition*, p. 108.

23 Barth, *Church Dogmatics* II.I., p. 177.

24 Gillian Rose, *The Broken Middle* (Oxford: Blackwell, 1992), p. 249.

25 Gillian Rose, *Judaism and Modernity: Philosophical Essays* (Oxford: Blackwell, 1994), p. 143.

26 Rose, *Judaism and Modernity*, p. 6.

27 Gillian Rose, *Mourning Becomes The Law: Philosophy and Representation* (Cambridge: Cambridge University Press, 1997), p. 37.

28 For an additional articulation of this same critique see Martin Kavka, *Jewish Messianism and the History of Philosophy* (Cambridge: Cambridge University Press, 2004) pp. 150–54.

29 Rose, *Judaism and Modernity*, p. 152.

30 In this respect, Rosenzweig's analysis resembles Derrida's analysis of the relation between justice and law. See Jacques Derrida, 'The Force of Law', *Acts of Religion* (ed. Gil Andjar; New York: Routledge, 2002). In this essay, Derrida distinguishes between justice itself and justice as law with the former working as the mystical foundation of a law that presupposes force. Law inevitably deconstructs itself so far as it is predicated upon an impossible and indescribably mystical foundation. Moreover, this mystical foundation both supports and undoes the character of law as that which claims to universalize standards and just behaviors. Justice speaks for the individual other who the law therefore neglects. The difference between Rosenzweig and Derrida on this point has to do with the fact that what for Derrida is a mystical foundation is for Rosenzweig

covenantal life. Consequently, Derrida's thought continues modernity's painful exile of the theological while Rosenzweig's, for all the reasons announced in this book, redeems it to its proper status.

31 One may ask then, in view of the earlier noted challenge to command ethics raised by John Milbank, whether Barth's dissolution of the self in the face of divine judgment results in the nullification of the self which Milbank finds in Levinas' work. Of course, what differentiates Barth's analysis of the self from Levinas' is Barth's doctrine of creation. More specifically, while Levinas' command ethics never returns to the self who in her service to the other completes her own particular destiny, Barth's obedient believer is restored to her creaturely status through her adherence to the divine command. While Milbank may be able to launch his critique against the Barth of *Romans* II for whom obedience to the divine command is concomitant with the death of the old man and the birth of a new man whose life, nonetheless, remains impossible from our current perspective, Milbank would have more difficulty arguing against Barth's position in the *Church Dogmatics*. Barth's doctrine of creation is more developed in the *Church Dogmatics* and obedience to the divine command does not result in the death of the old man but in the fulfillment of the creaturely character of the sinner. Barth's more developed doctrine of creation negates charges of nihilism like those advanced by Milbank and, while Barth does hold that the complete fulfillment of the person awaits the kingdom of God, the kingdom of God is not an imperceptible reality but the completion of the created order that we may, by the grace of God, perceive analogously through our world, our bodies and our experiences. Obedience to divine command offers life for the creature made in the image of God.

32 Barth, *Church Dogmatics*, I.II., p. 431.

33 Barth, *Church Dogmatics*, I.II., pp. 445–46.

34 By arguing that Barth's theology mandates the labor of justice, I do not mean to suggest that Barth was committed to a particular political program or that his commitment to a political program instructed his theological position. The latter position is advanced by Friedrich-Wilhelm Marquardt, *Theologie und Sozialismus: Das Beispiel Karl Barth*s (Munich: Chr. Kaiser Verlag, 1972). More specifically, Marquardt argues that Barth's theology is directly linked and influenced by his socialism. As George Hunsinger points out, however, Marquardt's reading of Barth anthropologizes Barth's theology. Hunsinger says, '[F]or Marquardt, the kingdom becomes a reality to be actualized in and through human action, not a reality to be actualized by God alone. God's "religious function" is ultimately subordinate to his "moral function"; justification by faith is subordinate to reconciliation in the world; God, to the kingdom of God; theology to anthropology . . . For Marquardt, God conceived as effective is identical with socialism. This theological contour has

little to do with Barth.' See George Hunsinger, *The Radical Politics of Karl Barth* (Philadelphia: The Westminster Press, 1976), p. 188.

35   See Miriam Peskowitz, *Spinning Fantasies: Rabbis, Gender, and History* (Berkeley: University of California Press, 1997) and Rachel Adler, *Engendering Judaism: An Inclusive Theology and Ethics* (Philadelphia: The Jewish Publication Society, 1998).

36   Both Peskowitz and Adler appreciate this aspect of the analysis of desire. For a detailed discussion of the relation between their hermeneutics of desire and the category of law see my 'Theological Desire: Feminism, Philosophy and Exegetical Jewish Thought' in Hava Tirosh Samuelson (ed.), *Women and Gender in Jewish Philosophy* (Indianapolis: Indiana University Press, 2004).

37   Adler, *Engendering Judaism*, p. 53.

38   This is the argument at the heart of Rosenzweig's essay, 'The Builders: Concerning the Law', *On Jewish Learning* (ed. N.N. Glatzer; New York: Schocken Books, 1965), pp. 72–92.

39   See Cornel West, *Democracy Matters: Winning the Fight Against Imperialism* (New York: Penguin Books, 2004).

40   See Peter Ochs, 'Israel's Redeemer is the One to Whom and with Whom She Prays', in *Liturgy, Time and the Politics of Redemption* (ed. Pecknold and Rashkover; Grand Rapids: Eerdmans, forthcoming 2006).

41   See Joseph B. Soloveitchik, 'Confrontation', *Tradition* 6, no. 2 (1964).

42   See John Locke, *Letter on Toleration* (New York: Hackett Publishing Company, 1983).

# Works Cited

Adler, Rachel, *Engendering Judaism: An Inclusive Theology* (Philadelphia: The Jewish Publication Society, 1998).

Althaus, Paul, 'Theologie und Geschichte: Zur Auseinanderetzung mit der dialektischen Theologie', *Zeitschrift für systematische Theologia*, I (1923/4).

Altmann, Alexander, 'A Discussion With Dialectical Theology', in *The Meaning of Jewish Existence: Theological Essays, 1930–1939* (ed. Alfred L. Ivry; Hanover: Brandeis University Press, 1991).

Aquinas, St. Thomas, 'Summa Theologica Part I', in Arthur Hyman and James W. Walsh (eds), *Philosophy in the Middle Ages* (Indianapolis: Hackett Publishing Company, 1983).

Bader-Saye, Scott, *Church and Israel After Christendom: A Politics of Election* (Boulder: Westview Press, 1999).

Barth, Karl, *Anselm: Fides Quaerens Intellectum: Anselm's Proof of the Existence of God in the Context of his Theological Scheme* (trans. Ian W. Robertson; London: SCM Press, 1960).

—— *Church Dogmatics: The Doctrine of the Word of God*, vol. I.I. (trans. G.W. Bromiley; Edinburgh: T&T Clark, 1995).

—— *Church Dogmatics: The Doctrine of the Word of God*, vol. I.II. (trans. G.T. Thomson and Harold Knight; Edinburgh: T&T Clark, 1994).

—— *Church Dogmatics: The Doctrine of God*, vol. II.I. (trans. T.H.L. Parker *et al.*; Edinburgh: T&T Clark, 1992).

—— *Church Dogmatics: The Doctrine of God*, vol. II.II. (trans. G.W. Bromiley *et al.*; Edinburgh: T&T Clark, 1994).

—— *Epistle to the Romans* (trans. from the sixth edition, Edwyn C. Hoskyns; London: Oxford University Press, 1968).

Batnitzky, Leora, *Idolatry and Representation: The Philosophy of Franz Rosenzweig Reconsidered* (Princeton: Princeton University Press, 1999).

Bergson, Shmuel Hugo, *Dialogical Philosophy from Kierkegaard to Buber* (trans. Arnold Gernstein; Albany: State University of New York Press, 1991).

Berkouwer, G.C., *The Triumph of Grace in the Theology of Karl Barth* (Grand Rapids: Eerdmans, 1956).

Bromiley, Geoffrey, *Introduction to the Theology of Karl Barth* (Edinburgh: T&T Clark, 1979).

WORKS CITED

Buber, Martin, *I and Thou* (trans. Walter Kaufman; New York: Scribner, 1970).
———— 'On Hermann Cohen', in *The Writings of Martin Buber* (ed. Will Herberg; New York: New American Library, 1973).
———— *On Judaism* (ed. Nahum Glatzer; New York: Schocken Books, 1995).
Carter, Stephen, *Culture of Disbelief: How American Law and Politics Trivialize Religious Devotion* (New York: Anchor Books, 1994).
Cohen, Hermann, *Die Religion der Vernunft aus den Quellen des Judentum* (Leipzig: Gustav Fock G.m.b.H., 1919).
———— *Logic der reinin Erkenntnis* (Hildesheim: Georg Olms Verlag, 1977).
———— *The Religion of Reason Out of the Sources of Judaism* (trans. Simon Kaplan; New York: Frederick Ungar Publishing Company, 1972).
———— *System der Philosophie Erster Teil: Ethik des reinen Willens* (Berlin: Bruno Cassier, 1907).
Cohen, Richard, *Elevations: The Height of the Good in Rosenzweig and Levinas* (Chicago: University of Chicago Press, 1994).
Derrida, Jacques, 'The Force of Law', in *Acts of Religion* (ed. Gil Andjar; New York: Routledge, 2002).
Ferreira, Jamie, 'Kant's Postulate: The Possibility or the Existence of God?', Kant-Studien 74 (1983).
———— 'Making Room for Faith', in D.Z. Phillips and Timothy Tessin (eds), *Kant and Kierkegaard on Religion* (New York: St. Martin's, 2000).
Fishbane, Michael, *The Garments of Torah: Essays in Biblical Hermeneutics* (Bloomington: Indiana University Press, 1989).
Fisher, Simon, *Revelatory Positivism? Barth's Earliest Theology and the Marburg School* (Oxford: Oxford University Press, 1988).
Gadamer, Hans Georg, *Truth and Method* (trans. Joel Weinhsheimer and Donald G. Marshal; New York: Crossroad, 1991).
Galli, Barbara, 'The New Thinking: An Introduction', in Franz Rosenzweig, *The New Thinking* (trans. Barbara Galli and Alan Udoff; Syracuse: Syracuse University Press, 1999).
Gibbs, Robert, *Correlations in Rosenzweig and Levinas* (Princeton: Princeton University Press, 1992).
———— *Why Ethics: Signs of Responsibility* (Princeton: Princeton University Press, 2000).
Glatzer, Nathan N., *Franz Rosenzweig, His Life and Thought* (New York: Schocken Books, 1961).
Gordon, Haim and Jochanon Bloch (eds) *Martin Buber, A Centenary Volume* (Ben Gurion University: Ktav Publishing House, 1984).
Gordon, Peter, *Rosenzweig and Heidegger: Between Judaism and German Philosophy* (Los Angeles: California University Press, 2003).
Greenberg, Yudit, 'The Hermeneutic Turn in Franz Rosenzweig's Theory of Revelation', in Stephen Kepnes (ed.), *Interpreting Judaism in a Postmodern Age* (NY: New York University Press, 1996).
Handelman, Susan, 'The Torah of Criticism and the Criticism of Torah: Recuperating the Pedagogical Moment', in Stephen Kepnes (ed.), *Interpreting Judaism in a Postmodern Age* (New York: New York University Press, 1996).

Hauerwas, Stanley, 'A Christian Critique of America', in *The Hauerwas Reader* (eds John Berkman and Michael Cartwright; Durham: Duke University Press, 2001).

Heidegger, Martin, *Being in Time* (trans. John Macquarrie and Edward Robinson; San Francisco: Harper & Row, 1962).

Hunsinger, George, *The Radical Politics of Karl Barth* (Philadelphia: The Westminster Press, 1976).

James, William, *The Will to Believe: And Other Essays in Popular Philosophy* (New York: Dover Publications, 1956).

Jungel, Eberhard, 'Von der Dialektik zur Analogie: Die Schule Kierkegaards in der Einspruch Petersons' in idem *Barth-Studien* (Zurich and Cologne: Benzierger Verlag and Gütersloher Verlagshaus Gerd Mohn, 1982).

Kant, Immanuel, *Critique of Practical Reason* (trans. Lewis White Beck; Indianapolis: Bobbs-Merrill Educational Publishing, 1983).

——— *Critique of Pure Reason* (trans. Norman Kemp Smith; New York: St. Martin's Press, 1965).

——— *Religion Within the Limits of Reason Alone* (trans. Theodore Green and Hoyt H. Hudson; New York: Harper Torchbooks, 1960).

Kavka, Martin and Randi Rashkover, 'A Modified, Jewish Divine Command Theory', *Journal of Religious Ethics* 32.2 (2004), pp. 387–414.

——— *Jewish Messianism and the History of Philosophy* (Cambridge: Cambridge University Press, 2004).

Kepnes, Steven, Peter Ochs and Robert Gibbs (eds), *Reasoning After Revelation: Dialogues in Postmodern Jewish Philosophy* (Boulder: Westview Press, 1998).

Levenson, Jon D., *Sinai and Zion: An Entry into the Jewish Bible* (San Francisco: Harper & Row, 1985).

Levinas, Emmanuel, 'God and Philosophy', *The God Who Comes to Mind* (ed. Bettina Bergo; Stanford: Stanford University Press, 1998).

——— *Totality and Infinity: An Essay on Exteriority* (trans. Alphonso Lingis; Pittsburgh: Duquesne University Press, 1996).

Locke, John, *Letter on Religious Toleration* (New York: Hackett Publishing Company, 1983).

Lowith, Karl, 'Martin Heidegger and Franz Rosenzweig on Temporality and Eternity', *Philosophy and Phenomenological Research* 3 (1942/43), pp. 53–77.

MacIntyre, Alasdair, 'What God Ought We Obey', in Michael Peterson *et al.* (eds), *Philosophy of Religion* (Oxford: Oxford University Press, 2001).

Maimonides, Moses, *Guide of the Perplexed* (trans. Shlomo Pines; Chicago: Chicago University Press, 1963).

Marquardt, Friedrich-Wilhelm, *Theologie und Sozialismus: Das Beispeil Karl Barth* (Munich: Chr. Kaiser Verlag, 1972).

Matheny, Paul D., *Dogmatics and Ethics: The Theological Realism and Ethics of Karl Barth's Church Dogmatics* (New York: P. Lang, 1990).

McCormack, Bruce, *Karl Barth's Critically Realistic Dialectical Theology: Its Genesis and Development 1909–1936* (Oxford: Oxford University Press, 1995).

Mendelssohn, Moses, *Jerusalem: Or on Religious Power and Judaism* (trans. Alan Arkish; Boston: Brandeis University Press, 1983).

Michalson, Gordon, *Fallen Freedom: Kant on Radical Evil and Moral Regeneration* (Cambridge: Cambridge University Press, 1990).

Milbank, John, 'Ethics of Self-Sacrifice', *First Things* 91, (1999), pp. 33–38.

——— *Theology and Social Theory: Beyond Secular Reason* (Oxford: Blackwell, 1993).

Milbank, John, Catherine Pickstock and Graham Ward (eds), *Radical Orthodoxy: A New Theology* (New York: Routledge, 1999).

Mosès, Stéphane, *System and Revelation: The Philosophy of Franz Rosenzweig* (trans. Catherine Tihanyi; Detroit: Wayne State University Press, 1982).

Myers, David, *Resisting History: Historicism and Its Discontents in German-Jewish Thought* (Princeton: Princeton University Press, 2003).

Niebuhr, Rheinhold, *Moral Man and Immoral Society: A Study in Ethics and Politics* (New York: Charles Scribner's Sons, 1960).

Novak, David, *Jewish–Christian Dialogue: A Jewish Justification* (Oxford: Oxford University Press, 1995).

——— *The Election of Israel: The Idea of the Chosen People* (Cambridge: Cambridge University Press, 1995).

Ochs, Peter, 'Israel's Redeemer is the One to Whom and With Whom She Prays', in Chad Pecknold and Randi Rashkover (eds), *Liturgy, Time and the Politics of Redemption* (Grand Rapids: Eerdmans, 2006).

——— *Peirce, Pragmatism and the Logic of Scripture* (Cambridge: Cambridge University Press, 1998).

——— 'Scriptural Logic: Diagrams for Postcritical Metaphysics', in Stephen Fowl and Gregory Jones (eds), *Rethinking Metaphysics* (Oxford: Blackwell, 1995).

Pecknold, C.C., *Transforming Postliberal Theology* (London: T&T Clark, 2005).

Peskowitz, Miriam, *Spinning Fantasies: Rabbis, Gender and History* (Berkeley: University of California Press, 1997).

Pickstock, Catherine, *After Writing: On the Liturgical Consummation of Philosophy* (Oxford: Blackwell, 1998).

Poma, Andrea, *The Critical Philosophy of Hermann Cohen* (trans. John Dunton; Albany: State University of New York Press, 1997).

Rashkover, Randi, 'Exegesis, Redemption and the Maculate Torah', in Peter Ochs and Nancy Levene (eds), *Textual Reasonings: Jewish Philosophy and Text Study at the end of the 20th Century* (London: SCM Press, 2002).

——— 'Theological Desire: Feminism, Philosophy and Exegetical Jewish Thought', in Hava Tirosh Samuelson (ed.), *Women and Gender in Jewish Philosophy* (Bloomington: Indiana University Press, 2004).

Rogers, Eugene, 'Supplementing Barth on Jews and Gender: Identifying God by Anagogy and the Spirit', *Modern Theology*, vol. 14, (1988) pp. 43–69.

Rose, Gillian, *Judaism and Modernity: Philosophical Essays* (Oxford: Blackwell, 1994).

——— *Mourning Becomes the Law: Philosophy and Representation* (Cambridge: Cambridge University Press, 1997).

——— *The Broken Middle* (Oxford: Blackwell, 1992).

Rosenstock-Huessy, Eugen (ed.), *Judaism Despite Christianity: The Letters on Christianity and Judaism between Eugen Rosenstock-Huessy and Franz Rosenzweig* (New York: Schocken Books, 1971).

Rosenzweig, Franz, *Der Stern der Erlösung* (Frankfurt: Suhrkamp Verlag, 1988).

—— *On Jewish Learning*, (ed. N.N. Glatzer; New York: Schocken Books, 1965).

—— *The New Thinking* (trans. Barbara Galli and Alan Udoff; Syracuse: Syracuse University Press, 1999).

—— *The Star of Redemption* (trans. William W. Hallo; New York: Holt, Rinehart and Winston, 1971).

Rotenstreich, Nathan, 'Rosenzweig's Notion of Metaphysics', in Paul Mendes-Flohr (ed.), *The Philosophy of Franz Rosenzweig* (Hanover: University Press of New England, 1988).

Schleiermacher, Friedrich, *On Religion: Speeches to Its Cultured Despisers* (trans. John Oman; New York: Harper & Row, 1958).

Schüssler-Fiorenza, Elizabeth, *Bread Not Stone: The Challenge of Feminist Biblical Interpretation* (Boston: Beacon Press, 1984).

—— 'Feminist Spirituality, Christian Identity and Catholic Vision', in Carol P. Christ (ed.), *Womanspirit Rising* (San Francisco: Harper, 1992).

Seeskin, Kenneth, *Autonomy in Jewish Philosophy* (Cambridge: Cambridge University Press, 2001).

—— *Searching for a Distant God* (Oxford, Oxford University Press, 2000).

Silber, John, 'The Ethical Significance of Kant's Religion', in Immanuel Kant, *Religion Within the Limits of Reason Alone* (trans. Theodore Green and Hoyt H. Hudson; New York: Harper Torchbooks, 1960).

Soloveitchik, Joseph B., 'Confrontation', in *Tradition* 6, no. 2 (1964).

Soullen, Kendall, *The God of Israel and Christian Theology* (Minneapolis: Fortress Press, 1996).

Stout, Jeffrey, *Democracy and Tradition* (Princeton: Princeton University Press, 2004).

Tillich, Paul, *Systematic Theology: Reason and Revelation, Being and God*, vol. 1 (Chicago: University of Chicago Press, 1951).

Von Balthasar, Hans Urs, *The Theology of Karl Barth* (trans. John Drury; New York: Holt, Rinehart and Winston, 1971).

Ward, Graham, *Barth, Derrida and the Language of Theology* (Cambridge: Cambridge University Press, 1995).

Weiss Halivni, David, *Revelation Restored: Divine Writ and Critical Responses* (Boulder: Westview, 1997).

West, Cornell, *Democracy Matters: Winning the Fight Against Imperialism* (New York: Penguin Books, 2004).

Wood, Robert, *The Ontology of Martin Buber* (Evanston: Northwestern University Press, 1969).

Wyschogrod, Michael, 'A Jewish Perspective on Karl Barth', in Donald K. McKim (ed.), *How Karl Barth Changed My Mind* (Grand Rapids: Eerdmans, 1986).

—— 'Why Was and Is the Theology of Karl Barth of Interest to a Jewish Theologian', in Martin Rumscheidt (ed.), *Footnotes to a Theology: The Karl Barth Colloquium of 1972*, Studies in Religion Supplements. (Waterloo: Corporation for the Publication of Academic Studies in Religion in Canada, 1974).

Zank, Michael, *The Idea of Atonement in the Philosophy of Hermann Cohen* (Providence: Scholars Press, 2000).

# Index